MOONDOG

THE VIKING OF 6TH AVENUE

MOONDOG

THE VIKING OF 6TH AVENUE

The Authorized Biography

BY **ROBERT SCOTTO**

PREFACE BY **PHILIP GLASS**

PROCESS

Contents

PART ONE: ROOTS (1916–1943)

>An account of Louis Hardin's childhood prior to his
>blindness; the various places he lived, his earliest
>proclivities and adventures; the family life that explains
>so many later developments will be explored.

>The accident causing his blindness; Louis' coping
>with his handicap; his discovery of his lifelong
>vocation of music; the dissolution of his family, his
>schooling, his first marriage, his growing independence,
>his decision to go to New York.

PART TWO: THE TREE OF LIFE (1943–1974)

>Louis' first decade in New York; his association with
>the New York Philharmonic; his pen name, Moondog,
>in 1947; his cross-country trip; his earliest successes,
>his earliest music and records, his life-style and growing
>reputation; his second marriage.

>His first albums, some on prestigious labels; the birth
>of his daughter; his court case with Alan Freed and
>WINS; the evolution of "the man with the face of Christ";
>his ideas and opinions; his New Jersey and New York
>retreats; his separation.

To Maddy and Mike

Fatti ... per seguir virtute e canoscenza

Remembering Moondog

by Philip Glass

The *Village Voice* had a piece about Moondog needing some-where to live, so I trekked out to his usual spot, in front of the Warwick Hotel, at 54th and 6th and invited him to stay at the house I was living in with my wife JoAnne Akalaitis. A few weeks later I get a call from Moondog from a pay phone; he sounded cautious but says he'd like to come check out the room.

I look out the window and the sight of Moondog crossing the street startled me. He was such an imposing figure, about six foot eight if you count his Viking headpiece, and he was so confident in his walk you wouldn't think he was blind. I wondered how, as a blind man, he managed to cross the street without an instant of hesitation until he showed me how he listened to the traffic lights; I had never heard them before in this way.

So here's Moondog at the front door, all stately and remark-able with horns on his head. I offer him our big room on our top floor. Moondog turns down the big room. He says he wants our small room, where he could stretch out his arms and feel the walls and ceiling. That's what he was comfortable with, like what he would eventually do in his tiny house upstate. The way he later described his upstate home, it sounded like a spider or an octopus, with small arms or corridors reaching out from the center.

He ended up living with us for nearly a year. I thought he was terrific, fascinating and musically very interesting. We formed a music group, Moondog, Steve Reich, Jon Gibson and myself. For a time, we had weekly sessions playing Moondog's compositions. We took his work very seriously and understood and appreciated it much more than what we were exposed to at Juilliard. Steve recorded many of our sessions.

Moondog came from a true American tradition; he personified the maverick, solitary hero composer, like Nancarrow, Partch, Ives, and Ruggles. He really impressed me with his work, and that he could play all of his music. Once he gave me a gift of a big composition with 37 parts. I still have the music.

I was particularly interested in the way Moondog could work lyrically with odd rhythms; in a way it wasn't dissimilar from what I was doing at the time with Ravi Shankar. Moondog was quite interested in our work, too, and seemed to appreciate that we were also finding our own voices compositionally.

When he lived with us, Moondog was very connected to jazz. He'd stand in the stairway to the jazz club, Birdland, and play along with anything they were playing inside the club. I was amazed at his facility for doing this, and the way he could make music of found sounds. I remember him standing on the roof overlooking the Hudson River, and when the Queen Elizabeth ship pulled into port blowing its horn, Moondog would toot along with it on his bamboo flute.

As amazing as he was, he was a difficult guy, and a bit of a racist, too. He spoke of not liking black or Jewish people. He asked me whether I was Jewish, and I said I was. He then wondered why this happened to him, why all his best friends happened to be Jewish and black. He seemed genuinely sad and confused by this unfortunate circumstance.

Though he spent a year with us, I gave him lots of privacy. Before he moved to Germany, it did become uncomfortable at times. It seemed that he felt entitled to grab hold of any woman he could. He told me, "I can't be prosecuted for rape because they can't do that to blind people." Another uncomfortable thing about living with Moondog was that he didn't pick up after himself or know how or bother to throw out the trash, so I spent some time cleaning up the fast food he brought to his room, like empty boxes from Dunkin' Donuts and half-eaten bones from Kentucky Fried Chicken.

I only saw him once after he moved to Germany. He came back once more to visit New York and we had a great dinner together at my home in the East Village.

Moondog lived a life of tremendous courage and discipline; he was an admirable, unique person and a personal inspiration.

Introduction

M oondog's incredible life was not only interesting, but also instructive, in many ways as much a cautionary tale as an adventure. Many remember him as the Viking of Sixth Avenue during the Sixties, a true eccentric in a city famous for every imaginable form of antihero and bohemian: his broadsides against government, the monetary system and established religions—coupled with his unconventional modes of dress in juxtaposition to his serious devotion to music—brought him both fame and notoriety. He appeared often in the media and was scrutinized from a variety of viewpoints: he was, in short, a sort of celebrity against the grain at a time when an anti-establishment stance had great appeal.

Moondog was, however, and had been from the start, a rebel whose roots were not nearly as shallow and ephemeral as some made them out to be, a man who had a religious devotion to, of all things, the past. Although he evolved despite his wishes into a cult figure, and welcomed, despite his deeper powers of discernment, his moments in the spotlight, his unpopular beliefs about Western civilization and his commitment to traditional tonal music, on the surface an unwieldy dichotomy, were the twin halves of a worldview he had built up steadily and laboriously for decades, and which he refused to abandon when they ceased to be fashionable. Although he will be recollected as the proto-hippie (or beatnik, if memories extend that far into the past) or remembered nostalgically as the consummate blind street-poet-musician of his day, the supreme loner articulating an extreme position, Moondog was quite serious about what stood behind him and what, as a consequence, he figured forth. Fortunately, many know him as a serious musician, primarily, and an interesting versifier whose work has evolved steadily through the apparent chaos of his life. Even after all of the images have been shed, and labels like "primitive" and "naïf" properly understood, his music may last. He was, in short, more than a symbol for a generation on the road or in revolt: he was a man of talent and discipline committed to living the life of the artist in order to make music when he might as easily have lapsed into bitterness or, worse, self-pity.

A biography of a life so variegated, filled with so many changes and contradictions, puzzles and paradoxes, must account for the growth of the mind as well as the adventures of the body. Music, therefore, is embedded in the text quite simply because Moondog's life breathes music. His search for his roots and his identity, which consumed so much of his time, he did for the most part alone, as he lived so much of life by himself. The alienation he experienced in childhood evoked responses that frustrated his orientation to the world; blindness made him more vulnerable and wary. Only a strong man, with a strong sense of self-survival and an even stronger commitment to his ideals, could have made it through unscathed, let alone remain sanguine, productive, optimistic. Out of the chaos of a life with challenges, hardships and disappointments, he found refuge not only in rebellion against the enemies of certain traditions but also in representing them to a hostile or indifferent present; he found comfort in perfecting established conventions; he found meaning in extending cultural artifacts.

Those who knew Louis as the Viking probably have little idea how long it took for him to arrive at his name, his dress and his credentials. His "conversion" to Nordic dogma and ritual, for instance, was not merely a pose nor simply a reaction against the faith he had surrendered at childhood's end, but an expression of concepts won through harsh experience and patient, if erratic, research. Louis

Hardin was not only searching through his bizarre childhood and paralyzing blindness for a sense of who he was: he was trying to find a continuum within which his hard-won ideas could comfortably fit. He became "Moondog" in 1947, at about the time he also began to compose music seriously, soon settling into a mode of life in New York City which he sustained, despite frustrations and partial successes, until 1972, for just under three decades: musician, poet, seer, and "beggar" (according to police records), living on the streets of Manhattan. His self-reliance, in light of his handicap, became legendary.

The patterns of his evolving dress are an interesting measure of his evolving philosophy of history. By the early Sixties he had become one of the most photographed street figures of his time, but his importance as a composer, and, to a lesser degree, as a performer, mattered more to him. He had to teach himself everything he later transformed, and in so doing created his own idioms. Philip Glass, an early friend and younger contemporary, said on the liner notes to one of his CDs *(Violin Concertos of John Adams and Philip Glass,* Telarc 80494, 1999), when asked about those who influenced him the most: "You know there is a maverick tradition in American music that is very strong. It's in Ives, Ruggles, Cage, Partch, Moondog, all those weird guys. That's my tradition."

The unusual, unclassifiable, strange and haunting originality in the best of Moondog's compositions certainly entitles him to serious consideration as an original American composer. Clothes do not make the whole man, though they do create an image which may become, for better or worse, indelible.

Moondog spent the final twenty-five years of his life in Germany, perfecting, if not completing, his life work. (For those into numerology, which Moondog certainly was—see his discussions in *The Overtone Tree*—it is a tantalizing but otherwise no more than titillating datum that his life falls into three roughly co-equal periods: his childhood and young adulthood, 1916–1943; his New York period, 1943–1974; his German period, 1943–1999.) Thus that singular man in the street and in the doorway, that bohemian Nordic rebel and antiquary, composed several huge tone poems celebrating Norse myth; that apparently improvisational jazzman (he almost never performed or conducted save with a minutely detailed score) settled down at peace with an ancient world-view, writing by admission in the tonal, Western tradition; that broadside balladeer took his ironies, satires and prejudices and honed them into a unified, imagistic—if bizarre—story of civilization and its discontents. He became in the eyes of many, especially in the Europe he chose to be a part of, something like an archetypical blind seer, respected with caution, poetically celebrating permanence through the fluctuations of the moment. Despite physical disabilities in his final decade, the creative spark remained as vibrant as it ever did, as did his devotion to loveliness and form in the face of the grosser realities of the quotidian. His idealism, though less naïve, was still as intense, and his diligence, patience and labor were if anything ratcheted up a notch. Like so many original people, Moondog seemed to grow younger with age.

THE BIOGRAPHY DELINEATES the stages of Louis Hardin's growth into Moondog, presents his ideas as he formulated them and interprets them in terms of the logic of his life; it also explores, in some detail where it is unavoidable (the Alan Freed case, the first Columbia album), the people and places, the masks and the faces. His development as a composer will be traced historically. Moondog himself participated from the start and cooperated until his death: this is an authorized biography. All of the passages not specifically cited in the text come from hours of personal interviews and hundreds of pages of private correspondence, some of it on deposit at the Oral History of American Music Collection at Yale University. His verse autobiography, which is frequently cited, is, like all of his other published materials, available from Managarm (managarm.com). Opinions and assessments are either those of Moondog or the author, unless otherwise clearly indicated.

I tried not to write a bloated, glacially-paced story, so I deliberately chose to omit scores of anecdotes, program notes and reminiscences, especially those which largely duplicated details already presented. (Moondog, for instance, in practically every one of his interviews, and there are many, said essentially the same thing about his working habits, theories of composition and philosophy of life.) Thanks to my editors, Shane Davis and Adam Parfrey, who pruned my academic tendency toward the prolix, the book has a lot less redundancy and fewer lists.

I beg the indulgence and forgiveness of my many committed correspondents over the years whose generous contributions of materials are, therefore, unacknowledged. Many people afforded me invaluable help, of course, in some cases beyond my expectations. Ilona Sommer (Goebel), first and foremost; Paul Jordan, Thomas Heinrich, Stefan Lakatos, and all of the other trustees of Moondog's legacy; June and Lisa, his two daughters; Hammond Guthrie (3rdpage.com) and moondogscorner.de for publishing parts of the biography on the web; the administration at Baruch College, CUNY, and Dean Chase, for their generous support, both financial and academic; the contributors who are cited specifically in the text and the scores more who gave anonymously.

To them, to Lu, my family (especially BJB), my colleagues and students at Baruch College, my friends—all of whom did more for me than they can ever realize, and I can ever adequately acknowledge: thank you.

— Robert Scotto, May, 2007

Prologue: Autumn, 1966

Moondog, who had recently turned fifty, gets ready to start his work day. In order to beat the oppressive and dangerous pedestrian mobs at rush hour, he rises early and dresses meticulously. It takes him some time to assemble his outfit, especially in the narrow confines of his dank Aristo Hotel room, and the baggage he must carry along with it. It is, for a sightless man who dresses to be seen ("Who ever remembers the blind man with a tin cup?" he asks), a diligent, patient and laborious act. When he is finished, however, he is like no one else: the Viking of Sixth Avenue. Nearly every layer of his dress uniform is hand-made; every bit of his accoutrement marks a vivid moment in his life, a gift, a discovery, a transmutation. As the look evolved through the years, the simple garments composed of squares sewn together gave way to tunics and cloaks of one piece or a leather cape and leggings. His head is sometimes covered by a flat cap that comes to a point above his nose or, today, one of the trademarks of his latest image, the horned helmet with a wrap-around turban. The cup from which he drinks or accepts donations alternates between a hollow antler and a hollowed-out moose foot. The look is seamless, homogenous, revealing a man arriving at a statement rather than a plea or a cry of defiance. Although it seems paradoxical to some that his arcane appearance can be thought to reflect a sober, carefully worked-out behavioral idea, nonetheless the Viking represents nearly thirty years of tangents aiming for a center, and he carries it with the assurance of a man who has earned the right to be outlandish in a very specific way.

The *New York Times* reported a year earlier (15 May 1965):

> His new outfit is a velvet cloak and hood of brilliant scarlet, lined with pale green satin, and two pieces of thronged cowhide that partly cover his feet. He abandoned his old costume, made up of surplus army blankets, to "get away from the G.I. connotation."

His dress, he tells passers-by, is "my way of saying no. I am an observer of life, a non-participant who takes no sides." Now, at the Avenue of the Americas and 54th Street, "his favorite corner at the moment," with the trimba alone of all his '50s innovations—"the only musical instrument I have here"—he has transformed himself from the person he was when he had first "established himself as a landmark in Times Square," standing on that traffic island and playing the oo and the uni.

Today, almost like a magician, he balances so much from leather lines. Over heavy, rough pantaloons goes a weighty brown toga, and over that the bright red woolen tunic. (Once he owned a bearskin as an outer garment until it fell apart from old age. A "berserker," he would say, in Viking lore, he who "wears the bear's shirt," was believed to assume the animal's physical strength: thus the legends of the ferocious special troops from the north. Alas, he would add, the word corrupted into a synonym for a crazy person, someone out of control, and the courageous warrior, like the pre-Christian Gothic world he defended, was buried by the victors.) The same red material wraps halfway up each of the horns of his helmet, which he affixes next. This is a complicated affair: bound by leather thongs, weighted with chain mail and sewn onto the hood cape of heavy muslin one shade lighter than the beige horns, it helps us focus on the particular charm of his face. His long, graying beard, his deep-set eyes, his chiseled, solid

cheekbones and nose, are there to impress. He appears more formidable and larger than his substantial frame is in reality—until
he smiles. Often the loose-fitting, heavy headdress falls over his
eyes, but it never seems to bother him. Suspended from the
thongs underneath his chin is a leather strap that secures his
spear, which always stands six feet straight up from the ground.
No other blind man has a cane quite like this. From his wrist
dangles an antler water jug. An inner series of pockets holds personal items like his Braille slate and "snatter," a Braille book to
read, some blank cards to write upon, some money. The payload,
however, is carried in the duffel bag which he hefts over his shoulder, his "walking office." Here is Moondog's plenty, a complex
blend of sophisticated survival tools and items for sale: his rack
for displaying poems, music and records, his donation holder,
announcements, booklets, curios, food, trimba. His last step is to
lace up his footwear—it is impossible to call them shoes, and
there are no socks—worn in a close wrap above the ankle. Thus
draped, cinctured, clasped, laced, packed and fitted, he is ready to
set out.

Upon leaving the Aristo, he walks carefully east to the Avenue
of the Americas and then north to the Warwick Delicatessen,
where he gets his take-out breakfast. Perhaps he may be slowed
down by an admirer or an inquisitive out-of-towner or an especially congested intersection. Even before 9 a.m. the midtown
area is a tangle of cabs, buses, trucks, carts, cars and pedestrians.
Before the office towers around him have filled up, however, and
after avoiding the low-hung parking restriction signs that used to
cut into his face until he took to wearing protective headgear, he
is at his station, 54th and 6th, a few yards down from the north-
east corner with the four-foot polished stone patio walls of the
MGM building to his back. There he breaks out his coffee (regu-
lar, with sugar), an orange, a sandwich (it looks like pastrami) and
a Danish (of course). Perhaps the city humming around him, the
sounds which have intrigued and inspired him for over twenty
years, suggests a canon (he always composes in his head, never at

an instrument), or a couplet, so he punches quietly into his slate with the sharp stylus beneath his cloak—a Braille manuscript that a copier will later translate, at great expense too often, into notes or print. The winds whipping across the street from the East and Hudson rivers, together with the shadows covering the sidewalk as the sunlight is cut off by monoliths of glass and stone, make a second cup of coffee welcome. It is too early and too cold to open up his outer garments, yet he stands erect, a living piece of sculpture, ready to do business.

The crowds begin to pass by, old friends and voices, new acquaintances; he sells a little poetry, an old record or two, his perpetual calendar; he passes out broadsides and announcements. He is at this spot because it is at the center of an industry (ABC, CBS, NBC, MGM, studios, record stores, agencies, all situated within a few short city blocks) and because he loves the people here, loves to talk with them, not at them, to listen, to cherish the novelty of sounds, to seek out new wrinkles in the fabric of the human garment. They come, but not all of his visitors are friendly or knowledgeable: a class of New York City schoolchildren files past him on their way to a museum or Radio City, giggling in the anonymous safety of numbers. One straggler, a boy of about ten, delivers a parting burst: "You ain't shit." Moondog laughs, a booming, uninhibited baritone. To some hecklers, though, his response is less emphathetic. One gentleman, baiting the Viking with digs about his peculiar dress, finally asks what the spear is all about. Moondog, annoyed that so much good time has been lost, retorts: "Why don't you climb up on top of it, and maybe then you will get the point."

Taxi drivers, truck drivers, secretaries from the surrounding offices, all send greetings. Nearly without fail he will recognize a voice out of the past. So acute is his sense of presence that many do not realize that he is blind; so down-to-earth is he with those who discuss less arcane matters with him that some are utterly unaware of his reputation as a composer and musician. Although he is wary of extending trust too far because he has been hurt in the past, he is nonetheless unafraid to share his earnest ideas, even with those who deliberately seek him out to mock him and, through him, the naïve, eccentric idealists he is thought to personify. However rich his innermost life, he knows he is a spectacle and he is proud of the fierce vulnerability that distinguishes him from the hucksters and hustlers he knows too well.

It is now mid-morning: between visitors, coffee-breaks and routine sales—Moondog tries to have something for everybody—he will take a swig of grapefruit juice. "I like a drinking cup made from horn," he has said; "it's as old as man." Since Moondog has no engagement tonight, no performance or appearance, he will stay at his spot for a good eight hours before packing it in. The sudden updrafts of wind cascading down the darkening Manhattan canyons can suddenly isolate him among a sea of faces. Underneath his tunic, however, he is patiently at work, clicking away. Composing in this way can be a very painful business: come winter, the bitter cold freezes the metal to the skin of his fingers. He cannot write in Braille with gloves on. In rain or snow, sometimes, he accidentally gouges the skin beneath his nails, an injury that is doubly troublesome: the same sensitive fingertips that write are also the ones that read and make music. Still, eyelids closed, as if in meditation, for minutes or longer, he works until a new voice apprehends him and fixes him in time and place once more.

Through lunchtime and on into the late afternoon he alternates among many roles: friend, oddball, composer, guru. Some come just to see him; others make sure they go that block or two out of the way to pass by; a few stumble upon him unaware and under-prepared. He is seldom flustered. Musicians pause to talk trade. A choreographer listens to him expound upon modern dance for half an hour. A couple of rockers improvise with Mr. Rhythm. On one such occasion, Big Brother and the Holding Company walked away with the madrigal "All Is Loneliness" and later recorded it, their lead singer, Janis Joplin, intoning Moondog's dark sonorities with her own peculiar edginess. The only thing they did not do, he notes wryly, is perform it in the 5/4 time in which it was written.

Toward dusk, a couple of college students come to hear Moondog on Vietnam and macro-economics. No stranger to these issues, nor to confrontation, he marries free speech movements on the campuses, the demonstrations against sending troops to southeast Asia and the imperial presidency into a dynamic, comic critique with eddies and undercurrents that answer some disturbing questions in some startling ways. He is sympathetic to their plight and to all the confused victims whose alienation he has sensed. He tells them how he, too, drifted away from family and faith, how he, too, came to loathe the abuse of power in high places, and he provides them with a lively counter-history of unacknowledged repression, immoral behind-the-scenes politics and an economic system armed for war. To them he is a vertical line in a world of horizontal planes, someone to be trusted even if he is not entirely credible. The violence implied by his costume is belied by his optimism. He was there, you can hear them saying, is there now; he *knows*. He sings with them a few of the songs they have come to identify with and a few of his own. A cynic might argue that this encounter was ephemeral in the long run, that little ultimately was changed by the noise and tears; nonetheless, few will easily forget this moment, even after they have hardened into middle age and, as one of the chroniclers of their generation has put it, fallen into place. It was not so much the role or the uniform that moved them, even if that was the reason they came. They will remember a strong yet sensitive man.

Then, soon after the last note dies, he is alone again. It is getting cold and he starts home, his gear in order, his burden shouldered. Too proud to use any of the standard paraphernalia of the blind, he walks upright and straight, though a couple of passers-by cross teeming Sixth Avenue with him. Back at the Aristo, he muses on the varied riches of the day: he made a few dollars, had a good time, broke no laws, avoided violence. His room is cold, but Moondog is used to the cold; in fact, he prefers his walk-in closet to the overheated apartments his friends and admirers offer him. To the hardened veteran of Wyoming winters, a man accustomed to living on the streets and sleeping in places few ever visit, the Aristo is downright cozy. And so, as night falls, in the drifting movement of his consciousness toward sleep, he carves out yet another moment for his work, punching quietly in the unlit room, playing.

Part One

Roots

(1916 –1943)

Chapter One

Archdeacon Prettyman's Animated Doll

(1916–1929)

I n little Plymouth, Wisconsin, is an Episcopal church, St. Paul's. The little brown church on the corner (as it is known locally) became a designated historical site in 1978 and has changed little since 1920. Although it is the oldest single-site church in Sheboygan County, it still has the same little bell to summon parishioners, the same pipe organ, the same cedar shingles. Built in 1858, in part with funds from New England, the myth grew up around the building that was propagated by the Easterners who moved into Plymouth and founded the parish. The folks up on Yankee Hill, still a well-to-do residential area with big houses and spacious lawns, perhaps believed that the structure was put together with pre-fabricated materials from back east; certainly the little boy inherited that belief. That was, of course, long ago, and times and surroundings are wholly changed. Plymouth is forty miles north of Milwaukee and just east of Sheboygan and Lake Michigan.

To those looking for stories of idyllic childhoods, that of Louis Thomas Hardin, Jr., later to be known as Moondog, might at first seem so. His father was the priest resident at St. Paul's, and little Louis was raised from ages three through five in the rectory, built in 1907 and also nearly unchanged. His mother, born Norma Bertha Alves, was the organist on Sundays. He had an older sister, Ruth Louise, a younger brother, Creighton, and maternal grandparents nearby.

Plymouth was a cheese town (cheese capital, by local reckoning) in the heart of the heart of the country. Next to the parsonage was the village firehouse, behind it a small mill stream, in front of it a tidy lawn. Across East Main Street was the library. For an artist as a young man, such a childhood might have become either the stuff of nostalgia or the tinder for rebellion. No self-respecting storyteller today would ask his readers to accept a fantasy of respectability so hackneyed. Nevertheless, the future Moondog, of all people, grew up here. Predictably, serpents lurked in the garden.

Louis was born in Marysville, Kansas, on May 26, 1916. The family moved to Clinton, North Carolina after his father had enlisted as an army chaplain for 1917 to 1919, just before the armistice. Plymouth was the family's third ministry. For Louis, childhood was an odyssey through America's middle with his itinerant preacher father for nearly three decades. After Plymouth and his earliest recollections, he lived in Wyoming (1922–1929), then back east in Missouri (1929–1933). After he became blind, he went north to be schooled in Iowa (1933–1936) before rejoining his family in Arkansas (1936–1943). A brief but productive ten months in Tennessee preceded his pilgrimage to New York at the end of 1943.

Seven states (ten towns), tragedy at sixteen, his parents' divorce and remarriages, and ultimately losing touch with all but a few of those who influenced him early: all these shaped the man who had played on the rectory lawn near the dairy lands of Wisconsin. Louis' later restiveness and drive to live in the middle of the action and noise, on the streets if necessary, are indubitably due to his unsettled childhood. His mistrust of solid, middle-class values also probably reflects the ambiguities and vaguenesses of his boyhood. Despite its storybook settings and some memorable joys, his childhood was not happy. It was exciting and challenging, its pains illuminating as well as embittering, but the conflicts he would later have with the adult world (oversimplifying) are re-enactments of conflicts he inherited from the complex, enervated generations that generated him. Mom, to the boy, would always be mom, as a madrigal written fifty years later makes clear: "All at once my mother's face appeared, the face I knew when I was two plus two makes four. Her hair a golden halo, two eyes of blue to see me, through and through." Grandma apparently was weighty enough to barter with the Episcopal hierarchy at nearby Fond du Lac in planning the career of her son-in-law (and why not: Bertha Alves, born Meyer, claimed to be related to Meyer Amschel, founder of the Rothschild dynasty) and insistent enough to appropriate the youngest grandson, Creighton, to herself. Louis always felt that his brother was more a cousin, groomed in years to come for the medical profession, outside the range of his father's lethal eccentricities.

His complex and compelling father was by far the most potent early influence, for better or worse, on the boy, who would one day become an even greater rebel and pariah than his sire. Louis Sr. was a minister who fell from grace, a man of wit and resource, an adaptive survivor with a hint of dangerousness. He had been born in 1886 in Lexington, Kentucky and raised on a farm in Indiana. Two weeks after his son's birth, on June 11, 1916, he was ordained a deacon in Marysville, Kansas, at age thirty. He had attended Valparaiso University in Indiana and Hamilton College in New York, where he received an LL.B. in 1915 before graduating from the Kansas Theological School. On November 30, 1917, in Wilmington, North Carolina, he was ordained a priest. He entered the diocese of Fond du Lac on December 9, 1918 and assumed the cure of St. Paul's on January 8, 1919 (earning $1,100 in 1920). His son's description of him ("an Episcopal minister, merchant, rancher, real estate and insurance agent") is tinged both with irony and respect. He gave his namesake and favorite child a healthy perspective on reality, for this student of Napoleon and Sousa marches, satirist of ministers on the make, and capricious yet loving parent was as surely out of place in his time as his son, who would grow up to be a living anachronism.

Louis' birth certificate says that his mother, age twenty-five, was a housewife. She was far more than that, even when and where that would have been enough. She shared her husband's irreverence and adventurousness, and together they would quarrel with the Episcopal Church through a satiric novel, the publication of which accelerated the family's dispersal and disintegration. She was at home in Wisconsin, born and raised near Plymouth. She married her husband while they were students at Hamilton, in 1913.

Louis' roots on both sides were Germanic. (In Chilton High School, German was still required in 1920.) Place names memorialize the first- and second-generation dairy farmers who had migrated in the 1800s from Northern Europe: New Holstein, Kiel, Pilsen, Kohler, Oostburg. The names of Louis' neighbors do also: the printer on the corner across Division Street from St. Paul's is still called Wandersleben and Schmidt, and next door was the family of Gustave Zerber.

Through his parents Louis inherited many of his later interests. Music, the primary one, came to him through his mother's training and performance as well as his father's fancy. (His sister Ruth also was musical, performing throughout her youth in song, dance, and band.) His parents gave him a love of literature, especially in the satiric vein, through their collaboration and in the glorious rhythms of the King James Bible and the Book of Common Prayer. Louis' devotion to percussion was born in his father's marches; his love of the organ came from his early immersion in his mother's playing; and his irreverent, jocular, rollicking verse, in some surprising ways, exemplifies the diction with which his parents celebrated the religion they were apparently ceasing to believe in. His devotion to folk music and to the counterculture he later symbolized might even have been sparked by the assertion on his paternal side that John Wesley Hardin, the famous outlaw, was a distant relation. Roughly sixty years later, Louis wrote a song about him.

From January 1919 until winter 1922, Louis grew in wide-eyed wonder as the world just beyond his perceptions began to constrict around him. Everything was gigantic, powerful, and obscurely meaningful. The mill stream was The Mighty Mullet, the firehouse a center of dynamism, urgency, and speed. The friendly fire chief showed him how the harnesses were kept suspended over the horses in their stalls, and the wagon waiting behind, ready to hitch up and gallop off. Some of his earliest memories were of local fires, one of them traumatic. One bright, hot summer day, playing with forbidden matches on the powder-dry lawn between the rectory and the church, Louis kindled a blaze that grew rapidly around him. The lawn, he notes, "that had been tan before was black," and as he fled in panic the neighbors came running, trying to beat down and contain the flames until the fire engine, fortunately next door, arrived "to keep the church from burning down." In retrospect, this might seem to be some kind of emblematic protest by a four-year-old unable to otherwise articulate his gripes, but this is both speculative and irrelevant. It remained curious, nonetheless, that he alone of the Hardin clan would continue to reveal himself through such symbolic situations.

Life swirled around, and Louis swept it in. As upon any child of four or five, the world of things fell upon him almost sacramentally, while his elders marked a mysterious perimeter to his activities. First, there was nature, and Louis from the beginning was a Wordsworthian who would always remain a flower-child. In the spring, with his mother, he would go in search of the wild violet, walking out of town up a slight hill into the woods. In the fall the two would again leave the beaten track to pick weeds with bulbous tops, which his mother would paint silver for decoration. Behind the parsonage was the parish hall, demolished in 1978 after it had fallen down, and a garden whose main attraction, in June, was a strawberry patch. Winter, with the deep freeze and monumental snows of the Great Lakes plains, was equally memorable. His earliest recollection was of the brutal cold outside tempered by his awareness of "the mystery and wonder of Christmas" and palliated by the variously shaped cookies his mother baked "in the manner Grandma taught her to."

Plymouth was all news: kindergarten at five; his first parade, Memorial Day, 1921, in which he marched with a toy flag. His earliest attempts at absorbing the larger world outside the rectory's protective shield occurred on his "funday" Sunday mornings, when he would spread the color comic strips on the parlor floor and then lie directly on the paper, moving his body from one picture to the next rather than moving the text before his eyes. He "sniffed" the ink from frame to frame, crying when he had finished all there was. One of the neighbors had an upright piano with the reticulated rolls that mesmerized him and Ruth. This, along with the church bell, the church organ as played by his mother, and his father's phonograph records formed his earliest musical perceptions: not profound, but rich and unforgettable.

Although Louis felt singled out as daddy's boy (or, as he put it, "a curled darling on display"), he was normal enough to be curious, mischievous, and more. His dabbling with petty crime and the inevitable stirrings of rebellion ripened into a pathetic attempt to run away from home. First he had dipped into the family money pot. Like Rousseau, who tried to steal the forbidden apples because he was hungry, he found his "borrowings" escalating. "*Gelt* is guilt," he was taught, so when his parents refused to give him some money, he was convinced that he must take it. There, atop the upright, one chair-boost away, was the kitty; unsurprisingly, if not commendably, his "profit motive grew." With his "last and largest hand" from the money-pot that seemed "open-ended," he decided to light out for good with a friend on the road to freedom. The scope of this, his first antisocial act, was small: it took him to a farm owned by his buddy's uncle, down the road. The two boys thought they had reached the promised land and gladly lent a hand with the chores in exchange for supper. Their shock began to set in when the farmer told them that he would drive them back to town, since it was too late for them to walk. Dad was "hopping mad," and with belt in hand he stood the quaking Louis on the kitchen table, making music enough, as his son wryly recalls, "to beat the band" on that rebellious hide.

Although strings might be pulled behind his back, the parsonage was his father's domain. Louis was called "Bus," short for Buster, until he was thirteen years old, at which time he claimed his given Christian name. The reason was the long locks that flowed over his forehead until his father took him, "unilaterally," to a barber. Mom cried in anger, but dad's "arbitrary" decision went uncontested.

Reverend Hardin was at the center of Louis' world. When visitors came to the rectory on church business, Louis would stand behind the big chair in the office and try to repeat his eloquent father's polysyllables ("parrot-like," as he later punned). Not only did Reverend Hardin deliver arresting sermons, but he also wrote a book and was a "giggle-good" speller. Growing up in a world charged with words, many of them magic, Louis was bound to be a devotee. He was also bound to make the mistake that made his parents roar. Despite some evidence to the contrary, Louis thought his father had an equable disposition because of the society he was a member of: the Knight's Templar.

His father played a dual role: irresistible beacon to his moth-like son, and omnipotent tyrant dominating a tender imagination. One Sunday morning, when the four-year-old was supposed to be tucked away fast asleep, Louis ran out of his house in his Dr. Denton pajamas, across the lawn to the front door of the church, where the early service was in progress. He marched down the middle aisle and climbed into the pulpit to daddy, who was preaching. Mom left her organ to lead the boy back home. But as father attracted, so could he repel. Louis' first memorable scare came at Christmas, most likely in 1920, when a man dressed like Santa Claus (dad) came to the door at night, grabbed the child and started to leave, taking him back to the North Pole. The onlookers thought it hilarious, but the terrified child missed the humor. The high cost of insincerity, which became apparent early in their love-hate relationship, soon touched nearly every corner of Louis' life. For the minister the world was filled with wonder and meaning. For instance, Louis loved to pore over the pictorial war books in dad's library, entering "a world more fantastic than fiction could ever be." Though a man of God, his father had Napoleon as his "second god" and was fascinated by all things military. His son was soon absorbed also in the battle scenes, which were not "something which had happened somewhere and somewhen" but fantasies, "ends" in and of themselves. Louis unsurprisingly struggled to reconcile the strict disciplinarian and military strategist (the preacher with a pipe and a book about Napoleon in his hands, as a later madrigal recalls him) and ecclesiastical pariah with the vocal altruist. This double standard ("my father asks, the people give—when I ask, he doesn't give") was the first of many contradictions the future iconoclast had to live with, and, like so much that was both attractive and off-putting, it also paralyzed and confused.

Family tensions grew despite Plymouth's idyllism. Grandma Alves, who had practically adopted the youngest son, Creighton, was a quiet but assertive matriarch. If Louis was daddy's boy and Ruth momma's girl, Creighton was indisputably grandma's. Louis was not only far from his younger brother for much of the time; he was also subtly excluded from conversations between grandma and mother in German. It would take him over fifty years to be reacquainted with the language and culture he would come to love.

Louis was afraid of his grandmother. Once, when the family visited Chilton, he accidentally knocked over a tub filled with clothes and soapy water and got his nose summarily pinched. He would, disguised as a thief, sneak into the cellar where the winter apples were stored and "pinch" one in return "when the coast was clear." His mother, backed by grandma's authority, could be as "unilaterally arbitrary" as his father, and perhaps more damaging to the marriage than any career manipulation was another secret Louis discovered years later. After Creighton was born, the two women decided that "mother must be sterilized at once." Grandmother's sister, Erna, had died in childbirth, so she was overcautious with her remaining child. Daddy was "unsuspecting," back in Plymouth parsonage, "in the dark about the pact."

The marriage, which was to last fifteen years more, was already showing signs of stress, mercifully invisible to the children then. Together mom and dad were working on a manuscript "they said would be a book," and their lives changed dramatically when it was finally published. In retrospect, it would appear that the Plymouth years were dominated by *Archdeacon Prettyman in Politics*, by its creation and its repercussions. To the boy who would drive the adults to distraction with his toy car while they worked, the withering stare he got did little to allay the enchantment:

Dad was Dad and Mom was Mom. I never could
have understood that she
was beautiful and he was handsome, not until
the time I couldn't see.

Although they were on their way to "semi-separation" even as
they collaborated, they "couldn't bear to say it," and he could not see
beyond the wall of solid domestic respectability that protected him.

These barriers began to fall in the coming years. First came the
book. They celebrated its publication in April 1921. By the end of
the year, however, when its open scorn for things clerical had alerted the inevitable enemies, the Reverend Mr. Hardin was on his way
to do missionary work in Wyoming. Louis soon learned that its
satire was not merely religious, but also topical, an obvious attack
on the local brethren. The author on the title page was Norma B.
Hardin, but Louis insists that the "lampoon" that turned into "a
lead balloon" arose from his father's animus and biases, that dad was
the one for "stirring up a hornet's nest." Louis also credits his father
with the four illustrations, caricatures. After all, Reverend Hardin
was progenitor in spirit of the son who would later come to personify anti-establishmentism: beneath the mantle of the ministry
was a rebel unable and unwilling to submit to the order, a Norse-
man under wraps. By becoming the Viking, Louis advanced the
rebellion his father had initiated, though never conscious of cause
and effect. He would reject not only the ritual but also the dogma;
he inherited an itinerant lifestyle, emulated its protagonist, and
tried to elevate it to art.

Prettyman attacks the rigid establishment in the church, with its
quibbles and backstabbing infighting, its vitality squeezed out by
bureaucracy. Since his father could not take direct credit for a satire
so transparent and scathing, he and his wife hit upon an ironic
solution. The dedication, dated April 1921 at "The Rectory, Plymouth, Wis.," seems to offer an ingenious escape route for the man
of God about to savage his fellows:

To My Husband
Whose Faith in the Final Triumph of Brotherly
Love over Bigotry and Ritualism in the Church
Has Won my Sympathy and Devotion, For
I Know it is Founded on a Rock
Norma B. Hardin

In hindsight the sentiments are sadly hyperbolic. Neither faith nor marriage survived the wake of the novel's publication.

One of the four cartoons depicts the stiff, otherwise nondescript Prettyman approaching the "majestic towers of St. Mark's," barely discernible through the foliage that dominates the landscape, while another shows a more robust archdeacon exclaiming, upon seeing his beloved swimming in a pond: "What a water lily." The bathing scene, complete with a menacing snake, is a mock-epic adaptation of the primal Garden of Eden scene. Unfortunately, the quality of reproduction is blurred and the printing sloppy. The novel itself looks rushed-out. It is incoherent, bombastic, wordy, often formulaic, and crude in its characterizations. As fiction *Prettyman* was little noticed and quickly forgotten, and as satire it was too dull to prick any but a few hierarchs (and grandma, probably). It is of interest only as an influence on Moondog and for what little light it sheds on the community it ridicules.

Despite the title, the Reverend Prettyman is not the novel's protagonist. As it develops, in a "broken-backed" narrative, he dominates the political and amorous intrigues of the first half, but in the end becomes antagonist and buffoon. The real hero and heroine are the Reverend Fletcher Lamont and his bride-to-be, Julia Skinner. To realize their love, he must reject the hypocrisy of his colleagues and their Keystone Kops antics, and she must reject the fool's proposal to live happily ever after with the true Christian minister. There are a host of pale Dickensian characters, meetings, trials, and letters that struggle feebly to hold the reader's attention through predictable plot turns.

Percy Prettyman is appointed Episcopal Archdeacon of the "conservative diocese" of Smithfield. He is "high" church, the service he conducts "beautified with the assistance of red-headed servers, incense and gregorian music." The bishop conveniently starts to die, and the ambitious prelate campaigns for the post, noting that instead of preaching the Gospel of Christ he gives the people what they like: "lectures, the 'mass,' lighter phases of church history and socialism." Various fools get in on the crooked election, and as the prelate campaigns he also courts the daughter of Judge Skinner, "as artless as a roe, a full blown Miss, with all the subtle charm of the twentieth century." (What are we to make of the fact that she is described early in the novel as one who looks like a "descendent of a Viking King"? Coincidence or foreshadowing?) After the first comic trial and a stolen letter fiasco, the good Reverend Lamont steals Julia from the crypto-Romanist Prettyman: "Lamont had been whipped to a finish in a wonderful game of ecclesiastical politics, a modern institution erected upon the ruins of a dying Christianity."

Although the plots, sub-plots and counter-plots can be funny, there is a bitter residue: bribery, snitching, backbiting, theft, and character assassination appear to be the norm. The burlesque even extends to the dialogue of the lovers. Julia to Fletcher: "I'll not quarrel with you again—until I feel like it." The bishop dies, Prettyman and Lamont fight for the job, and Julia (like this novel depleted by its own ominous undertones) flags. Several trials, restorations, excommunications, and elegies later, Lamont wins. From the mid-point Prettyman hardly appears again, as the prejudice of the author(s) becomes more evident: at a convention, we find "the Ritualists sitting at tables reserved for them, while the Evangelicals sit with the people generally." Wooing, Julia and Fletcher converse thus:

"I notice that the Archdeacon always calls the Lord's Supper or Holy Communion the 'mass.'"

"The Prayer Book says that 'the sacrifice of Masses, in which it was commonly said, that the priest did offer Christ for the quick and dead, to have remission of pain or guilt, were blasphemous fables and dangerous deceits,'" he answered.

"Do you know what I think about our Prayer Book, Fletcher?"

"Not particularly."

"It is the bulwark of the English Reformation."

"You are correct my dear," he replied.

At Lamont's inauguration he attacks "Churchianity," the "tendency to promote the interests of the Church or clergy, rather than the spiritual welfare of the people." One can almost hear the Hardins laughing at their superiors. Only after Julia and Fletcher are safely married does Prettyman voluntarily leave for England, where there presumably are greener pastures for the old-fashioned ritualist scorned by the egalitarian American mob. The novel ends in cloying romance: "The deep river roared and plunged in the distance, in its mad race to the sea, while a man and a woman knelt in a certain garden in the city, and returned thanks to an invisible King."

As Louis notes, dad "got into hot water with the bishop over it" and was transferred by year's end to "episcopal Siberia," Wyoming. In 1972, about fifty years after he left it, he returned to Plymouth as Moondog to hear the bell "that cast a spell" over him, "the first of all I could recall, the last of all I could forget." The pastor's little son was playing on the same lawn Louis had almost burned away that hot summer day. The rectory and the church were just as remembered. He was led into the church: "I played a few chords on the same pipe organ my mother played on. I stood in the pulpit and recited some of my couplets where he had delivered his sermons." The reverently elliptical "he" is revealing. Here was Louis' paradise lost, and its memories, torrential, ecstatic, and sad, lay at that moment too deep for tears.

WYOMING WAS A FAR CRY from the rolling pastures and stable town life of the Midwest. It was, to the Episcopal church at least, a frontier to which they forwarded their fallen angel: if the softer routines of a Wisconsin dairy town provided too much leisure for the cynical cleric, then perhaps the rougher frontier life would make him focus more attentively to his calling. The ordeal lasted seven years, and when the Hardin family came back east in spring 1929, Louis, Sr. found his position in the church precarious and his marriage, the one "built on a rock," in its final stages of disintegration. Rather than strengthening his faith, the Wyoming ministry had weakened it; rather than pulling the family together through adversity, it had hastened their dispersal.

Louis was six when he set out with his father, leaving mother, Ruth, and Creighton to come later; he was just shy of thirteen when dad, Ruth, and he settled in Hurley, Missouri. Thus the revelations of these transitional years were darkened by a maturing sense of frustration, vacillation, and insecurity. The lifelong wanderings of the later Moondog, whose roots were shallow until he had to dig them out of a distant past, and whose office was always "portable," continued into another dimension the western peregrinations of his father.

The trip out by father and son from Wisconsin to Wyoming was rough. Louis remembers the "rattletrap" with a whistle that sounded more like a moan, and the long and dreary "sleeping-waking-looking" routine of rail travel. But he remembers more vividly the awesome variety of wildlife in the great expanse of river and plain that awaited him like a revelation—the flowers, the fish, the camping expeditions in the near wilderness. Nothing in Wisconsin could prepare him for the monumental scope of the West: "I went wild over the riotous colors of the semi-desert flowers, especially the sand lily and the Indian paint brush," Wyoming's state flower, so "beautiful, exotic and arresting," under "so clear a sky." A collection of letters by Elinore Pruitt Stewart, a woman who settled in the same area as the Hardins (Burnt Fork) roughly a decade earlier (1909–1913), paints an equally exhilarating portrait:

> I enjoy the memory of that drive through the short spring afternoon—the warm red sand of the desert; the Wind River Mountains wrapped in the blue veil of distance; the sparse gray-green sage, ugly in itself, but making complete a beautiful picture; the occasional glimpse we had of shy, beautiful wild creatures. (*Letters of a Woman Homesteader*, rep. 1961, Univ. Nebraska Press, 122-23.)

But even here, in the virtually unbounded freedom of open spaces, a conflict arose between some instinct in Louis and parental authority, especially his father's. "Every new patch I would shout for Dad to stop," but how was the boy to know "my parents and the flowers were annoyed"? Eventually, dad refused to stop any more, leaving Louis to cry, like every other child so abused, at the injustice. "He should have told me that the only way to pick a flower was to leave / it where it was, alive."

Sounds, too, were lodged powerfully in the blind man's retrospective memory of his sighted childhood, as we might expect. Some of the sensual energy was transferred from eye to ear: "The piping of the toads along the roads we traveled on into the night,/ were stored away in memory of sound and not in memory of sight."

The outdoors enthralled him, with energy and bounty and with its seemingly fiendish indifference to human comfort. In spring mother and Ruth joined them in Evanston, in the southwest corner of Wyoming, where they settled for a few months. Daddy, ostensibly a fisher of men, was also a skilled fisher of fish, especially the sacred trout. Even though little Louis attracted merciless hosts of mosquitoes, he observed in awe the preparations (netting, lantern, rods and reels, the tent, the smell of kerosene and tobacco) and worked hard to become bait-catcher. When dry flying was impossible, after a rain had muddied the waters, he was drafted for grasshopper duty and enjoyed catching them once he learned to strike before the creature jumped.

Late one evening, during one of their long missionary trips to the north and east, at Cokeville in Lincoln County, his parents put Louis and Ruth to bed on an army cot and then struggled onto a beaver dam by lantern, catching with the Royal Coachman fly all the trout they could carry. Later as his mother cooked the fish in butter "its tail would rise to meet its head in an arch."

At Evanston the Hardins resumed normal family life. The Reverend, always off-center in his powers and passions, filled the air not with church music but with ragtime and military marches. As recorded on 78s, "The Stars and Stripes Forever" and "Sabres and

Spurs" made a deep impression on the boy, who remained hooked on marches ever thereafter (though he did not compose any until 1978, when he wrote nineteen in the "contrapuntal, canonic style"). He also heard "Alexander's Ragtime Band" and, appropriately for a flower child, Mac Dowell's "To A Wild Rose"—danced to by Ruth, then eight, in the local cinema, accompanied by her mother on piano. Music was a constant, if not an obsession, of his childhood from then on, yet few if any of his favorites are classical in any sense, and he received no rigorous training until after he became blind. Like his public persona, his preferences in music developed independently; more than the nature of the music, the quality and context of his experience of it formed his musical impulses. To Louis as a child, music was a natural backdrop for more momentous events. Only later what was once peripheral, ubiquitous, and ornamental became substantial, special, and central, but by then he was committed to creating music, not just consuming it.

To a child in 1922, technological wonders appeared like another form of magic, and the circus came to town. Never having seen so much magnificence in one place, Louis could only stare agape at "the antics of the clown" as the parade passed by. He saw the first of the "too few" motion pictures he would ever see in Evanston, the silent *Ben Hur*, for him a view into the modern age. One day, without warning, someone loaned the Hardin family a Model T, a Tin Lizzy, so that his father could make the long trips his ministry required, and so Louis' first automobile ride also took place during the memorable month of resettlement. So did his first close call. He can still remember the face of the driver of the other car, "as cool as could be," as he inched his way past in the opposite direction on the outside of a hairpin turn. Louis, whose car was safely tucked on the inside lane, perceived the two passing machines, an "inch" between them, "on the edge of Nothingness." The new age didn't merely emerge, it exploded upon him, with its miracles and threats.

Even as a churchman's son, with friends and playmates who were children of the clergy, Louis learned a hard lesson boys usually learn, that those immediately over one in the pecking order are meaner than those at the top. In Evanston, some churchmen stayed with them for a few days, one of whom had a son who bullied Louis. Once in a while Louis would get upset enough to run into the house crying "Edwin hit me," but with no redress from either parent. "Edwin hit me" became a household taunt for whenever he complained of bullying by other children. Such are the enduringly bitter moments of childhood. Instead of attention there were taunts; instead of warmth, distance.

> I know I was never taught how to defend myself, either ver-
> bally or physically. I could have used a few lessons in boxing
> and wrestling, but had no one to teach me.

Although his father's mission was religion, Louis thought his preparation for life strangely un-Christian. Many aspects of the preacher's difficult, sometimes treacherous livelihood suggested a double standard that no civilization, let alone individual, could resolve. Traveling around southwest Wyoming, preaching in the boondocks, was, in retrospect, "seeing what was left of the pioneer era." It was a far cry from Yankee Hill, "carrying the Gospel to the lorn," baptizing cowboys in their boots, in trout streams: daddy fished men with "book and candle" through a series of "one-night stands, / in services by lantern-light, baptizing and the laying on of hands." To Louis, this "high" church mission with an unexplained earthy dimension, at times exhilarating and at times insufferably boring, ultimately smacked of that hypocrisy most painful because most central, the minister's (and his family's by association). If the father-figure fails as father, if the magical bond of the family fails to hold, what of the avowed dogma? What of the converted when the converter has lapsed?

More troubling to Louis than the sins of mere church people was the rape of culture by culture, encouraged and empowered by organized religion. He would return as an adult to the plight of the American Indian; he would even try (and fail) to live among them about thirty years later. Their tragedy, he thought, was partly self-authored. (In 1949, though, when he attended a Blackfoot Sundance in Idaho, he was pleased that "their tradition of dancing three days and nights without food, water, or sleep" had persisted.) Yet through them he felt the sorrow of a civilization destroyed by the superimposition of another, by the "grubbers" who scooped out the "irrigation ditch" of the latest "happy hunting grounds." With them he could resonate, with the percussive rhythms of his later music, especially that of the 1950s, a conscious reworking of something plaintive, primal, brutal, and elegiac. To their moral and religious qualities he likened those of the Northmen he believed Western history had tried to bury. To the six-year-old the first contact was awesome—the Treaty of the Wind River Reservation (in west-central Wyoming), the Arapahos, "glaucoma-ridden," "reduced by gunpowder and seduced by whiskey." To their noble but pitiful world came the Reverend Hardin, a stranger in a strange land. Once a squaw threw a nice fat puppy in the pot, "hair, guts and all," in honor of the visit. When it was "done," she cut it open and offered it to the Reverend, who declined it, feeling uncharacteristically unwell. There, to the later Moondog, another paleface crime was allowed in the name of good intentions:

> While at the Arapaho reservation, during a convention of missionaries, bringing God and the blessings of Christianity to a people who had their own tribal beliefs as good or better than what we had to offer, I came in contact with a culture of a people utterly foreign yet fascinating. I did not know then that we were witnessing the dissolution of something fine and noble. What we called a reservation they must have called a concentration camp, captive audiences to our unwanted importunities and impositions. To the injury of being defeated was added the insult of forced indoctrination, with the sicknesses and diseases of the white man thrown in.

Perhaps the most memorable experience of his youth took place the day he had a lesson on the drums while sitting on "the leathered lap" of Chief Yellow Calf. Not only was this man unconvertible by the missionaries, but he also gave to Louis that most precious gift, an unforgettable moment that echoed down the years as the boy also grew up to be unconvertible, a one-man reservation in the middle of a progress-loving, hostile world. The chief was a noble, dignified reminder of the "recoverable" past; when Louis became Moondog and, later, the Viking, he, too, reclaimed a vanishing mode of perception, drumming along. Louis came out of the brief time he spent on the reservation with less to love about the cultural charge he had inherited and more to revere about the buried lives he would resurrect in the future. As his father created for him an itinerant life and modeled for him a rebellious stance, so from the Treaty of the Wind River Reservation he walked away with a new beat, a new instrument, and a new dimension to his world, including his music.

THE HARDIN FAMILY FINALLY settled near Burnt Fork in what a contemporary book called "the Godless Valley." (The author, Mrs. Honore Wilsie Morrow, and the editor, Arthur H. Clark, protested that the story was true despite local resentment. To many, however, *Judith of the Godless Valley*, published in 1923, was a novel.) Into this wild place came the minister with a troubled vocation and family. Burnt Fork, so named because forest fires had denuded its banks, held the new mission. Stewart in her *Letters* notes how only a decade earlier there was "no minister in this whole country," and when she was to be married there was, in her husband's Scots, "no kirk to gang to." (But the most complete local history of this entire period, *Uinta County: Its Place in History*, published by the same Arthur H. Clark in 1924 and written by Elizabeth Arnold Stone, notes that the Episcopal Church conducted "a prosperous Sunday school" at Burnt Fork.)

Legend and myth vied to vilify the place. Intermarriages between white and Indian thereabout are said to have produced excellent cowboys, some of whom became rodeo champions, while others became feared outlaws. Stories circulated that Butch Cassidy and his gang used the valley as a hideout, and in Uinta County he became the Robin Hood figure he remains in popular imagination. The idea that the place is evil persists even today. For the limited number of residents there is a high rate of violent crime, goes the superstition, and even where statistics prove otherwise, alluring falsehoods die hard. Late in summer 1922, though, after their travels through western Wyoming and peacemaking with the Episcopal ecclesiarchy, Father Hardin started preaching to the "unconvertibles," the "grubbers of the sage." Wyoming became "a very nice place to live" despite his parents' benevolent neglect. The settlers turned out to be friendly, the scenery lovely (it was in the foothills of the Rockies, after all), and the environment, ultimately, nourishing: he caught his first trout there, his mother was his teacher (in a log school house), and the family lived on the ground floor of a log community hall. The action was upstairs: church services, dinner-dances, conferences, and the special local gatherings called "blow-outs." Once a Bishop Thomas came to Burnt Fork to inspect the mission and was treated to a feast at the house of a neighbor. Afterwards he was invited to visit the community hall. The distinguished visitor faced the only way up, a flimsy-looking exterior staircase. When asked if he wanted to go up to see where the preaching was done, the bishop declined, saying: "No, I have a vivid imagination." This snub of their laboriously built and maintained worship place was "just the thing to turn them livid."

Reverend Hardin, an irrepressible groundbreaker, tried to be not only a pillar of the community on Sundays but also a productive worker during the week. He made the downstairs front room into a store, selling candy, tobacco, groceries, and ammunition. The supplies were trucked from towns about fifty miles across a semi-desert on a snaking road, via Horse Shoe Bend: "impassable in winter by car, impassable in spring because of mud, impossible in summer because of dirt." Louis recalls the "winding way to town" by the spectacular Twin Buttes.

Dad was not dismayed by logistics or by the warnings he got from his closest friends about how tricky going into business was for a preacher, and how inevitably the requests for credit would create painful dilemmas. His neighbor and confidante (and one of Louis' adult heroes), "Uncle" George, was direct: don't sell on "tick." "If you do or don't give credit, you will make enemies. Those who ask for and receive it, and are late in paying or won't pay, will dislike being asked for the money. It is better to have full shelves and enemies than empty shelves and enemies." Dad flourished until the credit gave out, defying not only sound economics but also pragmatic public relations. Forty years later, his son would be accused of infantile exhibitionism in playing like a child to the grownup world around him, adopting a stance grounded in history and formed by the dynamic, iconoclastic personality of his father. To twist the rules before finally abandoning them was a family tradition. Why shouldn't an Episcopal priest run a country store? Why shouldn't a blind musician make his living as a "beggar" on the streets of New York? When the children came in, climbing over the sacks of sugar for a peek at the candy display, and asked for some "ratbait," gumdrops, or "Black Jack" gum on tick, he had to say, "Show me your penny." When a certain Emma, the daughter of a rancher, brought a gift of bread and meat to the preacher, and then asked for credit, dad had to be guided by the profit motive. But not for long: after giving in and giving credit he eventually settled for payment in kind (once with a wagon and a team of horses), and left years later with many uncollected accounts. The dualism proved tedious in the long run. (As Louis put it: on Sunday you tell them it is more blessed to give than to receive and on Monday you tell them you can't get something for nothing.) Some of the parishioners summed up their objections:

"The Hardins never should have got worked in merchandising," some would say.
    "While he was preaching, she was teaching.
    Wasn't that enough to pay their way?"

Louis recalls: "I caught on to the idea of double standards early."

Mother was the only teacher. With the brief exception of his days in a Plymouth kindergarten, Louis' mother was his first and only for years, and of her pupils he thinks he may just have been "the worst," getting into mischief as he did even though all assumed he would "know better." She taught him the alphabet, how to read and write. She was—especially in the first and brightest Wyoming years—as much a constant in his life as his often absent father, and equally exemplary and demanding. Against such accomplished adults the boy felt inadequate and disappointing, a harsh chord in an otherwise harmonious symphony. Most of Louis' early relationships with women, in a pattern reaching beyond his thirtieth birthday, were attempts to recapture his lost mother: romances with older women sometimes twice his age, steady, self-supporting, musically and intellectually accomplished. They were all teachers. Just as Louis repeated his father's rebellion, he also searched for the anodyne to his mother's rejection. Although "Mom was Mom," Louis had few happy memories of her. Once a hay wagon "full of happy hearts" took off for a Lonetree dance without him: Mom was there, Ruth was there, snuggled under blankets, but he was left behind. In revenge, though alone and unseen, he put on one of his sister's dresses, indicating the attention he craved and appropriating an identity others might take seriously.

Near the end of Louis' first year, in the spring of 1923, his mother directed the children to gather the winter's trash and dispose of it in a bonfire. Unfortunately, the blaze was too close to the schoolhouse and carelessly supervised. After all of the other children had gone home, Louis, riding the family horse, noticed that the fire was still smoldering and that smoke was rising from behind the schoolhouse. Cords upon cords of stovewood had been ricked against the rear of the building. It was cedar, with its unusually inflammable bark, and a spark had blown over onto and ignited one of the pieces. Louis was paralyzed by two fears: a conditioned fear of fire and the fear of galloping the huge horse, which he knew he could neither control nor stay on top of. So instead of dousing the flames, he trotted after the cowboys he could find, in twos and threes, who hurried to the fire only to find it uncontrollable. This was not Plymouth, with its fire engine ready nearby; by the time the neighbors started to transport buckets of water uphill from the creek and little Louis pitched his cups in, his dad had seen that it was "no use." A huge crowd had assembled. Helpless, they removed anything portable, crowbarred the desks from their moorings, and surrendered to a "festive mood." Men then took the long poles that seemed to be everywhere and pushed in the walls; the blaze spoke with a roar, awesomely, especially to the child shuddering with guilt. Many years later Louis would be willing to share the responsibility with others, but the anguish of the moment was exclusively his. If mom had not built the fire so close, if the school board had not foolishly had the wood stacked next to the building, and if Louis had not panicked, then the structure might still be standing.

> If I'd used the wood-pile as a platform,
> both for getting off and on
> the saddle, so's to kick the burning stick,
> the schoolhouse never would have gone.

But he had been too human.

A colorful and delightful neighbor in Burnt Fork, "Uncle" George, the "star of the piece," lived two hundred yards down the road. It was he who fêted Bishop Thomas, cautioned the minister about going into business, fiddled at the blowouts. He came visiting some evenings to spin tales. As he started a story he would fill his pipe, light a match and hold it poised, then become so absorbed in what he was saying that he forgot it and burned his fingers. In the course of the tale this would happen repeatedly: he would fish out a new match from his vest and soon drop it with a yelp. His characteristic punctuation, for emphasis, but also to be sure his listeners were paying attention, was to say continually "Don't you know." In front of Uncle George's ranch, out in the middle of the county road, was the biggest cottonwood tree Louis ever saw. Its commodious shade was a haven for many summer travelers. Moondog, in 1971, remembered it in a madrigal flashback, dreaming of how he showed a friend the great tree of his childhood: "See with me an unforgotten cottonwood standing where it stood, yonder?"

Another madrigal (from 1968) recalls the "big event" of the ranchers' summer, hay-making. "On a summer's day in '23, Uncle George was making hay, the western way, with pine-pole stackers, made by hand, in height about sixty feet or more. It seemed higher to me." The farmer's life, filled with "jack-pine runners-up" and "pine-pole pulverizers," monstrous machines on enormous stretches of land in the burning heat of the summer, is the legend of the West as personified in Uncle George, part harsh reality, part myth, all magnified in recollection:

> A study in geometry, the stacker stood its
> groaning ground, a pair
> of nine hypotenuses making no excuses
> in the upper air.

Louis' contradictory perception of childhood is nowhere more apparent than in this period: although Burnt Fork was a nice place to live in and the people were good, he was vexed by his family's problems and his own insecurities. Years later he would become a living paradox, a conspicuous rebel, yet so conservative that the liberals who revered him were left aghast. His internal struggles gave rise to the temptation to become two people, two irreconcilable sets of attributes that comfortably accommodate both ends of the spectrum, that please both mom and dad, church and state, life and art. (Besides, he would point out to those who cared to know, he was a Gemini.) What to others was a maddening bafflement of contradictory impulses came to him through his nature and his nurture. And even if, upon reflection, the sun did shine often, the flowers bloomed, the taste buds watered, and the music played, the price was high.

The road to his home, as he recalls it in 1973, was alive with his favorite things: "Pussy willows pussying every branch along the road" and "flowers where the purple sage was growing," hiding nasty ticks for the unsuspecting. "Let me sing the praise of watercress, ... of crystal clarity in motion," he also notes, celebrating his "allegiance" to the plant he always loved: "let me pluck another sprig and revel in its tangy taste again," or in its green color, "reflected in the icy pool below." At home there was "Godless Valley ice cream," the best he ever had, made from Hereford cream, vanilla, whole eggs and sugar or fruit, packed in ice and salt and churned inside the freezer: "Stoll's delight," as it was known locally, named after a neighboring family, was a memorable "ritual in the ranchhouse." (The Stolls had raised a huge Hereford bull from a calf and asked Louis if he wanted to sit between the enormous horns, which he did, amazed. He noted with amusement, in reference to the headgear he would sport in the Sixties and Seventies at the apex of his Viking uniform:

> I never knew I'd have to wait threescore of
> years before I heard it said,
> "I never shall forget the day I sat between
> the horns of such a head."

Winter brought joys with its hardships, the teams of horses "jingle-jangling" through "trackless fields of newly-fallen snow." He and Ruth would carve a snow house out of a large drift that had formed a foot-thick crust from the alternation of thawing and freezing; with door and roof and floor it was "the Whitest House you ever saw." When the snow thawed and rolled down the hill "in haste," Louis was there, "channeling the flood": "Who cared about the wet and cold? I had an engineering job to do." In the backyard was a Rocky Mountain peak, always capped with snow. A 1970 madrigal recalls: "Well, Old Baldie has himself a snowy rain. Down, down, down it came. Above the timberline the raindrops fell in the form of snowflakes."

For a boy who loved to fish, the confluence of Burnt and Henry's Forks was paradise, well stocked with trout.

> In the twiggy branch behind the hall I hookt
> a trout and yanked him out.
> Be it e'er so small there's ne'er a prong
> of Henry's Fork without a trout.

The colorful locals held exciting celebrations. For July 4th the ranchers carved out an island "in the middle of the purple sage" for a track and a picnic area. There the entire Godless Valley would go to sport, see the races, wave flags, and shoot fireworks. A 1970 madrigal describes "[f]lags in the meadow," which he hoped were "standing there still, pale blue." What would become a day with tragic connotations nine years after his first Wyoming Independence Day was then the pinnacle of childish ebullience. There were also those "blow-outs" right above his bedroom on the versatile second floor. The dances, usually held on Saturday night, included young and old, in winter and summer, fair weather or foul. Whole families came, even the babies, "generally in farm wagons full of warm hay and blankets in winter." Stone's book on Uinta County notes how the scattered settlers had "all-night parties to which they would gather from far and near to dance to the music of volunteer fiddlers." When the little ones tired of the festivities, they were wrapped up and placed along the benches that ringed the room. During the whole long evening, until three in the morning or later, the horses were tied to the hitching post, out in the cold or heat, in ice or snow, "with nothing to eat or nothing to cover them." Since "no one gave them a second thought," they "had to take it, and did." Inside, Louis, bigger than a child for the night, was an intimate part of the action:

> By word of mouth it got around, "There's
> gonna be a blow-out Saturday
> night, eight-thirty sharp. The preacher's
> wife, her son and Uncle George'll play."

Play he did, performing for the first time in his life, doing what he would do so often later: drumming in front of a live audience, accompanying mom's piano and Uncle George's fiddle. The primitive materials were presciently appropriate: half of his "set" was a steamer trunk, which he would straddle and kick; the other half was a snare drum, donated back east and kept through high school, which he struck with shoe-shapers. Throughout his long career Moondog invented new percussive instruments from odd materials in strange shapes, his own versions of found art, so his eccentric childhood was a prelude to his even more eccentric maturity. It is clear with hindsight that his "musical career," however humble its inception, evolved in a warm environment, and the deep memory of it was more important than the quality of the music then produced.

He was a boy, too, experiencing the awkwardness and shock of coming of age. When the gelding, Ethel Welch was riding spread his legs and urinated, the boys who had surrounded her, "chivalrous in front of blushing maidenhood," pretended that nothing was happening. As they grew soggier, though, she turned crimson, yet horse, damsel, and knights rode out the moment to its conclusion. (Ethel's father was so heavy, so "full of self-importance," that the chairs of Burnt Fork were said to groan whenever he approached. One such seat in the Hardin household had held a treasured and ill-fated old 78.)

Along with awkward dismantling of naïveté and innocence were somber glimpses of gratuitousness and injustice. Not only did con artists and bullies beat and trick the unsuspecting preacher's son; those he trusted betrayed him. Louis was shocked one evening in the upper room before a dance when a "friend" took him for a ride on the shoulders, then bent over suddenly and "floored" his unsuspecting passenger. Louis' nose took the stunning force. Howling, with blood and mucus dangling from the wound, betrayed and in agony, he later wondered what his "mother must have thought, for she was there and saw it all." In time he "came to expect it more and more" in order to deal with it. Cynics are forged by experiences such as these. If punished for something he had done, he was not informed about it; if he was unpopular, the reasons were never articulated; if he was being singled out as a target, no one explained the rules of the game or afforded him methods for settling grievances. He was a little like the horses who had to take the treatment they got.

Even the pleasanter memories were soiled by shameful acts. Yet his deviancies, no more serious than other children's, were mainly cries for attention, arising from his need to be considered alive, vital, and flawed rather than merely an "animated doll." He stole, items sentimental rather than exotic or opulent. He hid a part of himself as well as his loot, alienated and ashamed, feeling like a forgotten failure. Now and then, "but mostly now," Jean-Jacques Hardin would help himself to his dad's candy "on the sly," without much guilt. Throughout his adult life, since possessions were morally tainted, he almost perversely did without them, traveling ever lighter and freer. The saddest memories are of his alienation, from his parents first and foremost, but also, through them, from the world that frustrated and excluded them. Louis was, it seemed to him, the "funny bunny" that didn't quite make the grade, rather than the trusted companion growing in competence under loving guidance. No one told him "what was going on." When he had gone down a row of potatoes picking all of the attractive blossoms and presented his bouquet to dad and Uncle George, they were irritated and told him not to do that again. He does not remember being told why. Louis was in awe of his father's horse and seemed to be drawn to the animal that loomed as big as an elephant. There he was, tethered on a long rope out back, eating a disk into the long grass around him, making rings through the meadow until the autumn snow. One fateful day he noted that the horse was saddled and bridled, so he led it up to a platform in front of the community hall and mounted. The ensuing ride cross- country took him past corrals, sheds, pens, hills, yet he rode without stirrups (he couldn't reach them anyway), relying on the horn of the western saddle for balance and support. A neighbor sent him home via a "short cut," but forgot to tell him that a pole gate blocked one leg of the trip through Uncle George's fields. Like the cowboys he imitated, he dropped a couple of the poles from the saddle, but he was too small to stretch down and put them back in place, nor could he hope to remount were he to dismount. Later that day a dejected Uncle George came to report that six of his milk cows had gotten into the alfalfa, bloated, and died. Uncle George, a "good tracker," probably knew that whoever was on dad's horse had left the gate open, but never directly accused Louis (who never confessed). Why wasn't he told the consequences of his actions? "Even then I knew enough to know they knew / I didn't know what I was doing," he puts it, but responsibility somehow slipped through the net of circumstances, amorphous, as he slipped through the web of events, uninformed, unformed, and adrift.

Even though the natural wonders around him were his solace, the joy that sustained him through the turmoil of treacherous relationships, the inhabitants of the place, remained strangers: if not hostile, at least indifferent. The local cowboys, whom he often imitated as any child might, in reality disappointed as much as appealed to him. The profanities they taught him drew laughter from adults. For such a little one, the son of you-know-who, to say such things! Everybody knew what was happening except his parents, who were unaware, always "wrapped up in their own activities." So while a seedy element had him "on a string"—asking the seven-year-old, "Are you getting any?"—he went unsupervised and unwarned. When the riders coughed and spit they disgusted him; when they took the gumdrops they had just purchased in dad's store and threw them into the air, waiting with gaping mouths to devour them on the fly, their pride of accomplishment turned his stomach. He felt, more strongly than necessary, that he undermined his father's mission and that his parents simply allowed it to happen: he was a "sapper," since it wasn't piety but notoriety that began at home, and thus dad's "impregnability" was eroded by his bad example. "Buster," "Flopsy," the "animated doll," though well provided for in some ways, was left to his own devices, and often chose poorly.

The Hardins, moreover, were never accepted except as visitors by most. In a land conspicuous for its lack of ministers, a godless valley, they were always on trial. If the inhabitants resented the holy man telling them "how to live the good life" in the first place, as Louis always felt they did, how cynically must they have viewed his son's running with the wrong pack?

It is hard to explain the preacher's seemingly arbitrary and offhandedly dismissive treatment of his son. But ultimately he measured his worth against his father, who dominated his moral perceptions, his (un)awareness of inequality, injustice, and disproportion. Perhaps he asked too many questions, so answers ceased; perhaps he was left to his own wits in accordance with some inscrutable philosophical principle; perhaps inaccessibility was both cause and effect—in other words, he was "delinquent" because he was ignored and pushed further away because he was different, not an integral part of a design he failed to construe. He got into hot water, but what child doesn't? When he needed to be treated decently, however, he was inevitably disappointed. One day, while Louis was wandering around the old dirt track behind the schoolhouse he spotted a dull round thing on the ground, a muted silver dollar "corroded into gray." He took the prize proudly to the preacher, who promptly pocketed it. No matter how hard the boy cried, he never saw the inexplicably confiscated coin again. He was "hurt terribly" and began to distrust. In his desperate adolescent search for models, he found a void he could not fill: he was neither the man of God's son nor much like the female Hardins, and quite unlike the shiftless cowboys. What, then, could he become?

The Burnt Fork years ended abruptly when "transfer time" came again. Louis never got explanations, just the facts. There was no farewell party, for everybody was "busy saving everybody's face." So, be it self-imposed or not, they pulled up roots and drove Lilly-Vory's team (a payment for groceries) out of Burnt Fork, heading north and west toward their new home, Fort Bridger.

Father Hardin's career, according to the annual journals of the proceedings of the Wyoming Episcopal Missionary District, followed some strange ellipses. He is noted several times in the list of "non-parochial clergy," the earliest on July 5, 1922, and the latest on July 8, 1929, as having arrived from the Diocese of Fond du Lac in March 1922. Bishop Nathaniel Seymour Thomas, S.T.D., entrusted him with the "Unorganized Missions" of Burnt Fork and Fort Bridger for several years, until 1925, when the prelate in charge of reporting on missions noted the following:

> I have made two visits at Burnt Fork to consult with the missionary, the Rev. L.T. Hardin, and the mission committee on building plans for this mission. The progress and permanency of the work at Burnt Fork demands a proper plant and it is planned to build a log church and rectory and to repair the parish hall, an old two-story log structure of historic associations.... Mr. Hardin ministers also to Fort Bridger, where he is temporarily in residence.

In 1924 he even presented four candidates for confirmation in Evanston. But before he moved his family to Fort Bridger, he commuted regularly for several years, and by 1924 his affairs were clearly troubled. In the journal he is no longer listed in connection with a specific mission, and one Mr. Roeschlaub has apparently taken over for him at Burnt Fork, building a "comfortable four-room log rectory with some assistance… There was a good Confirrmation class at Burnt Fork. No services have been held at Lone Tree or Fort Bridger in this field." Father Hardin mysteriously and cryptically has disappeared from the record, although he was there preaching, for his name doesn't appear at all on the roster of the clergy. Moving to the rhythm of his own drummer once again, in a frontier fort, he was invisible to his church. In the 1929 journal, after a gap of four years, he appears on the list of Non-Parochial clergy once again, just before his departure for points east. The effect on the family of these climbs and falls, traumas, relocations, breaks, and reconciliations was profound.

FORT BRIDGER WAS ALREADY FAMOUS in 1924, when the Hardins settled there for a year, a living remnant of the romantic nineteenth-century exploration of the northwest. By 1929, when they left Wyoming, their acquaintances had begun to turn the property over to the public domain as an historical landmark. For Louis, fresh from the living West and its rural frankness, this brief immersion into history and dense public activity was when he was happiest.

If Burnt Fork was where the spirit of the wilderness spoke to a young boy, Fort Bridger awakened his consciousness of an immediate and thrilling past. There the Lincoln Highway "snaked itself around my psyche" (a telling metaphor in light of what he called some of his earliest rhythms: snaketime). Founded by Jim Bridger (1804–1881), one of the heroes of westward expansion along the Oregon Trail, the fort and its environs were well-preserved in 1924, and the town that had grown up around it was lively. Its history included much of the traffic that led to the early settlements in what later became Wyoming, Nevada, and Utah. Bridger was a mountain man whose knowledge of the stupendous, unexplored West, and its indigenous inhabitants (he had three successive Indian wives) was legendary. He was reputedly the first white man to see the Great Salt Lake (in 1824), for instance, guiding settlers and the military through the Rockies and beyond; a fossil-rich rock stratum in western Wyoming became known as the Bridger formation. He founded the eponymous fort in 1843 as a way station on the Oregon Trail and fur-trading post. After he left it in 1858, by then the famous old man of the mountains, the army ran it until 1890, after which it remained a stop on the Lincoln Road. An 1849 government report vividly describes it:

> A drive of thirty miles during which we crossed Ham's Fork three times and Black's Fork once, brought us to Fort Bridger, an Indian trading post, situated on the latter stream, which here divides into three principal channels, forming several extensive islands, upon one of which the fort is placed. It is built in the usual form of pickets, with

lodging apartments and offices opening into a hollow square, protected from without by a strong gate of timber. On the north and continuous with the walls is a strong, high picket fence enclosing a large yard, into which the animals belonging to the establishment are driven for protection from wild beasts and Indians.

As it grew and evolved it acquired striking and original additions: stone boulder storehouses and barracks, for instance, an impressive stone chimney, rows of trees along the creek and numerous outbuildings.

One Will (William A.) Carter (Jr.), son of "the distinguished pioneer Judge W.A. Carter," sold Reverend Hardin a trading post made up of three stone buildings, a section of the original fort, possibly part of the estate later conveyed by Mr. Carter to the Historical Landmarks Commission of Wyoming, where it is preserved at the Museum. There, besides running the post office, for hot tourists in need of cold drinks and ice cream, arriving in Pickwick buses "so long they had to swing out before they turned the corner by the monument," or locals in need of supplies, the minister set up shop once again when "there wasn't any mail to sort." Louis watched the comings and goings from the square, across from the stile in the fence of Carter's house. He would never see another. There, despite contrary signs and opposing impulses, his father decided to preach on Sundays in a small, empty store. Mrs. Hardin still taught school, her "normal" degree adequate enough to serve the community's requirements.

Louis' paradise was shattered briefly by a visit from the East. Grandma, Grandpa, and Creighton (who had never lived in Wyoming) came out, not on vacation but to build a home on Hardin land. It wasn't too long, however, before they "missed Wisconsin" and headed back, leaving Creighton at last with his parents. Deeper problems evolved, incidents engraved upon the memory of the peculiar and hypocritical injustice done to Louis by his parents, whom the world regarded through different eyes than his. One stands out, vividly: his mother held an Easter egg hunt at the school and whoever discovered the designated lucky egg won a big basket of goodies. Louis, looking for something special, passed over a smashed, half-hidden egg which another boy retrieved. When it was announced that the reject was, of course, the winner, he could not be consoled, crying out that he had spotted it first. "But you didn't bring it in," his mother had replied, disclosing for him a lesson in pragmatic Christianity: then and forever the significance of the paradox "the first shall be last and the last shall be first" was made manifest. At any rate, the consolation that others might construe the contest as fixed should he have won did little to fill up the void. Though no one could say that "mama's boy was privy to the prize," a certain theme, a bitter taste, ran like a bass line beneath his growth to young adulthood. It seemed that he must be, because of who he was, somehow better. To his sorrow, as his scarred memory attests, he all too often came to see himself as somehow worse.

Buried at first by the onslaught of new and vital impressions, his awareness that the novelty had a destructive side developed gradually. Before he earned his own shotgun, he learned how to shoot by training his BB gun on "anything that flew." To his regret, the carnage he left in his wake permitted him to glimpse a darker side of himself that Buster's curls and Flopsy's tail had disguised. "Following a farmer's plow, that showed the other side of life, I saw / spent cartridges and worms come up together."

Dad, meanwhile, was "trading more and more and preaching less and less." One traumatic day in 1925, the Model T was reclaimed by the mission. With the car, it seemed to the boy, also went "the yen for preaching." Behind the failing ministry, it became clearer to Louis, lurked the failing marriage. One reason Louis found out years later, when his dad admitted to making passes at a woman who took care of the Hardin children during summer when his mother went to Laramie. Although the advances were rejected, his mother probably found out, and there was a "blow-up" upon her return, "another cause for eventual separation." Dad was looking to trade the store for a ranch soon. The pace accelerated: the Hardins moved twice during 1925 to 1927, neither move secured by an Episcopal sinecure.

First came the Workman ranch on Beaver Creek, near Lone Tree, not far from the land originally traded for the Bridger property. During the two years Reverend Hardin lived there, Louis was his only companion—mom, Ruth and Creighton stayed in Bridger, coming to the ranch on holidays, and otherwise rarely. In 1927 they came to the Hickey ranch on Henry's Fork, closer yet to Burnt Fork and bigger, apparently another even trade. Mom and siblings returned for two academic terms while she taught in Lone Tree. During the second semester the four of them traveled from the ranch to the school in a covered wagon school bus. In 1928 Louis was again alone with his father, and life was "hard" but "good." Dad hauled the mail halfway to Bridger, the distance being too great to be made with horses, especially in winter. He would meet the other driver at a noon rendezvous, lunch over a wood-burning stove, and then return, putting the letters in the ranchers' mailbags hung at the side of the road, arriving home, if he was fortunate, by nightfall. In the meantime, before Louis could ride to school in Burnt Fork in the morning, he had to make breakfast for the two of them and run his trap line. Despite the demanding routine, the "sights and sounds of Beaver Creek and Henry's Fork will always be a part / of me, no matter where I go, no matter what I do," he later reminisced, celebrating further with a madrigal: "On a tributary of the Green, more specifically the rivulet of Henry's Fork, my dad had his family. A cabin of pine was our humble home, but it was happy in spite of all...." He loved the "open range," the "feeling of unlimited freedom" there, where he was his "own master, and comparatively independent." It was picturesque despite some erosion, even if the old log bridge was waiting to be washed out in a spring flood. Reverend Hardin might have been taken in by shrewd bargainers who saw in him a soft touch, but he purchased for his son vivid and undiminished memories of labor polished into joy: "We had to get up so early that the pre-dawn sky was alight with the brightest stars I ever saw, and the air was so cold your nostrils stuck together. I had to take an ax and chop a hole in the thick ice in the stream to get a bucket of liquid ice for the horses and the cows to drink." Throughout his life Louis could endure punishing hardships in primitive environments; he also survived in New York City as a blind man. The skills he developed on the frontier, and his insistent need to homestead, brought him solace when all else failed. Nature for him was like the magpie's nest, improbable, and, like its call, unforgettable. Out of the crazy quilt of experience would always come the urge to make beautiful songs, and in moments that would test the patience of the hardest minds and bodies, he made some of his loveliest music.

By the time Louis was twelve he was old enough to see how the settlers' attempts to domesticate the land made for both high romance and back-breaking labor. The high point of the year was haying, which he now joined for the first time. The enormous stacks were estimated for tonnage after a rancher tied stones to tape measures and threw them over the top in a crisscross pattern. The big sheep companies then bought the hay and drove their herds into the fields to winter there, sheltering in the willow groves and eating down the hay. One Ben Romero, from Taos, impressed the boys by living out of his covered wagon throughout the harsh winter, eating for the most part a "very, very hot" chili as sustenance. This demanding country, this "primitive" environment, often called forth inventive, explosive responses for survival. Thus Louis became a proficient trapper (beaver, muskrat, and mink) and sharpshooter: he shot mallards on the wing, rabbits from the hip, and once even a pair of rabbits with one bullet. Bill Luckey, a former hunter and trapper, taught him many techniques. He would also park his covered wagon between the willow groves and allow the boy to ride his mare, which could single-foot. Many years later Louis would recall the comfortable ride this gait gives in a tender madrigal. He was raised in what seems in retrospect like a Hollywood western.

His coming of age, or, rather, becoming twelve, also brought him size. He had been the little guy, the new boy who always changed schools, whose mother was often the teacher: in other words, the easiest to pick on. In 1928, in Burnt Fork, however, he was all of a sudden the biggest boy in school and his mother taught at Fort Bridger. Nevertheless, his troubles only went "from worse to bad," because he still had not yet learned a valuable lesson about pushing little ones around: there are bigger ones waiting in the wings, brothers, cousins, who know how to fight.

With size and bruises came the first stirrings of romance. He worshipped his teacher, Jesse Chip, "the blue-eyed blond with turned-up nose," who danced with him once and whose proximity induced his first ecstasy. His crush went unrequited, however, and he soon learned how dreams are dashed. One day in school she smelled skunk, and he had to admit that he had caught one that morning. He was "excused" for the day. His second crush, with a woman his own age, turned out to be even more painful. Her name was Madeline Smith, and it was she who spotted Louis with a friend's sister in a haystack. The romance ended abruptly when she rushed off to tell his mother, at the ranch for a brief stay. That evening Louis got another memorable beating. Disbelief and disillusionment set in when disappointments struck, when cynicism about ideals took hold. Once a friend shocked him by telling him casually that there was no Santa Claus. Only a few years later, after his tragedy, the last delicate strands of his faith would be cut, and no firm beliefs would hold his imagination until decades later, when he became the Viking of Sixth Avenue. He would of course come to be suspicious about intimacy and dubious about absolutes. Among natural wonders, as he grew into young manhood, his world was falling apart.

As always, his interests and activities orbited his father. More and more as the years passed he lived apart from his brother and mother. Reverend Hardin, though, was always there, model and tyrant, hero and betrayer. He was flawed but always acted with panache, was memorable even in his failures, was nothing if not ambitious and controversial. How often was the boy trapped, unresolved, within his father's paradoxes, and, what is worse, moving around with a man aimless but blessed with a preternaturally clever twelve-year-old? What was he to make of this man? Dad had encouraged Louis to save the money he made selling his pelts to the fur companies. In the Mountain View Bank was an account in his name with over a hundred dollars in it, of which he was rightly proud. One day dad asked him for a loan. Louis was reluctant, remembering his silver dollar, but ultimately surrendered his hard-earned savings. Shortly afterward the ranch was sold, and the family was heading back to Wisconsin. When Louis finally asked after his money, his father explained that he had spent thousands and that Louis really ought not to expect anything back. How about a bike, then, the boy countered, something he had always wanted? He never got the bike. With great understatement, the man looking back on his childhood noted how these "unhappy incidents … did not inspire confidence" down the road.

Reverend Hardin was a mark. The "country slickers" probably took him on the ranching deals, but more definitely they often traded "something for less than something" with him. One incident illustrates not only his father's naïveté but also his ability to get the last laugh. Jody Pope offered to trade a strawberry roan, right for the boy (it was said), for the twenty-one-jewel pocket watch Hardin had had since a young man. As soon as Louis mounted, he was thrown, for the roan was a "no-good, worth about four dollars." Months later guests were over to dinner at the Hardin home, some of whom had been amused at the roan transaction. The main course, enormous, juicy steaks, was delicious, if a bit sweet. To appreciative laughter, dad announced that they had just eaten the horse. He may have made a poor deal, but he certainly closed the circle with a touch of class.

On winter evenings dad read before the fire (Napoleon was still his favorite subject), pipe in hand. Louis sometimes asked for information, which his dad would give, usually correctly, a half-hour later, long after the question had been forgotten. But such endearing moments do not outweigh the traumas of arbitrary laws and harsh reckonings or the anxieties of separation and loss. There was no stable center for the boy's growing needs, for in this family nothing was secure.

The final months the Hardin family spent in Wyoming, in spring 1929, proved to Louis, now edging closer to his thirteenth birthday, how little was left of the marriage founded on a rock. His mother, sister, and brother came only during the summer or on holidays. Although they did not divorce until 1937, the cycle of separation and reunion undermined confidence. Once Louis was dropped off early Monday morning at his school, two hours before class began, so that his mother could be on time for her students at Fort Bridger, and he remembers rolling on the ground as they pulled out, "crying and crying for the mother I didn't see." Everyone knew that she wanted to go back to Wisconsin, to be near her parents once again. Louis, however, loved his ranch, his freedom, his life. Then a shattering, illusory choice was presented to him so as to make it seem as if he held the balance of fate in his hands. One day he and his father were working in the meadow. Dad turned to his son and said that he had received an offer for the ranch and couldn't decide whether to sell or not. "I will be relying on you more and more," he observed. "It is your decision to make: shall we stay or sell?" Louis did not want to go, but he was old enough to realize that this move was inevitable. "Let's sell," he answered, not quite thirteen.

Father, mother, sister, brother, and Louis, together again, decided to make the trip back east leisurely. They bought a car in Salt Lake City, where Louis saw his first talking movie (Al Jolson sang "Sonny Boy"), and headed toward Chilton. Dad professed to look for a farm thereabout after they arrived, but found nothing. Louis and Creighton, innocent, spent the summer fishing and swimming at grandma's little house on Spring Street, now filled to bursting. It was the year the stock market crashed, that Reverend Hardin left the ministry in deed if not yet in fact and set out again for new places, and that Louis returned briefly to the earliest memories of his childhood, wiser and sadder.

Chapter Two

The First Violin

(1929–1943)

ouis' odyssey continued in August 1929, when the Hardin family found a farm in Hurley, Missouri. Since he could find nothing around Chilton, and since he was still enamored of farming, the Reverend Hardin unenviably had to ask his mother-in-law for financial help. He was at this time a minister without a ministry and thus without an income. Louis was certain that grandmother ran the show and held the purse-strings. (Grandfather was little more than a shadow, conspicuous by his absence. More than forty years later, in 1971, when he wrote some madrigals about his past, in one of the very few about Hurley, he told of grandpa's death, after the Autumn 1929 crash: "When mother said, 'Your grandpa's dead,'" I shed no tears at all; but when my dog Lindy died, then I cried and cried.") The Alves family very probably were glad to see the irreverent and troublesome preacher move several states away, but neither were they bashful about holding on to the Hardin who mattered to them: Creighton, as usual, stayed on in Wisconsin, except for the year he and grandma lived in Hurley after his grandfather's death. Another year later, after the family moved to Arkansas, he became in practice what he had always been intended to be: his mother's and his grandmother's son. Louis' mom, while the marriage spiraled toward its demise (in 1937), stayed on with her husband except for a short time in 1930, when she went on the road as a saleswoman for a book (*The*

Lincoln Library). Louis, as always, lived with his father; he and Ruth went to school in Missouri that fall.

In hindsight, Louis' youth had two halves: the idyllic half ending in 1929, when he was thirteen and the family came back East, and the tragic half ending in 1943, when he was twenty-seven. Never normal or mainstream, he was moved by dramatic events during these years closer to the moment when he would assume responsibility for his own self-expression. While the events were occurring, of course, their effects were obscure. Moondog had just become a teenager in a mobile and unusual family, with a rich childhood behind him. He did not know what he wanted to be when he grew up, what he wanted to do for a living (other than avoiding the clergy), or even where he would be living a year later. No one could have predicted even roughly the arc of his future from the narrative of his past. Many years later, shortly before she died and long after she had last seen him, his mother remarked, upon hearing his music on a recording, that she could not believe her son had created such a thing. The Louis she had known, wild boy, random drummer, made in his father's image, was not the Moondog he had become, and she could no more understand his latest incarnation than his earlier ones. His father, who had died earlier, might have nodded in appreciation, if not approval, of the Viking. But his parents were probably too self-absorbed to notice what was blooming under their care, because it was an alien species. Ruth would disappear soon, forever, a rebel in her own quiet way, and Creighton would become a prominent surgeon. Louis would, in his own time, come to live on another planet.

Despite the Concord grapes, strawberries, blackberries, apples, plums, walnuts, and persimmons, Louis felt "confined" to forty acres—after Wyoming, Missouri made him feel "fenced-in," "hemmed-in," and "out of place." Coming out of the North and the West, the Hardins were again outsiders, viewed with suspicion if not hostility. Louis felt the antipathy, but he didn't help matters by boasting about the feats he had performed back at the frontier. He deservedly acquired the nickname "Windy." Although friends were hard to make, nonetheless Louis was fortunate in many ways. Dwight Parsons saved him from drowning after a deluge hurled him into the stream behind the Hurley canning factory; Ruby Eaton, the most beautiful girl he would ever see, starred opposite him in *Picture Girl*, an eighth-grade play; June Young, the school's best student, displayed the finest penmanship Louis would ever decipher; Edgar Ragsdale, as Louis' well-traveled and oft-battered nose will attest, was the best boxer, weight for age, in his time. He and Creighton had some rare brotherly moments together fishing in the mill pond behind the barn from a boat they built. Once Creighton tended a boil on Louis' neck so fastidiously that he seemed to Louis even then to "have the feel" for healing that led to his becoming a doctor. And, of course, there was the bulldog Lindy, who came with the place, so loved that he inspired Louis' *nom de plume* nearly twenty years later. His howling at the moon, reproduced in Louis' first 78 with the Spanish Music Center as *Moondog Symphony*, would also lead to the entertaining lawsuit he would file against Alan Freed a quarter-century down the road.

Tops and yo-yos were hot then. He grew from thirteen to sixteen and into high school. Along the way he met the second great teacher-love of his life, one for whom he had no romantic attachment but with whom he had the longest association, Ruth Sloan. Despite Louis' bizarre career and the distances between them, the two managed to stay in contact through fifty years. "Sister" Sloan he called her because of her patience and quiet inspiration, for he came to love her as dearly as he loved his sister, the two Ruths merging into the mother who was slipping out of his life.

He also felt the direct influence of musical training for the first time. Mr. Thomas formed and led the high school band, with Louis drumming. Mr. Graham came from Springfield to lead the community orchestra, Louis again drumming. Although he could read only values, not notes, he made up for his imprecision with enthusiasm on the set his mother had bought him. Once Mr. Graham brought his bigger and better orchestra to do a local concert, "to show us what it was all about." "The precision was a revelation to me..." Mr. Thomas picked Louis to go to a band concert in Springfield to see "bigger and better bands play bigger and better music," not just the simple marches such as "National Emblem" that they performed in Hurley.

Louis had always tinkered; his earliest efforts had led to original percussion instruments that served him until he finally had a drum set. Throughout his New York period he would forge one unique instrument after another, mostly percussive, building upon his earliest impulses for self-expression and continuing a lifelong, desperate quest for originality. He was "keen on making models out of wood" in his little workshop in the basement or in the barn loft, using designs from *Popular Mechanics* and *Popular Science* magazines. His freedom, craftsmanship, and curiosity—the strong sense he had of shaping the world because he was so often alone in it—led to the greatest catastrophe of his life, which severed him from the normal and the ordinary. No other event could have precipitated Moondog out of Louis Hardin more directly; in fact, Louis might never have even pursued a career in music, let alone the career he did, had he been fortunate enough to survive adolescence without this punishing trauma. After this, most other events in any life would seem inconsequential.

In spring 1932 the mill pond burst its banks, washing away a couple of shops and part of the mill. Louis was walking along the railroad tracks a few days after the flood when he picked up an interesting object and brought it home to his toolbox to scrutinize later. On the morning of July 4, 1932, shortly after his sixteenth birthday, he began to tinker with his discovery. It was a detonating cap, carelessly left behind by a construction crew, and he was blinded instantly and permanently when it exploded in his face. His left eye was so badly damaged that it was removed in Springfield by Dr. Kemp, who helped to make Louis' hospital stay a "joy" despite being the messenger with terrible news. Through his efforts the boy was taken to St. Louis, where Dr. Wiener tried to implant an artificial lens in his right eye. The operation, however, was "as painful as it was unsuccessful." Louis had to face the incredible reality that he would never see again. The physical pain was close to unendurable, unrelenting, a paralyzing torture. So many of the underpinnings had been knocked away; so little stood in their place. He was a healthy youth one day, curious if somewhat adrift, playful. The next day he was handicapped, dependant, confined. Few can empathize with such a loss, but to understand what it was like to absorb the punishment and move on is important, because of its role in what he became.

He described the first days of his blindness as like being "smothered alive." With nowhere to turn and his home in limbo, Louis drifted. One day a lady came by the Hardin house saying that she was working for the state. Louis never found out her name, but she did more for him in that one visit than did all the others with good intentions but no plan of action. She left him a metal Braille alphabet after teaching him how to use it. Out of the darkness began to emerge possibilities. For the rest of his life, no matter where he lived and in whatever conditions he worked, he would read and write with his fingers, encoding melodies as well as words.

The repercussions of his being blinded are hard to describe, because it is almost as though a new person emerged out of the experience and a second life struck out on its own, carrying only vestiges of what went before. One of the first things to go was his religious faith, which he had trusted because his father had preached it. It had obviously let him down. He couldn't know then that the old one would someday be replaced by what he came to call "the Alpha and Omega Tribulation Trail." In 1932 there was a void. Nor was his the only life transfigured. In Wisconsin Creighton wept; those closest to him remade their lives.

In his forty-second month in Hurley his dad swapped the farm for one in Shannon City, Iowa. Louis, meanwhile, was learning Braille in St. Louis from February to May 1933, not only adjusting to a new way of learning but also being humbled by what he didn't know about music. After rehearsing with the school orchestra, he was told gently he wouldn't be needed; he played too loudly and too often, as he was used to doing in the band, and not according to the written parts. He was hurt by the rejection but knew it was just. He did not understand symphonic drumming. In that summer of 1933 Louis registered at the Iowa School for the Blind, in Vinton, and there he came to understand his new place in the world a little more clearly. Everyone agreed it was his best shot.

That summer of 1933, when Louis turned seventeen, was momentous in a number of ways. Before he started at his new school his sister initiated an almost daily ritual of reading aloud to him that would continue for several years whenever he came home during school breaks, a cherished and unforgettable kindness. One of the earliest books she chose, Jesse Fothergill's historical novel *The First Violin*, electrified the blind proto-musician, "something in it making Buster bust the banks of his creative inactivity" long before he came to learn any of the specifics, "the score," as he puns, of what makes musical composition. As with so many books that mysteriously redirect a life, its effect, considering its style, content, and form, is hard to explain. It is a conventional first-person *bildungsroman* about a young English woman studying music in Germany, with enough romance and domestic intrigue (the enigmatic widower-violinist of the title, for instance) to support the lengthy passages on musical themes. Perhaps the novel aimed to inspire young musicians by providing a pleasurable (if conventional) edifice upon which to hang the lessons. If so, it worked for Louis. Here, for example, is the last paragraph:

> Between me and Eugen there has never come a cloud, nor the faintest shadow of one. Built upon days passed together in storm and sunshine, weal and woe, good report and evil report, our union stands upon a firm foundation of that nether rock of friendship, perfect trust, perfect faith, love stronger than death, which makes a peace in our hearts, a mighty influence in our lives which very truly "passeth understanding."

Out of this Louis somehow felt his "youthful spirit soar," and he resolved then to become a classical composer. As at many other turning points, his faith in himself triumphed over logic and prudence—to his credit and our enrichment. The irony of the resemblance between the diction in this novel, with its eulogy of the rock of friendship, and the boast by his parents in *Archdeacon Prettyman* that their marriage was built upon the rock of faith, eluded him (as did the literary inferiority of the two most important books in his young life). Reading *Beowulf* a year later convinced him that he would compose opera—especially after he had listened to Wagner on the radio, the *Ring* cycle on Saturday nights from the New York Metropolitan opera house, that work's "thunder-lightning" stunning him into a rare silence. Only in his final years in Germany, over fifty years later, did he realize this dream, because only then was he able to gather together the various parts of his enormous saga of the Creation. Though never fully produced, in its spaciousness and scope it answers Wagner and completes Moondog's celebration of Nordic culture, but the blind young man in Iowa could not know that he would have the audacity to challenge the master. He was merely absorbing the first inklings of a lifelong, evolving creative act. At the same time he began to write poetry. His first effort, a blank verse epic set in Alaska about a mythical-symbolic White Owl, unfinished and long lost, prefigures some of the amazing verse he published years later.

Altogether, the three years at Vinton (he graduated in 1936) were, despite momentary embarrassments, disappointments, and frustrations, fertile. A despondent boy, suddenly handicapped, became an increasingly self-sufficient young man with big and definite life goals. There, most importantly, Louis' musical education commenced. He studied piano, violin (within six weeks playing in the second violin section of the orchestra) and viola (later playing in the string quartet). He sang bass in the choir. Later still, during his summer vacation in Arkansas (where his dad had been forced to relocate), he took up the pipe organ. In Vinton he heard his first classical records and came to love the classical music broadcast over the radio: Wagner, Beethoven, Brahms, and Tchaikovsky entered his life for the first time. Most of the boys in the dorm wanted to hear about sports, but Louis, more and more the "loner" and "oddball," asked for the "heavy stuff," often in vain. He pushed himself so hard that he spent two weeks in the hospital as a result of severe anemia. But for the first time in his life he was driven, and it manifested in ways that became permanent personality traits. He would dress differently, look at things in a different way, and work hard at being original without breaking any of the rules of craft. At Vinton Louis became an endearing and challenging individual.

His instructors were characters worthy of a Dickens novel. First, there was the teacher-love indifferent to her pupil's star-crossed importunities. Louis wrote one of his earliest love sonnets to Daphne Evans, the third instructor he fell in love with, but not the last. She taught violin. Rather than confront the boy directly, she allowed the English teacher, Mrs. Koenig, to explicate proprieties and realities: Daphne, among other things, was engaged. Undeterred, Louis went to the source and knocked on her door to invite her to listen to some recordings. She confronted him with what he considered a condescending recommendation to mingle more with students his own age. When Louis, in the throes of romantic agony, replied that Beethoven didn't mingle, her reply dwindled to contempt: "You're not Beethoven." He thought, but didn't say, that Louis and Ludwig, at least, were the same name. Instead he recognized wisely that this door was closed.

Next, there was the autocratic but inspiring Prussian orchestra leader, Bernard Schaefer, who "had an Old World atmosphere about him, very Germanic in his precise manner and his attention to detail." Louis was rightly afraid of him, because he was very strict, but nonetheless recognized a "fine influence" when he encountered one. One Saturday afternoon, when he was in the basement practice room sawing off a hillbilly tune on the viola, he heard a tap at the window followed by clipped words: "Not that. Learn your parts." Louis did. Mr. Schaefer and Ms. Evans played violin in the Waterloo Symphony, and from his window Louis would hear them return from rehearsal, wishing himself by their sides.

Then there were the sinister overseers, Mr. and Mrs. Ryan, the dorm supervisors. The God O'Ryan, as Louis dubbed him, and his mate Vendetta Etta, a "spiteful nun," seemed to have it in for him: they reprimanded him when he was late for typing class, complained about his hair (grown to such an "arty" length that his peers christened him "Longfellow"), and once even recalled him from an unapproved trip to hear the Chicago Symphony Orchestra at a nearby college, "to leave all the fun and excitement and go back to the dull, drab, regimented existence" at school. But their authority was not absolute; once, when Mr. Ryan would not let Louis go to town, Mr. Palmer countermanded the "martinet" on the staircase. When Louis' dad was forced to move, Ryan was all for sending Louis packing, since he no longer officially resided in the state, but Mr. Palmer bent the rules to allow him time to graduate.

Among influential persons early in Louis' second life, one stands above all: Anna-May Sansom, the organ teacher, his first serious love. Louis fell in love with his much older teachers for reasons then obscure but in hindsight clear. Not only was this an unconscious attempt to relocate his lost mother, his first teacher-love; it was also a desperate attempt by a vulnerable boy with a brash public persona to find the secure home his parents had failed to provide. Since he could not see, looks were not important, and appearances otherwise irrelevant—the public be damned. Such women dominated the first decade or so of his blindness. By graduation day, in 1936, when he was twenty, he and Anna-May were, as he puts it, "on the same wave-length." She, however, was twice his age, and the hesitancy he showed just before he left to go home proved crucial. She was willing to get married; she only asked when. He said he had to go to college in order to be able to support her. The affair was left dangling until he was talked out of it back in Arkansas. Anna-May wrote to him, in Braille, corroborating his decision, one that he regretted then and believed until the end did not express his best self.

While Louis was finishing school and learning about music and love, Reverend Hardin was once more on an elaborate adventure of self-discovery. The first thing he discovered was that he had not yet become a farmer. Apparently Grandma Alves did not wait to act upon the news: she sold the farm in Shannon City and converted the money into an education loan to fund Creighton's medical studies at Madison a few years later. The preacher once more took to preaching. The 1935 edition of the *Presbyterian Journal for the Diocese of Arkansas* lists him as rector of Trinity Church, Van Buren (near Pine Bluffs). Louis, at home for vacation, practiced on the church's pipe organ every day, memorizing a Bach prelude and fugue in Braille, and also played at the Sunday services. He thought his Bach was pretty good until Anna-May told him to concentrate on exercises back in Vinton. For well over a year father and son lived in separate states until, after graduation, they reunited again in a new homestead, this time in Batesville, Arkansas, where from 1936 to 1938 dad was rector of St. Paul's Church.

The next couple of years brought many dramatic and drastic changes. At Batesville the Hardin family finally broke up. After Louis left for New York (1943), he never again met with his father, mother, sister, or brother, and scarcely ever wrote to or spoke with them. His parents both remarried and died, his sister disappeared, and his brother, after becoming a surgeon, ended contact between them. When Reverend Hardin came to Arkansas from Iowa, Louis' mother, as usual, stayed behind out west, teaching. During the 1936–1937 academic year, when Louis was a freshman at Arkansas College, a small Presbyterian school in Batesville, the family was briefly together one last time as all three Hardin children attended the school. Louis looked especially well-groomed in his yearbook picture. But soon mom was gone for good, the Hardins were officially divorced—a quarter-century after they were married and fifteen years after they published *Archdeacon Prettyman in*

Politics—and Creighton was in premed school near grandma. Ruth stayed, becoming Louis' surrogate mother, a relationship that both troubled him and soothed his wounds, as ambivalent as the one with mom: uncertain, necessary, and ultimately broken.

If Louis' dad was the major force in his life, then after his blindness Ruth ran a close second. When he was still at Vinton, Ruth would take him to hear concerts. She even bought him a new suit—charged to his father's account. Then, as later, her gifts were double-edged: she charged so much and in so many places that her father told the stores to close her out. Once Louis had given her some money to get a book on orchestration from Chicago, which he patiently but excitedly awaited. Every day she would visit him during his practice with an ice cream cone, and every day she answered him that the book had not arrived. After a month or so she finally broke down, admitting that she had spent the money. The ice cream cones had seemingly been a daily atonement. Although he loved her, and would forever appreciate her indulgences, Louis distrusted her, much as he distrusted his father. She had learned from a master. Such early insecurity within the nuclear family and under the auspices of a religious life hardened in him a cynicism that marked his dealings with people in New York. What role models for a young boy, later a blind young man, were Louis' family members, especially the minister. He grew up on a muscular but uncaring Christianity.

Other sureties also were undermined. In Batesville, he learned to doubt the faith of his father, in part because of the books Ruth read to him. The two would get up early, pack a light lunch and some paperbacks on philosophy and science, and walk to a favorite reading place on a wooded hill outside town. Before his twenty-first year he had not seriously questioned the existence of the Christian God, although he had his doubts; after these sessions he would never again believe, no more so than in Santa Claus or the Easter Bunny after the age of ten. "I thought that if the God my father preached about was good, He wouldn't have let it happen to me. And if He was all-powerful and looking the other way at the time, He would have restored my sight. But He did neither, and I lost my faith." Into the vacuum created by the negation of his inherited dogma Louis would later pour patterns of belief that he had scarcely entertained in 1937, "a new outlook on the world based on the so-called laws of nature and one's relation to them." Nearly thirty years later he would will into belief a divinity of his own choosing "on discovering the Nordic pantheon, through the *Eddas*, which became meaningful because I wanted them to be." In his first year in Batesville, however, there was a profound loneliness, an emptiness without an explanation.

Louis was resourceful nonetheless, and tried to fill his life with meaning. Ruth's compensatory kindnesses as his world (sight, family, faith) crumbled supported his spirit for a time: she took him to hear the St. Louis Symphony, constantly supplied him with new intellectual materials, and even wanted to join him when he went to New York. But her love was too possessive, too disorienting, too smothering, and Louis fled, in large part to shed his old skin, to develop a new man out of the old boy. He needed "freedom of choice and action," "independence of thought and feeling." He had a lukewarm conversation with Ruth in 1948, in Santa Fe, after he had put off seeing her in New York. After that he never heard from her again. Of course he missed her. He recalled that she had been the best euphonium player in the Hurley High School Band, and he remained partial to this instrument, the cello of the band, ever thereafter: some of his later marching band music must have been silently dedicated to her. He could never forget her reading *The First Violin* to him, or how it changed his life. She had a "lasting influence" on him where it really mattered, more good than bad.

Louis' music grew in importance. Besides learning Braille and then music in Braille, he had to train himself to listen to music (on the radio at first) and transcribe it. As he put it much later (in the *Christian Science Monitor*, Sept. 3, 1970): "At first I didn't reproduce it exactly, but gradually by doing it over many years I developed an ability to write down what I had heard, so that if I could write down what I heard on the radio then I could write down what I heard in my head." He needed time to build upon what he had learned in Iowa, but what he needed more than anything else was another teacher, someone who could instill in him a devotion to what became a constant in his career as a composer: counterpoint.

Bess Maxfield was the last great teacher-love of his youth. At Arkansas College and for six years afterward, she helped him more than anyone else did. Patiently, after class, Bess would read and dictate music to Louis that was unavailable in Braille. In her family's 1880 home, with its "one of a kind" hexagonal front room and surrounding porch, she had, according to one contemporary, "more impact on Louis Hardin's life than any other." (Letter, Conway Hail, Jr., March 24, 1979.)

> Often I would see Louis and Miss Bess walking past on the way to her home where she gave him music lessons for several years. In the summer months she would read to him for hours. He would take notes on his Braille typewriter.

Another student recalls their "gifted and caring" teacher and the intimate classes. She also recalls how surprisingly "normal" Louis had become in so short a time:

> Some of the non-music related things I remember include walks with Louis out to "the bluff" where we talked of our dreams and I would sometimes describe the valley below. I remember one "daring" walk back along the railroad track. The most surprising association was the date we had to go "see" a movie. I had not known a blind person before and it had not occurred to me that he would enjoy a movie. I even hoped, perhaps, that it was my company he wanted to enjoy. I was a bit anxious and remember waiting for him to pick me up. He walked the five or six blocks to my house and I heard him come tapping up the front walk. From then on it was like any other date with an interesting young man—a movie, a Coke, a slow walk home. (Letter, Frances Pultz, May 3, 1979.)

One day Louis awkwardly handed to this young lady a sonnet, titled "No. 7," the earliest surviving piece of Moondog literature, printed here with minor corrections.

> Relinquish not thy post as Nature's bard,
> Oh lovely muse of pure angelic song?
> Continue in that stead, fair loveliness, and do
> Not lavish thy sweet murmurings amiss,
> Upon a wanton flower's standing guard
> As through thy measur'd haunt all Nature's throng
> Does bow with crowned heads to let thee through,
> Whilest from thy blushing lips descends a kiss.
> With humble Reticence beside me, quite
> Observant of my doing, I am leashed
> In chains of cold repression. 'Tis not my lot
> To be a river of clear revelation.
> My heart can but proclaim a part of that
> Serenity that lofty souls have known.

While life for Louis, after a bleak interruption, seemed once more to be filled with potential, dad still had a trick or two up his sleeve. In 1938 Louis had four years before permanent estrangement from his father. In the quiet years after he left Arkansas College to work at odd jobs on his and other farms, little of consequence occurred. It was, however, a pregnant stillness, because psychologically Louis was moving beyond his handicap toward a striking break from his past. At first it was painful, the insecurity paralyzing at times, the inertia frustrating. After the divorce in 1937, Rev. Hardin was still permitted to preach. Coming secretly to him, though, was a widow by the name of Mary Altman, whom he married in 1938. This was, finally, one step too far beyond the rules, even for the protean survivor who had bent them for two decades, and he was formally defrocked at a ceremony held on December 19, 1938 at which he voluntarily renounced the ministry. Soon his new wife bought a farm, and there dad and son lived until, to the great relief of all, Louis left. Before he did he began once more to grow his hair long and, for the first time in his life, a beard which he would never shave off. He also began to make his own clothes, another trademark of the image he would grow into. Although dad complained, he didn't force a change. Ruth, who had dressed him for years, was upset at the ponchos he fashioned out of square pieces of cloth in memory of the Indians he had known as a child, and she never could bring herself to approve of this mode of self-expression. During most of this time Bess Maxfield was the one joyous constant in his life, and it was fitting that she introduced him to the woman who finally helped him to fuller freedom and independence, his wife-to-be.

Virginia Sledge came from a prominent family in Memphis and was, like Louis' other loves, nearly twenty years older than he. She taught singing and had been commuting to Batesville weekly when they first met. Louis had been going through a second crisis, almost as bad as his first, at "the very edge," in his own words, when she "rescued" him. "If it hadn't been for her I don't know what I would or could have done." She loved him when all the love seemed to have slipped out of his life and much of the hope along with it. She also found him a sponsor in Memphis, the music lover and phil-anthropist I.L. (Ike) Myers, who was willing to pay for Louis' schooling and even support him afterwards. From February to November 1943 Louis studied at the Southern College of Music under Prof. Tuthill, and he and Virginia became lovers. During this time he befriended the photographer Saul Brown. Saul remembers Louis posing for life-drawing class at Saul's school—a sideline Louis found helpful later on in New York.

It was a long eight months, and Louis had little money. He often went to Saul Brown's for dinner. His friend even bought him a pair of treasured tennis shoes. Virginia found him lodging in a shack behind a boys' home whose director, Father Lane, turned the children into tinker toys (so Louis was convinced). The two became inseparable: on a bus she defended his grooming and dress against some giggling Memphis mothers: "In twenty years you'll be glad you saw him." She introduced him to some of her wealthy friends as "the young composer." Finally, she proposed marriage. It had to be secret because of her family, so they went over the line into Arkansas for a simple, quiet ceremony. The marriage itself, after the prolonged courtship, was brief; both came to realize that it was a mistake for many reasons. She knew that she would never be able to assume a role in her social world with Louis as her mate, and he knew that the bohemian yearnings he now felt so strongly would force him to lead a life she would find uncomfortable and perilous. Thus Louis' first marriage, at the age of twenty-seven, scarcely survived that summer of 1943.

By November Louis had come to a startling decision. He had the support of Ike Myers (who generously agreed to continue his modest stipend), his sister Ruth, and Saul Brown, who sent a few dollars from time to time. (The money stopped when Louis sent back some of his early poetry, which Saul thought anti-Semitic. When Ike Myers also received the verses he considered Louis ungrateful, but this was after he had stopped sending money. Louis wrote some early anti-Semitic poems he later published in New York in *The Milleniad*, a work of which only poor copies survive.) Though the impulse can be explained as an autodidact's inability to distinguish history from myth, Louis was rightly embarrassed later by these inexcusable juvenilia. What Ezra Pound (repentant of his own Axis propagandizing) came to call a "stupid suburban prejudice" was exposed as such, and he was confined to an insane asylum rather than executed for treason. For Louis it was probably a misguided attempt to draw closer to his Nordic roots.

With his aggregated allowances, Louis made the first of several geographical leaps: irrational, perhaps, and probably irreversible, but supported by faith in himself. He, a poor music student who did some modeling, blind but fiercely independent, would move to New York City. He would become an artist, a composer. He left behind his family, whom he would never meet again. His confidence must surely have been mind-boggling to his friends and loved ones, but despite Virginia's "tears and fears" and all the predictable warnings, he was committed to going to

Babylon without an acquaintance to call up or safety net of any kind. Until November 1943 Louis had been, in some form or another, a child of his father, a victim of circumstances, a student of several formative teachers, a lover, a husband, and a composer in training. He had never, though, been alone. Childhood's end can come in many shapes and sizes and at any age, but few have known one as dramatic as Louis', his face in the window of a bus heading from the Mississippi to the Hudson, to a brave and utterly unpredictable new world.

Part Two

The Tree of Life

(1943–1953)

Chapter Three

Snaketime

(1943–1953)

New York City is a frightening place for a stranger just off the
bus, poor and poorly connected. For a blind musician new to
being on his own, only a few months away from his father's house
and days from his first wife, the experience might seem overpower-
ing. But Louis adapted quickly and well to big-city life, and within
days was on his way to becoming self-supporting. More important
for the composer-to-be, he began to make music. The next decade
was eventful: a romance, an exciting association with the New York
Philharmonic; a cross-country trip; his first parcel of country land;
his earliest recordings and first street performances; and his second
marriage. He would become soon what he was to remain for a long
time: to some, a genuine and original artist; to others, an affected
eccentric; to still others, an enigma and even a threat. In 1947 he
would christen himself Moondog, the only name he would use pro-
fessionally, emerging, as he saw it, a new man at thirty-one, making
a fresh start out of much loneliness and pain. From the moment he
stepped off the bus, he was indisputably in charge of his own life.

It was chilly that Saturday morning in November 1943 when he
"hit the sidewalks of New York." After staying at a hotel for a few
nights (at two dollars per night) he realized that his pocket money
(sixty dollars, some of it from Ruth in Texas, and some from I.L.
Meyers) would soon run out, so he set out to find a room and a job.
Fortunately, he met an art model, who introduced him into several

academies, including the Phoenix School, where he made some money posing. The same young man also found him cheap lodgings in Midtown. Like all of his New York apartments, it was not luxurious, but it became his home for the next four years, a tiny skylight room at five dollars per week in a building at 332 West 56th Street (long since demolished). It was, to a visitor who followed him up four flights of stairs "two at a time" (Natalie Davis in *PM Magazine*, Jan. 13, 1945), cold and small, decidedly uninviting (cold because Louis kept the skylight open always, and as small as a "large closet," with a padded sleeping bag on the floor beside a portable organ). Some crates, Braille books, and a tiny electric stove filled the little remaining floor space. In such Spartan digs, eating in was usually confined to porridge in the morning. His diet when he dined out consisted mainly of raw vegetables, fruit, and black bread.

In a second-floor studio was the much older Anna Naila, who became first his best friend and then his next great love. Their relationship lasted for most of the four years they spent living in the same building and until 1947, when Louis pressed his desire to marry her. It ended when he decided, for the first of many times, to leave New York. She not only was yet another mother figure, but also influenced his early music. She was the first of several committed copyists—intelligent, devoted musicians who, often gratis, worked painstakingly for the artist they believed in. Anna transcribed the music he wrote at a desk or table, without an instrument, one note at a time: "He has to read each note to me," she said. "He has to say 'half note third line, full note first,' and so forth. It takes a long time." To an eyewitness this "small, sallow-faced woman in slacks" with her "long black hair neatly rolled into a bun" was visibly tired by this effort. To Louis she was a revelation: a classical dancer, a ballet teacher, "quite oriental-looking," laboriously transcribing his work at a card table. To her he dedicated his earliest "classical" pieces, "Callisto" in 1946, a twelve-part canon on an eight-bar theme, and "Portrait of a Monarch" around 1945 (conceived then and worked out several decades later). Two rhythm pieces recorded in her dance studio during a lesson appeared on albums in the late Fifties.

From the beginning he wrote as much music as he could in as little space as possible, rounds and madrigals that yielded the most sound for the least ink. One work, "Lullaby," music by Louis, words by Anna, and dedicated to "Wendy's doll, Margaret," survives in the possession of a mother, Magda Luft, whose daughter danced to the efforts of the collaborators.

Louis quickly became a social animal, even a minor celebrity, in a midtown bohemian circle. One young lady, Barbara Prentice, was so taken with Louis when he modeled in her art class in 1944 that she began taking him out. Since her father was an editor at Time-Life, these were exciting and glamorous events. A singer at the Abyssinian Baptist Church in Harlem, Elsie Marcello, befriended him and enriched his quest for a musical identity, introducing him to the Negro spiritual. They went to Coney Island several times. Two young women from Princeton who sang in a chorus with the New York Philharmonic one Easter took him on a tour of the Cloisters. A bohemian poetess with a social statement to make, Mary Siegrist, arranged a party in 1944 for Louis and another honored guest, Raymond Duncan, the brother of Isadora, who also dressed in clothes of his own creation. Unlike Louis' utilitarian squares, Mr. Duncan's were "elaborate and expensive," wool woven into a classic toga. Ms. Siegrist often entertained Louis in her Carnegie studio, and she composed the first poetic celebration of the new force in town, "Young Blind Composer."

> Lone traveler on your mountain height
> Enshadowed in what depthless depths of light,
> Leaning against what darkness,
> Taking the darkness for pillow for your head—
> As pillow, softly encompassing you
> What inner light irradiates all your world,
> What inner gleam shines to the far-off worlds,
> What unspent inner flame is burning through the night?
> How came you here, staffed Wayfarer,
> Part plunged in what a darkness,
> But with remembered joy still singing in the heart?

Though this cannot be taken seriously as verse, it articulates the frenzied adulation Louis would always elicit from some. His energy, creativity, and inexplicable self-assurance cowed the weak and awed the strong. Since he was then (July 1944) a set of characteristics in search of a character, self-definition often came in strange, unpredictable forms and from exotic directions.

Sometimes independence causes trouble, as Louis soon found out. Throughout his life in New York he would have legal troubles of varying seriousness: the first one came in the mid-1940s, when he was selling his earliest broadside, "Pen and Sword," on the streets. It contained social criticism by Louis as well as some excerpts from leftist writers, came out "irregularly" in editions of one thousand, and sold for a nickel from 1945 through 1948. Although all copies now seem to be lost, it is clear from interviews taken not many years later that his ideas were then crude and less idiosyncratic than his thought in the Sixties. (In 1946 he and Naila wrote a United Nations march hymn which he either sold or gave away; all thousand copies of this work are also lost.) One day a policeman led him into a side street. When he asked why, after waiting a couple of minutes, he was answered by the arrival of a paddy wagon into which he was pushed. By the time they reached the station house, one of the policemen had a torn shirt. The night court judge fined Louis two dollars after the arresting officer charged him with causing crowds. With the money Louis left a copy of "Pen and Sword" with the judge. His first, he notes wryly, "but not last, brush with the law."

The single most exciting and long-lasting encounter of his earliest years in New York, though, was his romance in many keys with the New York Philharmonic. There are several accounts of these four years, including Louis', a reporter's, and that of Halina, the wife of conductor Artur Rodzinski (*Our Two Lives*, New York, 1976, pp. 247–248). Louie (as he preferred to be called then, because "people get Louis mixed up with Lewis") was conspicuous: "His face was long, pale, ascetic, his cheekbones were high. The hairs of his flowing brown beard glistened.... His long thick hair was tied in a knot at the back ... and a brown kerchief knotted about his neck was decorated by a silver chain from which hung an Indian arrowhead." So he was noticed his first Sunday in New York, when he sat front row center at the Philharmonic broadcast concert, Bruno Walter conducting, Joseph Schuster cello soloist in Richard Strauss' *Don Quixote*. Here the accounts differ. According to Louis, smitten with devotion, he found the stage door entrance one day soon afterward and managed to climb a flight of stairs before the doorman, Joe Nelson, soon to become a close friend, stopped him. The orchestra rehearsal was at intermission, and Mr. Schuster happened along to notice his admirer. He had no trouble recollecting the singular man in front row and asked Louis if he would like to attend the rehearsal. Louis had hardly replied when maestro Rodzinski was fetched to make the invitation official. Then, in a "monumental moment," the conductor led Louis down the center aisle of Carnegie Hall to a seat and said, "Enjoy yourself."

According to the Philharmonic press agent in the 1945 *PM* article, Artur Rodzinski noticed Louis at the stage door entrance and was so impressed by this man "with the face of Christ" that he allowed him the unique privilege of attending all rehearsals, and also gave him some new clothing. Soon Louis befriended many in the orchestra, even becoming something of a good luck charm, a "mascot." They took up collections to supplement his meager income from modeling or, according to Halina Rodzinski, "making leather belts." Under the patronage of the conductor, who was then undergoing a religious conversion, Louis had great privileges, but, even more important, he witnessed the day-to-day business of making music. For a while, all was bliss. Summers, there were concerts at Lewisohn Stadium in the Bronx; for the rest of the year there were the rehearsals, which he never missed, when he met many musical luminaries, some of whom he would work with later.

There were internationally famous soloists such as Schnabel and Elman. There was a dazzling constellation of conductors, Metroupolis and Szell, for instance. Szell asked the orchestra's trombones to "sound like granite" during Brahms' Fourth Symphony, and Louis wrote a letter noting that playing without vibrato would do it (he always preferred pure, straight tones). Szell agreed. Leonard Bernstein, at the start of his fabulous career, once conducted Louis to the men's room. Later he called one of the compositions Louis submitted to the orchestra "Schubertian," but never chose for performance any of the scores Louis sent him during his long tenure. In 1945, at a grand affair in Madison Square Garden, Arturo Toscanini conducted the combined Philharmonic and NBC orchestras in an evening of Wagner. There the great one spied the anomaly, and when Artur pressed Louis upon Arturo, the young devotee was moved to press the maestro's hand to his lips. Toscanini pulled it away, however, observing wryly that he was "not a beautiful woman."

Louis made many friends in the orchestra, talented musicians who were mostly "princely" toward him. Bill Lindser played first viola on the two suites recorded on Epic in 1954. Julius Baker, the renowned flutist, recorded the album *Tell It Again* in 1957. The Weiner-Sabinski duo recorded several compositions on the first Prestige album in 1957. Harold Gomberg was so friendly that Louis would later write a madrigal about him and his instrument: "Mister O, Mister Boe, Mr. Oboe player, the orchestra would like to have an 'A' before it starts to play."

The smooth and the sweet relationship, however, soon soured, because of both professional jealousies and Louis' growing independence. According to Mrs. Rodzinski, Louis sold a suit, an overcoat, and a walking stick that Artur had given him. Louis countered that a thief broke into his room and stole the goods. The real issue, though, was not how the conductor's clothing disappeared, but why: Louis, on "the crest of an independence kick," would stand firm about his right to dress as he wished. He would take the handsome shoes Halina purchased for him and treasure the gifts from her husband, but he relied less and less on garments not of his own making. As soon as he first cobbled together his own shoes (in April 1944), he "hobbled" over in them to the Lotus Club to join the orchestra at its annual affair. On the drive home, as the Rodzinskis took Louis to his door, Artur asked him if he wanted to come live with them at their Massachusetts farm and their East 84th town-house—against the wishes of his wife, who objected that there wasn't room enough. If she had not presented logical objections, Louis might have accepted. As it happened, though, a distance grew between the two men, exacerbated by grumblings from the orchestra, some of whose members resented Louis' privileges and the collection taken up for him. When Artur insisted that they have a long talk about clothes, Louis shortened it to the rejoinder that he would dress in his own style. Although he was permitted this license, attitudes cooled. Against the "bitchiness of frustrated players," and against what appeared to be a wife's desire to prevent her prominent husband from being seen as eccentric, Louis had little recourse. But while he was there he learned much: "orchestration and administration of same," and, up close, the quality and the variety of the music that would be his lifeblood through the challenging years ahead. His favorite composition at this time was Mozart's G Minor Symphony, because of its "perfect blend of the classic and romantic ideal." These Philharmonic years were a time of synthesis, acquisition, and growth. Afterwards he would write more and more of his own music, "write my fool head off," and develop his own interests, models, and idiom. His years of attending rehearsal, of not only listening to what was being played but also learning what went into the playing, fueled rather than deflected his ambitions. He would always cherish these moments and these people; he would always be grateful to the Rodzinskis. Moving on, he glanced fondly back.

Although Halina Rodzinski and Louis differ on the course of events in these years, it seems to be not out of rancor. She genuinely gave much of herself to Louis: she tried to get him into Juilliard (which was not equipped to handle handicapped students, he was told) and took him to a noted eye specialist in a vain attempt to appropriate the latest technology. But later she snubbed or misunderstood him. Her book's tone in describing Moondog and his music is condescending. She erroneously attributes the "jukebox hit" song "Nature Boy" to him (another New York street character, eden ahbez, wrote it). Once, in the late Fifties, after Artur had died, Louis was passing through Lake Placid, where he knew she had a vacation home. When he phoned, she told him only that she had no car, and he moved quietly on. In 1969 they met on a Manhattan street, but she avoided his admittedly lukewarm attempt at rapprochement. It was, after all, Artur's visitation that opened the door for Louis and Louis himself, more than any other, who closed it. But not everyone saw him in the same light.

In 1947, thirty-one years old, in New York four years, drifting away from the Rodzinskis and soon to journey cross-country, Louis made a singular decision. He was at another crossroads. Much impressed by Omar Khayyam, as by exotic and original authors throughout his life, he set several dozen quatrains from *The Rubaiyat* to music. He also wrote his first cycle of canons for two violins and viola, performed for friends in Naila's studio. All of this music is lost. Although he was stepping out, independent as he was, he was still too closely allied with the past. Unknown, except as an eccentric with musical talent, he lacked direction and definition. So he would give himself a new identity, thereby breaking the tyranny of naming. One day, he mulled over the possibility of a pen name for himself in his skylight room and finally hit on one suggested by an old friend. Lindy, the dog that came with the Hurley, Missouri farm, always howled at the moon. Hobbling on three feet (the fourth being lame from early on), running circles around Louis, Lindy was a meek, mild mongrel. Calmly, with great self-assurance, he walked downstairs and told Naila, "I am Moondog." Although he would remain Louis to his friends, it was as Moondog that the world would come to know him. Only later did the full potential of his *nom de guerre* emerge: to the Eskimos the moondog is a moonlight rainbow; in the Edda it is a fierce pack of wolves with flaming tails of comets circling the earth; in the sagas it is a giant of tremendous power. There is even a whiskey in Kentucky called Moondog. He knew nothing of these resonances at the time, but in choosing such an identity—primitive, suggestive, melodic, combative—he began to shape the music he would make and the man he would become.

With the renaming came many other changes. It was as though once he assumed the right posture he became more aggressive in claiming his place. 1948 brought Moondog movement, and 1949 brought him land. After the leisurely pace (in retrospect) of the Rodzinski-Naila years, change accelerated, and Moondog was constantly innovating to keep up with it. When it was clear that he and Naila would not marry and that his long association with the Philharmonic had come to an end, though not necessarily as a result of these closures, he decided to leave New York for another life, an alternate route to his musical future. He cannot be accused of a half-hearted effort, yet his break with Gotham was short-lived, and for good reasons. Much happened in a couple of years, each event a crucial ingredient in the recipe for his identity as a New York fixture and a serious musician.

In the spring of 1948 he left for the Southwest, planning to live among the Indians. With a little hindsight he came to call this venture, which he didn't complete until 1951, with interruptions, his Portland- (Oregon) to-Portland (Maine) trip. The main reason for the change was what he learned when he got to New Mexico and sought out a people he had always considered his mystic kin. His childhood encounter had left an aura that the adult believed would illuminate his calling. When he left, he assumed he would leave behind the "cocacola culture" for one more primal, radical, and essential. Upset, perhaps, disillusioned slightly, motivated by an inner vision, Moondog would return to his past and discover the key to his future. It didn't turn out that way.

He was Moondog in June 1948 when he boarded the Greyhound bus for the West. As with all of his public acts thenceforth, the trip is well documented. Moondog would always be a favorite of the press, not only because he looked different, but also because whenever he opened his mouth something interesting, and usually something controversial, came out; he was articulate as well as eccentric, intelligent as well as imposing. He would leave in his wake many friends and good memories, pleasant feelings and earned pleasures. He would impress public officials and important musicians. But his mission to the West failed. There had been hints:

his friends in New York had cautioned him that he really wasn't cut out to be a missionary (even those who were unaware of his father). A woman in Texas, riding beside him on a bus across the Panhandle, wished him well after he told her his destination, but also hoped that he wouldn't be disillusioned. In New Mexico, he camped outside the Navajo reservation by the highway, wrote some songs, and made contact. If not hostile, his reception was at best lukewarm.

> I couldn't reach the old ones who were suspicious of me as a white, to say nothing of the language barrier. The young could speak English but they were looking over my shoulder at the culture I was leaving and I was looking over their shoulders at the primitive life they wanted to leave and forget, so neither of us saw each other in the process.

He had been so "arrested" by their "out of doors concept of living" (which he would always practice as well as preach) and by the "dim and distant past" that had shaped them and their customs, traditions, and language as to only belatedly realize that he was not welcome. Yes, he could play his flute at public performances, but he could get no nearer. To his dismay—how could he have been so naive?—he saw such marked internal discrimination, enforced by a rather cruel community pecking order (such as he was also to observe in the black ghettoes of Los Angeles), that he felt more than rejected: he felt "thrown back on his own ethnic past." The first murmurs from the old Norse in the man with the face of Christ, the "square" man with homemade clothes, sandals, and beard, might have occurred the day he was led out to an island in the highway by some peculiarly vindictive Indian youths and left there helplessly stranded between two busy streams of traffic. After his rescue, he left for Santa Fe.

The disappointment and frustration, however, did infect the rest of the trip, and until September of 1949, when he returned to New York, most of his adventures had been benign and enriching. One sad moment occurred in Santa Fe, though he couldn't know it at the time, when he talked to sister Ruth on the phone: it was the last time he

would ever hear her voice or, indeed, hear of her. She simply disappeared. He did see Leonard Bernstein, who quipped that he had a
date in Israel and Santa Fe was on the way, and he did meet a young
lady with whom he briefly fell in love. Jeannie was "the girl with the
velvet voice," as he celebrated her in song, who "may be a hermit" but
who made his heart "sing / like a hermit thrush in spring."

On he went: in Salt Lake City a policeman helped him make his
first pair of square drums out of pine scraps and leather oddments
from a company that made artificial legs. In Los Angeles he wrote
words for the tune he had composed in 1947, "Moondog," about
that dog howling at the moon, and a dance step, called "L'Ameri-
cana," to accompany the piece in 5/4 time. Even before he recorded
it several years later, therefore, snaketime went public. (When a
ballerina first heard the slippery, pulsing five or seven beats to a
measure, she had called it "snakey.") It stuck. The dance, he advised
those who interviewed him, would end the tyranny of "backward
dancing by women" and "replace the waltz in popularity." In one
newspaper, he is quoted: "No cheek to cheek will do... It will be
brush forward with the feet and dip... It can't fail. It will be to this
century what the waltz has been in the past. It has boogie beaten."
Although he created animated responses to his new wares, no new
dance sensation erupted unto the scene due to his efforts. He did,
however, meet and impress Duke Ellington while in Los Angeles, a
significant achievement indeed. The Million Dollar Theatre held an
amateur contest that Moondog tried out for and won, playing "a
little waltz-like piece in the Chopin style." The Ellington Band was
playing the theatre at the same time, and the great jazz figure asked
to meet the winner backstage. Moondog met not only the Duke,
but also Al Hibler, the blind singer, soon to record several big hits.
All of his new friends never failed to look him up whenever they
came east. The list of celebrities at "Moondog's corner" in the Sixties often reads like a Who's Who of the entertainment world. He
knew all of them by voice, and they couldn't miss him if they tried.

Wherever he went he attracted crowds, so it was always with a
little trepidation that he entered a strange, new place.

In traveling around the country like I did, sort of barnstorming, not knowing anyone, you could never tell until you got to a new town what the reaction would be. I am not talking about the reaction of people, as such, but rather the business community, by and large hostile to any outsider coming to town ... cutting down on sales. After all, they are paying rent.

Despite some resistance, he encountered little difficulty and no harassment. Willow Springs, California did send out a cop to ask him to leave, and Moondog was very fond of the argument: "You're too rich for our blood." More often than not he met marvelous people who treated him to unexpected bounties: Dolores House in Taft, for instance, invited him to her desert home for a few days, and there he went for walks "into the desert evenings, barefoot on the sand." There were others, nearly all female, who entertained him in a string of towns and cities in the west.

North to Portland, Oregon he went, via Eugene, where he was reportedly "selling his sheet music as he goes from city to city," and impressing the residents as "that man in square clothes." "My earrings, shoes and even my tent are made out of squares. I make all these things myself." Moreover, he declared: "I do not dress differently to get noticed. I get noticed because I dress differently." Casuistry aside, Moondog picked up his pace. Though he rarely hitchhiked (it being dangerous), he did arrive at Idaho Falls, as he puts it in one of his madrigals, by "rule of thumb" rather than by bus. There he picked up a tanned elkskin, which he sent to a taxidermist to become his new cape. On to Cheyenne and other points east. In Rochester, New York, he purchased maracas and clavas to replace the knobbed wooden sticks he had used for over a year. By September 1949 he was back in New York City.

If his jaunt cross-country had proven anything to him, it was that he was "determined to make a noise" upon his return: he would "waylay them in doorways"; he would "make things happen" on the streets. Since the traditional routes to success, through offices and auditions, hadn't worked, he needed a new offensive, bolder and fresher. Thus snaketime came alive on the streets of New York, exotic rhythms translated by the performer's commensurate skills. "Mr. Rhythm" would be one of his sobriquets, the off-beat percussionist who not only created odd music in 5s and 7s (and who knows what else), but who also fashioned new instruments to lend the rhythms greater distinction, thereby, intentionally, attracting even more attention. First came triangular drums (later called "trimbas") because they held their shape better and longer, then wilder percussive mutants with names such as "oo" and "uni" and "utsu." Also, for the first time in his life, Moondog began to live on the streets and make his living through the lawful occupation of begging. It was a full-time commitment to an artistic way of life he came to emblematize.

Life was hard but stimulating. With no home and little money, he rented an old panel truck parked alongside some other wrecks near the Polo Grounds in the Bronx from a garage man for fifty cents a night. He went regularly to the 51st Street Greyhound bus terminal, checked his baggage in a locker, and spent twenty-five cents on a shower. At night, he played snaketime in the doorways. The first time he dared perform was on 32nd Street west of 8th Avenue, in front of a bank, but an official soon came out and dispersed the early evening crowd. Then he moved uptown, into the Fifties, and worked at night, before larger and more appreciative audiences. One evening he "trommelt" in a doorway on the west side of Sixth Avenue, between 51st and 52nd Streets, when the owner came out to quarrel with the intrusion but wound up instead asking Moondog if he would like to make a record at his studio. Though his music itself was never left to chance, many other aspects of his artistic development were. The man was Gabriel Oller, proprietor of the Spanish Music Center, who soon became a patron, partner, and friend, as did his wife, Inez. Since money was a severe problem (Moondog only earned about five dollars a day on the streets, and he now had to pay to get his music copied), he accepted the offer to sleep on the basement floor during the day, because he was then free to record and perform at night. Within months, over winter 1949–1950, four 78s were produced, most of the music on them later remastered or rere-corded on the albums Moondog made in the mid- to late 1950s: *Snaketime Rhythms* (SMC 2523), side A "5 Beat," side B, "7 Beat"; *Moondog Symphony* (SMC 2526), side A "Timberwolf," side B "Sagebrush"; *Organ Rounds*, 1 and 2 (SMC 2527); and "Oboe Rounds," "Chant," "All Is Loneliness," and "Wildwood" (SMC 2528). Through what was then unusually complex over-dubbing, Moondog played all of the instruments, including drums, hollow logs, cymbals, trimbas, and maraccas, and of course he sang. In one newspaper interview he stated that he was "studying every instru-ment in the orchestra" in order to "record a whole symphony by himself"—something he came close to, though modestly, with *Theme* a few years later. By 1950 he was composing rounds and madrigals with such regularity that it took on the fervor of commit-ment, and he would write them for the rest of his career.

In the program notes of his later albums, and especially the lavish *Around the World of Sound* in 1971, he would expound his theory of composition, which he knew to be necessitated by eco-nomic realities: much music in a minimum of space. "All Is Loneliness" is his first and most famous, written on 51st Street between Broadway and Seventh Avenue, a melancholy, dirge-like tune in 5/4, like many of his earliest lyrics, as he told one reporter, "quite bitter." Here are two others: "You the vandal, plunder the vil-lage as you will. The earthworm will pillage you, the vandal, when you are under." The second could only have been written by some-one who had come, literally, to live in shadows: "You remind me of someone that I know." "How could you?" "Just look a little closer and you will see that I am the one I remind you of."

The young Allen Ginsberg, in his journal entry for April 17, 1952, wrote:

> Tacked on wall—Song by Moondog—
> "I won't go to your dark bed,
> if I do there be many eternities
> of night I'll regret it—"—a round.

Years later, the same poet, now a prominent voice in American letters and far more famous, appeared onstage with Moondog in an anti-Vietnam war protest rally. He even held the microphone. Moondog was becoming by the early 1950s an underground star.

Notoriety came, but it never brought him riches. Living on rooftops (his favorite was the YMCA on Broadway) or in a van, writing in a special pouch during cold weather to prevent his fingertips from freezing, eating chocolate bars and whole wheat bread stashed in the folds of his poncho—all took their toll. By March of 1950 he was ill from exposure. A friend was able to get him an inexpensive room at 101 West 44th Street, the Aristo Hotel, where Moondog would stay on and off for almost twenty years. When he played his music, however, not only musicians (old friends from the Philharmonic, new acquaintances from the world of jazz) but also the press listened, the media recorded. Art Ford and Jazzbo Collins first played his music on the radio. Dorothy Kilgallen sent her husband Dick to fetch him for an appearance on *The Breakfast Show* along with Henry Morgan and Henny Youngman. Walter Winchell and Jack O'Brian regularly reported on his activities in their newspaper columns, thus elevating him to the rank of "kerrikter." He even got his own radio show briefly on WNEW (called "Music and Moondog") Sunday nights. He refused to take money because he didn't want his artistic integrity compromised (see *Newsweek*, 24 December 1951, pp. 64–65). There was even a thoroughbred that ran at Aqueduct under the name "Moondog" in 1952.

For years he had been the pilgrim; now he was the object of a sort of pilgrimage. The list of his visitors and supporters is luminous: Duke Ellington, Benny Goodman ("I find Moondog's music arresting"), Dean Martin, Tony Martin (who perspired through a "ball hot summer" day as he slipped Moondog a ten), Sammy Davis, José Ferrer (who asked Moondog to play drums at his wedding to Katharine Hepburn, a deal that fell through), and Charlie Parker (whom Moondog later celebrated in music, as he did Benny Goodman); politicians (Percy Sutton); actors (Max Baer); fighters (the boxer then known as Cassius Clay, who always called him either "Moon" or

"The Dog," never both). Joan Baez named her dog Moondog; the Pentangle, a folk-rock singing group, had a song named "Moondog" on an album in 1968, calling him "son of rhythm"; the Beatles were called "Johnny and the Moondogs" before they chose their more famous name. One evening in 1950 a passer-by struck up a conversation and accompanied Moondog back to room 11 at the Aristo, where the two men sat on the bed and played music for hours. The young actor was "pretty good" with the bongos, on which he played some nifty rapid runs. He was quiet, introspective, and warm. Only later did Moondog know who Marlon Brando was.

Also in 1950 Moondog met the avant-garde composer John Cage, whose works he admired for their "atmosphere," especially one piece for percussive piano, but little came of it. (Later, when he met Edgar Varese, few sparks were ignited. In the Sixties, when he lived with Philip Glass, Moondog was the influence on the younger and soon to be famous composer.) On April 13, 1953, nearly ten years after he first came to New York, he was recorded live at the Pythian Temple as part of the program *Jazztime U.S.A.* (Brunswick 54001). It was not his first theatre concert (in 1950 he had appeared at Town Hall in a benefit for the New York University summer camp in the "Folklore of New York City" series), but it was the first time he was recorded with others. He was now clearly a member in good standing of the New York jazz community. His "improvisations" were very much "in" then: Marshall Stearns, later to compile a dictionary of jazz (with an article on Moondog) called his polyrhythms "the new trend in jazz," drawing on "Afro-Cuban" roots among others to forge an exciting and vibrant synthesis. In 1950 also he met, by chance (in front of a sexy lingerie store), a man who would be a fellow player for many years to come, Sam Ulano. Sam, having returned from Japan after World War II with some Japanese drums he'd learned to play at a kabuki theater, was a polished percussionist who also lived at the edge, experimenting with strange rhythms and stranger instruments. Moondog was fascinated by the new sounds, and the two were akin in the extremes to which they would go to hone their craft. Moondog would say, as reported by Mr. Ulano, that "the human race is going to die in 4/4 time." The two worked together on concerts throughout the 1950s and 1960s, and Sam appeared on many of Moondog's American recordings.

While he was generating excitement in New York, Moondog had the foresight to secure a retreat in case things got too hectic. Not long after he had returned from out West in 1949, with the first $600 he had earned on the streets, he purchased (over the phone) a three-acre lot in Mount Pleasant, New Jersey, a hamlet near Clinton, in the Delaware Water Gap area. For a while he would take the two-hour bus trip every other weekend and walk the three miles to "Sandalwood of the Barrens," as he called it, and he named one of his earliest rounds after it. At first he pitched a tent on his land.

> It's covered with maple, oak and dogwood trees and they say you can see the Delaware River from it. I wanted a spring, but you can't have everything. It's nice. I can get completely detached and lose myself in art.

The tent soon gave way to a long pine box. Building it in one day, Moondog had originally intended it to house his "personal effects," since he had no place to store them in New York. One end was closed off with firewood; the other was hung with a tarpaulin (the door). For months before winter, he slept in this unfinished rectangle no more than two feet high. But in the meantime the "Hunterdon Hermit" (as his neighbors got to know him) was digging steadily his more striking quarters. His "cave" was ready by the winter of 1950—he called it that and his friends in the area, the residents of which loved to talk to him and follow his strange progress, got to know it as such. A decade later, in upstate New York, he was to produce a startling variation on this approach to wilderness living, but an iteration nonetheless. Like his "square" clothing, certain ideas remained constant, and one of the most rigid was his insistence on living close to the ground. He learned how to rough it in Wyoming as a child and had come to believe that the Indians were better off for being children of nature. He would maintain throughout his life (especially after he became the rugged

Viking), that hardiness was one of the best correctives for hardship. Even though he wasn't there often, he managed to keep a Cornish game hen in a basket made out of twigs, "log-cabin style," and to build a fire-pit for cooking. He had big plans: he would build earth-drums. "You dig a hole twelve feet deep, build a frame, stretch a bull hide across it, and you can dance on it." His home would become "a mecca for musicians."

> Eventually, he hopes Sandalwood could be a place for exper-
> imental concerts, as Tanglewood is a place for conventional
> concerts. Along with earthdrums, he wants a pit 40 feet
> square, with a lower pit in the center for drummers, for
> primitive dancing.

None of this came about, although a humbler version of the dream came true in the early 1970s on his New York property. Soon he was "pestered by the curious" when he was there and "robbed by the kids" when he was gone. After his marriage he seldom appeared. But in the first flush of activity he wrote some of his earliest madrigals, one of his favorites picking up an image from his desert love of 1948: "Let me identify myself now: Songsters both, and both clad in brown, the hermit thrush and I dwell out of town." There, "one cold night in December," over a campfire, he wrote his "Organ Rounds," which he quickly recorded at the Spanish Music Center.

One unfortunate footnote to his Jersey adventure occurred in 1950 after he visited some friends in nearby Easton, Pennsylvania. The family thought it would be good for Moondog to take Peter, twelve years old, back to New York City, since he had shown great interest in performing music. Moondog, however, was not fully aware of the possible repercussions of such an apparently benevolent act. A concerned woman spotted this mini-Moondog on the street one day (for the boy, as might be expected, dressed like his mentor) and turned the adult in. Before he had time to respond, he was arrested, charged with kidnapping (crossing state lines with a minor), and entrusted to Bellevue for a week of observation. In the meantime the parents came and explained the escapade to the authorities, but not before Moondog received a sentence of thirty days, suspended. None of the psychiatrists at Bellevue could explain to him why he was there, but no one found anything amiss in his head, other than, perhaps, a persistently naive corner in his personality.

Moondog did something else while he was getting media coverage in New York: he took time out in 1951 to complete his Portland-to-Portland jaunt. This time he concentrated on upstate New York and New England, getting as far as Lewiston, Maine, beyond Portland, before being dissuaded by a cop from trying for Bangor. In Portland he visited Longfellow House and held an old flintlock whose heft impressed him. (The butt was thick to serve as a club when ammunition or reloading time ran out.) Wherever he went, columns of print followed him with sentiments such as "He will not soon be forgotten here" and "We've never seen anything like Moondog." On the trip he had his first SMC 78s to sell (*Snaketime Rhythms* and *Moondog Symphony*), but he made little with them. In Newburgh, New York, he was stranded with 47 cents; the local police not only fed him and put him up for the night but also took up a collection to help send him on his way.

One last grand event rounded out his first decade in New York. Moondog's first marriage had been as brief as it was unsuccessful. He had had several serious near-misses before and after Virginia Sledge, but he had also acquired some hermit-like habits that deterred prospective mates. This ended in 1952, when he married again, this time for eight years.

He met Mary on the street; the sparks flew, and the courtship was quick. According to his daughter, June, Mary was struck by his appearance and moved by his music; Moondog was stirred by the music of her voice. As with so many of his other lovers before and after, he was the passionate aggressor, igniting her interest with his creativity and overcoming the obvious objections of her long-suffering mother with his intelligence and wit. Into the complicated extended family of his bride-to-be strode this eccentric and irresistible colossus. He "knew" she was his "soul-mate" and she, lonely and dependent, though mildly rebellious, was entranced. Two arduous journeys converged at this moment: Moondog's out of the American heartland and domestic melodrama, hers out of the wreckage of World War II. Mary Whiteing's father had lived in Japan before World War II, met and married a Japanese girl, fathered a daughter, Suzuko (Mary), spent the war in a concentration camp, and inexplicably disappeared. In 1952, on their voyage to the U.S. to find him, Sakura Whiteing and her daughter were quarantined on Ellis Island for a long while before being set free to live on the upper west side of Manhattan. Mary had by this time a little girl of her own, Betty, born out of wedlock.

What a striking, gorgeous couple they made! She was delicate, slight, with Oriental features; he was tall, dark, and handsome. They were a photographer's dream couple, a study in contrasts. The June 4, 1952 issue of the *New York Journal-American* features a shot of Moondog playing a horn on a rooftop while Mary fawns: a "skyline serenade" to a "June bride." They married in a style worthy of the principals. On the top half of a large piece of card stock is a picture of the composer looking spiffy in a light cape over a dark tunic, holding a walking stick; beside him his wife wears a sparkling wedding dress and a tiara of flowers. The bottom half is a Moondog round, in snaketime, "You Who": "You're just as big as a minute, no? Time has stopped, and it is you who stopped it for me since I have been holding your minute hand."

Soon they were living in the Aristo Hotel, with Mary assuming the role of a full-time partner to her husband, making music on the streets on a variety of instruments, suggesting, adding, copying with a touch observers called artistic—in short, the younger version of the older women Moondog had courted for many years. Finally he had found the lovely helpmate with new energies, new ideas, and worldly beauty. Daringly Moondog broke free of old restraints and compulsions, marrying a lover rather than a mother-surrogate, someone outside his ethnic and artistic heritage. She was pregnant within months. When Moondog's first daughter, June Hardin, the only child he would ever father as a married man, was born on June 1, 1953, he had just turned thirty-seven.

Chapter Four

Moondog Symphony

(1953–1960)

After a decade in New York, Moondog had assumed a public life, tracked his creative impulses into a rich private world whose vitality and originality would mature with him, and renamed himself. Marriage sobered him, though he never was a candidate for domesticity. He had lost and found many roads, identities, and loves, but his tortured path now led definitely to one goal: composing.

Even in a life so eventful, the five years after his marriage and the birth of his daughter must have seemed exceptionally bright: he recorded albums on prestigious labels and won a decisive legal battle. Opting for eccentricity (a respectable position for the avant-garde artist), he also chose, consciously or not, to be "in" to a select few (novelty-hunters, slumming culture-addicts, and gossip columnists, unfortunately, along with the musical cognoscenti).

It is easy, and sometimes useful, to make enemies in New York. Many entertainers have made careers out of shock and insult, and have seeped into the mainstream from the most unlikely corners of a city that offers a bewildering mix of talents and posers. Moondog's style tended toward the assertive, even the aggressive, but his peculiarities and beliefs tended to mitigate his seriousness. Independence is one thing, almost always admirable, but living anomalies who are deeply committed to positions articulated in arcane formulas, despite the vital signs they flash, are another commodity altogether. Even when he might have chosen otherwise and had been advised to compromise, Moondog managed to live outside the consensus that could have altered his life. His changes came in his own tempo, like his compositions, or like his signature animals, snake and dog, that curled about and howled at the symbols we all live by.

But another "new" life began for Moondog in 1953, as it had in 1932 when he was blinded, and in 1943 when he set out for New York (and as it would in 1974 when he went to Europe). To prove his ability despite his handicap, and to prove his originality and independence from the complex of social, religious, and moral values he was raised in, moved Moondog to ever more startling heights of independence. His temperament usually survived the inevitable anxieties and disappointments. He could laugh at poverty and missed opportunities, reserving his righteous anger for grander targets. Outrageous acts trailed him to substantiate his claims. Look, Christianity, there are alternate rituals and dogmas and living spirits; look, mother, I, too, can make music, created in mind as well as by hand; look, father, I live where I want, sleep where I want, work in the echo of the sounds that feed my self-expression; look, complacent, "honest" middle America, while I draw my strength up through the pavement of Times Square.

Albums seemed to proliferate around June Hardin's June 1, 1953 birth like signs. Less than a month before, his first LP appeared with a modest flurry of publicity. Before she was a year old, one more and part of another appeared. When she was between the ages of two and five, four more albums came out; on one, she was even featured as the auditor of a lullaby. Her earliest memories, therefore, were not only circumscribed by the two addresses she grew up in but ringed also with seven albums by her prolific father.

Moondog's reputation rose from the sidewalks onto the airwaves. A "kerrikter" he would always be, but now he was also a serious musician whose compositions were going to appear on the radio, a personality the press came to admire intelligently rather than patronize or fawn upon. When June was seven and her parents had separated permanently, she knew a certain electricity that haunted her. In 1971, when she was eighteen, she asked her mother to be reunited with her father, even if briefly. As a student at New York's celebrated School of Performing Arts, she had met her father's music not as one familiar with it but through the advocacy of her friends; in the intervening eleven years they had neither met nor spoken. But when they finally did meet, it was, in one of life's pleasanter ironies, to work on an album. In 1971, she was a principal performer on Moondog's last American recording. The time between her birth and her majority limns his mature New York period.

Little is known about Moondog's married life, as both preferred. They seemed happy to most until they separated. Early on, when they worked on music as a team and June was still an infant, Suzuko (Mary) seemed to blend into the background, a shy, exotic beauty. There can be no doubt of her influence on his work, however. It is there both in its living presence (she was his copyist, transcribing his music artistically from Braille to score, sometimes, according to several eyewitnesses, writing down what Moondog would sing to her, and she was often his accompanist, on location and in the studio) and in its subtle shadings (much of the music's eclectic power comes from touches obviously hers). She was, though more comfortable off center-stage, a potent presence.

Their eight-year marriage spanned many creative endeavors. Mary was a quiet but energetic mother and partner. She attended Moondog's concerts, interviews, and other appearances; she performed with him on the streets, including the crowded pedestrian island at Times Square; her voice and playing are found on all but one of his 1950s albums. They were a striking pair: he long-haired, bearded, blind, and dressed in homemade capes and togas; she slight, delicate-looking, meticulously made-up. They lived in the Aristo until 1956, for four years; after staying for a few months at 449 West 56th Street, they moved to the Lower East Side, 179 East 3rd Street. There they stayed for the second half of the marriage, until April 1960, when they separated permanently. Moondog in one conspicuous instance probably sacrificed an excellent chance at the big time to preserve his marriage, but he also caused its failure.

Moondog's association with Tony Schwartz then was his most important professional relationship with anyone other than his wife. Mr. Schwartz, who became a seminal theoretician on the media (his books include *The Responsive Chord* and *Media: The Second God*), "discovered" Moondog on the streets of New York when he did his innovative work with portable sound equipment. He produced the first Moondog LP, made possible the second, and encouraged and promoted the music, which he genuinely admired. Unlike many of Moondog's early publicists (columnists, commentators, and disc jockeys), however, Mr. Schwartz was not out to make claims. He brought sensitivity to his craft, the novel skill of on-location recording, and a genuine interest in the performers. As later with Paul Jordan, Ernst Fuchs, and others, Moondog's association with fellow artists created vibrant and unusual products.

They met in the hubbub around Mr. Schwartz's earliest recordings. The producer first heard the performer when Moondog appeared at Town Hall in the 1950 "Folklore of New York City" concert. When Folkways Records commissioned several albums of music and sounds from the streets of New York, who better than Moondog to fill a track? *New York 19* (FD 5558, 1954), "conceived, recorded, edited and narrated by Tony Schwartz," was (say the program notes) an attempt "to channelize my recording activities to a thorough study of the folklore of the community in which I live": the west side of Manhattan "bounded on the north by 60th Street, on the south by the Times Square area, on the west by the Hudson River and on the east by Fifth Avenue with the exception of Radio City." On side two, band 1 ("Street Musicians"), between Professor Giuseppe Ravita, the "Carnegie Hall Fiddler," and band 2 ("the calls and spiels of…vendors, barkers and pitchmen"), is Moondog, "one of the most unusual street musicians" who "conceives, builds, writes music for, and plays his own instruments." The selection, untitled here but called "Fog on the Hudson" on the Mars album, "was made one foggy night against the background of the boat whistles on the Hudson River." On it Moondog played two of his trademarks, the oo (described by Schwartz as "a triangular wooden frame, each leg of the triangle about 18 inches long, with piano wire strung across and struck with a 6-inch dowel"; Moondog explains further that it is based on Indian scales, with five tones, the five black keys of the piano dropped into C major) and two triangular wooden drums, later to be christened the trimba. "Trimba" is often spelled with an "s", though it is not plural: as the instrument evolved and changed, so did its name.

Thanks to the "Magnamite," a "completely portable, light-weight tape recorder, which makes the world your recording studio and a little hand-held box your control room," Mr. Schwartz found Moondog often, unrehearsed. One other selection appeared on Folkways. In the 1957 *Music on the Streets* (FD 5581), "a Fascinating Collection of music and musicians recorded on the streets of New York," Moondog was taped in a doorway on 52nd Street between 6th and 7th Avenues, not far from the spot he would make a living landmark a decade later. The untitled piece ("Avenue of the Americas" on the Mars album) is the first of several oo-and-trimba improvisations.

The most sophisticated celebration of Moondog live *in situ* was *Moondog on the Streets of New York* (MREP-A2), produced by Tony Schwartz and Howie Richmond for Mars Records, Woody Herman's label. This album, Moondog's first, appeared slightly less than a decade after Louis Hardin first arrived in New York City, a bit more than five years after his renaming. It was the most ambitious vehicle thitherto designed for his music, and the first non-self-produced commercial offering. Unlike his SMC 78s, the Mars album enjoyed professional production, and was, though a financial disappointment, well received. The journeyman beggar with a "crazy, variant brilliance" (the phrase is Schwartz's) gained music-world credibility from this serious kind of exposure.

The record cover depicts Moondog kneeling on a blanket, displaying his wares on a sidewalk. His long dark hair, combed straight back, falls inside the lowered hood of his full-length cape. In a typical pose (also pictured on the Brunswick album cover), he is leaning over the oo, about to strike the board with the clava in his left hand.

Behind his right shoulder are records for sale; in front of them is his walking stick suspended from a string running above his head; by his left knee is an empty paper bag. Above everything is the yellow lettering of the title. John Briggs, who reviewed the album favorably for the *New York Times* (Sunday Arts and Leisure, May 31, 1953, p. 6), writes about the "nondescript brown robe and sandals, a flowing beard and uncut hair in two braids." More disparagingly, he goes on: "Moondog 'squats...like a street musician in some Oriental bazaar.'" Despite the natural tendency to think the image was staged for the advertising campaign, the photograph, by Benn Mitchell, is true to Moondog's life then.

The brief notes on the back of the slip jacket, by Tony Schwartz, are straightforward. Beyond the normal biographical survey is the claim that Moondog is the "most unique" of all the New York street musicians, influenced by Occidental and Oriental, primitive and classical "elements." Most of the music, from on-site tapings taken over several years, was transcribed by Suzuko, who also "sings and accompanies him."

The music is a strange and striking amalgam, eight selections that demonstrate Moondog's resistance to classification—a point Philip Glass would underscore decades later. To some this is a blessing, innovation at its unpredictable best. To others it is raw talent dispersed on too many fronts to concentrate with any success on one. To Moondog in 1953 it was a terse musical summary of his career: snaketime percussion with Amerindian roots, improvisational jazz affinities with Hispanic overlays, music born of and echoing the sounds of New York, vibrating with the Japanese influences of Suzuko. *Moondog on the Streets of New York* was his first harvest, in some ways prototypical: plangent chants and wistful melodies, implying tragedy and sadness, played against an effervescent, life-affirming percussion.

This unusual recording was unusually well-received. The trade magazines hyped it. *Billboard* broke the story first: "Moondog May Be Next Hot Wax Artist" (March 28, 1953). Several weeks later, on May 9, both *Billboard* and *Melody Maker* printed portraits, the former's of Moondog about to "pound 'oo' and 'utsu,'" the latter's captioned "They Call Him Moon Dog." *Variety* (June 10, 1953) followed, reciting the "Moondog Saga," or the rise from "doorway performer" to recording artist. Another piece, percussively called "Oo, that frantic snaketime, as Moondog rises on discs," was written by Leonard Feather (*Downbeat*, July 1, 1953), early in his career but clearly a Moondog fan from the outset. The most ambitious and serious review by John Briggs in the *Times* ("Blind New York Street Musician Heard in Sampling of Own Inventions") extols the "unexpected sonorities" of the "odd, exotic sounding tunes" of Moondog's snaketime: "a peculiar, slithering movement hard to describe and impossible to write down in musical notation." The record is "unique, individualistic," neither "primitive" nor "sophisticated, yet a little bit of both." The article mentions "large-scale orchestral composition" that Moondog was dictating, and a large work for voices ("The Cosmicon"), written in "tempo di serpente." Moondog had never been taken so seriously, or recognized in so respected a publication.

Moondog contributed in his fashion to the press conference announcing the record. As it is recalled by Tony Schwartz and Al Brackman, of the Richmond Agency, who helped produce the record for Mars and Hollis Music, this was a media event with Dali-esque touches, a happening before such events had such a name. The sheet music said, "Moondog on the Streets of New York Suite," and so the eight pieces were named later when Kenny Graham re-arranged them for studio band on MGM Records. They handed it out along with free orange juice at the Nedicks restaurant near Carnegie Hall. It was a weekday, from 2:30 to 4:30, a few days before June was born. Fifty publicists, newspapermen, and photographers attended, among them Dave Garroway, radio and TV host, Jim Moran, a flamboyant publicity man noted for getting his clients media coverage rather than paying for advertisements (and charging comparable rates), Schwartz, Brackman, and others. One unidentified critic sat at Moondog's feet while the composer expostulated on Asiatic music, rhythm, and scales. Mary, silent and loyal, whose scripts were praised as "artwork," out of both temperament and delicate condition, remained in the background. The event might have achieved more exposure, had it not been in Midtown Manhattan.

Moondog on the Streets of New York, though never popular, was the first of a string of critical and artistic successes. He made, through 1974, dozens of records, yet none enriched him in any way. At the time of June's birth, though, life seemed sweet. His first album had been well-received. Prospects were good. Tony Schwartz had introduced him to Goddard Leiberson at Columbia/Epic Records, and George Avacian would soon agree to produce an LP. His performance at the Pythian Temple was about to come out on Brunswick, and his Mars record was on its way to England to be re-issued as jazz. *Variety*, on June 10, 1953, cited his accomplishments in the plural: Moondog's "Major Disc Releases" were industry news.

His associations with Tony Schwartz and the Richmond Agency continued for several years before fading, gently and without rancor. (Mr. Schwartz was even responsible for finding Mary and Moon-june, as the child was then called, a temporary apartment at West 56th Street, next door to his own home, before the family moved to the East Village.) Moondog always felt that when two partners went in different directions agreements were dissolved and legalities were for the suited or the sighted who hung on the written word. To all and for all, the simpler the better; the fewer the restrictions, the fewer the problems. Before drifting away from Tony Schwartz, however, he would be enriched. On at least two occasions Mr. Schwartz used Moondog's music on radio and television commercials. In the American Airlines "Sounds of the Cities" series, the San Francisco trolley was really Moondog's oo. The royalty for that spot alone was between $800 and $900. A Moondog drum pattern accompanied a Kaiser Aluminum commercial, his rhythms generously accommodating its quickening tempo. To this day, his estate's rights to royalties from the commercial uses of his music have not been settled. Modest successes such as these convinced Mr. Schwartz that Moondog could have a wide appeal. Mr. Schwartz backed him in print and in action, because what he said in print he really meant: Moondog was an "explorer" with a "charming sense of humor." One day he saw Moondog play a four-foot flute with, and in the same key as, the whistle from the docking *Queen Elizabeth*: it "blew" the blind man's cool (and appeared later on the second Prestige album, *More Moondog*). Years later, when the CBS building was going up on 6th Avenue, Moondog complained to Mr. Schwartz on the street that he was "blinded" by the background noise. When others talked to fill in time, before a session, perhaps, or during breaks, Moondog silently thought.

Before drifting away from Al Brackman and the Richmond Agency, Moondog was well-served also. In a sense, since the Mars record was their property (like its MGM spin-off), promoting the unmanaged Moondog fell to them. They lost some energy and time trying to make Moondog a star, and in a year the parties were estranged. Moondog was loved by all and charmed his supporters, as always, but his "wariness" and his "distance," the other side of himself that he held back from possible exploitation, made certain transactions difficult.

Moondog went from one bizarre circumstance to another, sometimes needing help in strange ways. On May 25, 1954, the New York Percussion Society held its annual concert at the YMHA on 92nd Street and Lexington Avenue and asked him to be a guest soloist. (This concert was the first of many shows and recording sessions he shared with the drumming guru Sam Ulano, who organized the event for sixty of his students.) Although he readily accepted, he noted the difficulty of traveling through New York City traffic up to the Y with the instruments from the Mars album. To honor the commitment, he had to take his trimba, oo, uni, utsu, and samisen (the last, a Japanese guitar-like instrument, an awkward traveler because of its very long neck). Mr. Ulano agreed to help, but first he had to deal with an emergency. On the day of the concert, Moondog awoke with his jaw swollen from an infected tooth. Sam took him to a dentist, and the patients marveled at Moondog, always in costume when in public; Sam soon marveled at Moondog, who, without anesthesia (unavailable because of the swelling) had the bad tooth extracted. That evening, he was ready to go, and Sam appeared early at the Aristo. Suzuko had the instruments lined up in the room, and, since June was a baby of several months, the quarters were cramped. Mr. Brackman found a taxi with a sliding roof, secured the driver's services for both legs of the trip, and packed Moondog, his family, and his instruments, the samisen poking through the opening. The performance, according to several admittedly biased viewers, was more breathtaking even than the April session at the Pythian Temple. Moondog, using hands, feet, and individual fingers and toes, was at the top of his street musicianship, keeping four, even six rhythms alive simultaneously. He never played his early music with greater focus or effect.

Within a week, Dave Garroway, host of NBC television's *Today Show*, had contacted the Richmond Agency to set up an on-the-air interview. Mr. Garroway had been at Nedicks, but he thought it would be worthwhile for his viewers to see Moondog in his natural habitat, the noblest street musician, making his living. They planned it and got the help of the police; the interview would take place on the west side of Sixth Avenue, between 50th and 51st Streets, in front of the Spanish Music Center. In 1954 the row of old six-story buildings had not yet been torn down to accommodate a corporate headquarters. Moondog had many reasons for this choice of location. First, he wanted publicly to thank Gabriel Oller, who had helped him in so many ways; second, he loved the rumble of the subway as percussion *sui generis* (although it would not occur every few minutes as it did during daytime); and third, this was and would remain for two more decades his turf, where he was recognized, supported, and admired. The police had only one reservation: since Radio City Music Hall was just down the block, the filming could not take place until after midnight, when the last performance was over and the streets relatively clear. So in the earliest hours of a fall morning the scene was set for the first of Moondog's three appearances on *The Today Show*. (The others were in 1964 and 1969.) Moondog was in top form: for about forty-five minutes he talked theory, demonstrated his instruments, responded to questions, and reminisced about the good old days at the Spanish Music Center. When asked what his favorite instrument was, he responded with a favorite slogan: "the box that catches the coins." Although in a new medium, he was not out of his element.

One of the problems his supporters encountered over the years was that Moondog was so at home doing what he had done so well and for so long that expanding horizons meant tilling the ground beneath his feet. Moondog was happily married, the father of an infant, and the mainstay of his family. He made his money on the streets for the most part: royalties, performance gratuities, and residuals were marginal in the best of times. He was not anxious to give up his way of life, therefore, when another alternative—however attractive—came along. Almost incomprehensibly, Moondog at this time turned down an opportunity to become a famous performer, giving as reason that the trial period was too long for him to go without income. That his income came from "begging" was beside the point to him, nor was he familiar with Orwell's spirited defense of it in *Down and Out in Paris and London*; he had always been attached to his reality, not yours or mine. Here is what happened.

After the Mars record had been out a while, Joe Glazer, a successful theatrical manager, saw Moondog as an exciting new entertainment property. Mr. Glazer was no stranger to the rags-to-riches story, having guided the career and magnified the fortunes of Louis Armstrong, among others. They worked out the details in rough strokes: Moondog would put together a professional orchestra, and the "act" would, after a period of rehearsal, play at a New York club for a few weeks before heading out on a carefully arranged cross-country tour. Although no written agreement survives, it is obvious that all involved hoped the record would be promoted and Moondog would become a famous entertainer. Agents, managers, and performers were enthusiastic, at first. The Village Vanguard was booked and the demanding rehearsal schedule about to begin. Then Moondog decided to go his own way, and the enterprise fizzled out. One onlooker said he got cold feet, another that he thought only of himself. But he had worked through the initial stages without making a dime, and he had other mouths to feed. Could he sacrifice his immediate joys for an attractive but risky venture? Could he give up a comfortable livelihood as a beggar for the often short-lived glitter of show biz? More fundamentally, could he surrender his fiercely guarded independence, his hard-won privacy, to the commercialism he had mocked both in words and by example for a decade? Some saw an opportunity lost in his decision; to others it was principle triumphant. To Moondog the truth was probably less extreme: fearful of the music industry, wary of deals, conscious of his obligations, concerned for his integrity, and taking refuge in a stability he had shaped through numerous obstacles, he chose to stay where he was. Caution is not necessarily a Moondog virtue, but in this instance it seems to have melded with his remote, world-wary persona.

The music world continued to try to legitimize Moondog: his music changed dramatically during 1953–1971, the years of his first and last American albums, but it was usually tantalizing enough to convince at least one producer to attempt yet another assault on the public. They never succeeded (despite coming close in 1969), so Moondog's development as a composer never had to halt in order to accommodate fame. His music evolved in concert with his life, which was at times grim and frustrating, but Moondog danced to no other tunes than his own. Only once was there an attempt to "adapt" Moondog's music into the mainstream. Other than an occasional soundtrack, commercial, ballet score, or popular song, no musician would ever take a Moondog composition and present it in a new idiom, except for a British jazz composer and arranger, Kenny Graham. Several years after the Mars record, the "Moondog Suite," property of Hollis Music, was recorded in England and packaged in America by MGM Records. It was Moondog's last contact with the Richmond Agency. But it was their property, not his, and other than being informed he had nothing to do with the project. Nor did he gain more than a few dollars from it. The performances are slick, but Moondog's music does not fit comfortably into a jazz band format, even a "progressive" one. The smoothness of the studio irons out the very wrinkles that made Moondog's early music more than just a historical curiosity, as the MGM record now seems to be. At his most powerful, Moondog does not translate well.

Moondog's next recording was a stellar vehicle for his talents in the 1950s. A logical outgrowth of the Mars release, the ten-inch Epic album *Moondog and His Friends* is a much more elaborate, polished package. Much of the music is performed in the studio, by respectable ensembles. Most of it was intended to be orchestral, not conceived in miniature, and although Moondog does most of the actual performing, he assumes more weight as the composer rather than as the virtuoso. The polish here differs from that of Kenny Graham's record insofar as Moondog was allowed to smooth out his own edges.

Tony Schwartz was "instrumental" in making the deal and also provided some of the tracks in the album from his file of Moondog tapings. The negotiations are forgotten, and the working arrangements among the personalities buried by the performances themselves. This is, though, an anonymous production. His "wife" is mentioned once, not by name, and none of those responsible for the conception, production, and packaging (Goddard Leiberson, George Avacian) is identified. The cover does no more than vaguely suggest those who made the music: "members of the philharmonic-Symphony Orchestra of New York" and "two of the country's best young concert artists," among others. The pieces recorded at the Columbia studios were added to the selections from Tony Schwartz's library, and the entire program assembled and released in spring 1954.

The cover manufactures mystique. Moondog, black hair brushed back and tied in a glossy ponytail trailing over his left shoulder, handlebar moustache waxed, dominates the right foreground. Photographed from the waist up, he is playing his trimba (called, on this album only, the "dragon's teeth" drum) while behind him a slight, androgynous adolescent plays what looks like an oboe. The program notes on the back of the cover do little to explain the music. Moondog's "tonal pictures with new sound variations and new tempo variations" make up a "complex" idiom whose "sophistication…belies its seeming simplicity." Because the music is both experimental and "solidly grounded in classical form," it is now taken seriously by "ranking professional musicians" who respect Moondog's theories and "ingratiating ideas." The remaining space (two of the three columns of print) offers brief notes on each selection.

In addition to being virtually anonymous, the album is eclectic. The compositions on side one resemble those on the Mars album: with two exceptions, they are brief, mostly percussive and improvisational, with Moondog as the dominant performer. The second side is made up of two lengthy (for Moondog) orchestral suites, the only demonstration before the grand 1969 Columbia album of his abilities as a composer on a large scale. Despite the three Prestige albums' appearing several years after the Epic LP, they are more representative of him as a street musician, an image he would spend two decades trying to retouch, if not erase. The Epic venture is, in this sense, more generously suggestive of his wider scope.

By 1954 he had been composing orchestral music for almost a decade, but if it weren't for "Oasis" and the two suites, few would know. Not until the mid-1960s did Moondog conduct concerts of his more ambitious work, but nonetheless, and without deviation, he was always trying to become a serious (as distinct from a regional or a merely eccentric) musician. As he admitted on several occasions later, openly, even with the suggestion of a twinkle, the short "experimental" fusion compositions of the 1950s were his apprentice work, aimed, moreover, at making a publicity splash and a name for their creator. His long-range goals were bigger.

The Epic album, however, went nowhere and did nothing. It was not reviewed, got little publicity, caused no ripples, and barely sold. But the music ("Theme and Variation," "Oasis," "Suite No. 2"), the most forward-looking of any he recorded before 1969, opened up possibilities he only fulfilled in old age. Though the work was hard and recognition painfully slow to come (it was fifteen years before he recorded with strings again), he eventually became a composer for symphony orchestra.

ON NOVEMBER 24, 1954, the New York State Supreme Court delivered a triumph for Moondog's integrity and prestige. Poor but proud, armed only with principle, evidence, nerve, and endurance, Moondog had challenged the hottest new disc jockey in New York for appropriating his name, and won. After the last legal firework had sputtered and the journalists had moved on, the court ordered Alan Freed, soon to become the crowned prince of "rock 'n' roll," to announce on the air that his broadcast could no longer be called "The Moondog Show," and that he was not really "King of the Moondoggers" and their even younger groupies, the "Moonpuppies." Although Moondog's intransigent, perhaps misguided, position probably lessened his damages, his was still the clear moral victory: *he* was Moondog, and no upstart could take that away. The proceedings took months (years counting the aftershocks), but the high points occurred between November 1954 and February 1955.

Soon after the release of the Epic album, after celebrating two years of married life at the Aristo and his daughter's first birthday, Moondog was shocked to hear that a new Moondog ruled the late-night airwaves, a high-velocity guru of the new-wave teen music on WINS. Alan Freed was, in the early days of the "beat," spinning records and hosting a TV show in Cleveland. Lured by the romance and money of Gotham, he signed a lucrative contract with WINS on August 10, 1954. With guaranteed minimums and scores of spin-offs (concerts, dances, endorsements, and the like), it was an impressive package for a new face in town. Starting on September 7, 1954, the new "Moondog Show," as daily newspapers listed it, became outrageously popular. The borrowings, which Mr. Freed had worked out in Cleveland, were bold: in addition to the blatant eponymity, each program would begin with the opening howl from "Moondog Symphony." To thousands of teens and pre-teens it was the primal scream of a new sect. To Moondog, it was plagiarism.

While Moondog was initiating litigation, Alan Freed had taken a giant step into the big time. Popular reporting on his entry was rhapsodic. *What's Cookin' in New York* of September 25, 1954, features a picture of Alan "Moondog" Freed on the cover, eclipsing one of

Eartha Kitt. "Moondog House," as the new program was called by the WINS management in the article, has "aroused" the dormant rhythm and blues audience in the metropolitan area. Freed's "Moondoggers" had already lit up Ohio: "The 'Moondog' monicker, which when freely translated [!] means a modern day advocate of Blues and Jazz, became famous throughout the area." So famous and "powerful" had that shock wave become that the Moondog "Balls" drew over 87,000 paying customers, 25,000 on one notable occasion alone, before Freed headed east. His "Coronation Ball" in Newark, New Jersey, as reported over three lavish pages in the black-oriented pictorial magazine *Our World* (August, 1954) hit even giddier heights. During his last days in Cleveland (at station WJW), and while his first tapes for the Newark-based WNJR made headlines, "Mr. Moondog" in the flesh "packed" 11,000 euphoric spectators into the Sussex Avenue Armory. Vaughan Monroe (8,000) and Martin and Lewis (4,000), two of the prominent stage acts of the day, hardly held a candle to this skyrocket: the disc jockey, no longer a quiet employee who introduced music or "killed time," had become a superhero to his dogs and puppies, the best of a new breed of "Number One hucksters." Almost lost among the twenty or so photographs of the concert, the performers backstage, the fans at home or in various candid poses, and the billboard in front of Bamberger's (Freed's is the only white face in all of the crowds) is a telling headline, followed by an even more telling paragraph: "Moondog Theme record, copyrighted by Cleveland disc jockey, catapulted him to top of field."

> Except for his "Moondog" theme record Allan [sic] Freed might still be just another disc jockey. He had been on radio 10 years, starting as a sports announcer, before "Moondog" turned the spotlight on him. It was one afternoon a few years ago when the record came to his attention. Out of curiosity he put it on the turntable and as it played, he talked. That did it. Audience response, in the form of calls, telegrams and letters, was immediate. Quick to take a hint, Freed copyrighted this record which had been made by a blind New Yorker, also nick-named Moondog.

Moondog was on top of his case from the beginning. In July, when the August issue of *Our World* appeared, and he had listened, stunned, as someone read the Coronation Ball article to him, he retained the services of a copyright lawyer, Abner Greenberg. Before Freed even signed a contract or went on the air for WINS, he received a letter, dated July 13, 1954, which began:

> I have been retained by the original "Moondog" who alleges that you have appropriated his trade or professional name in your activities as a disc jockey and promoted [sic] of dances etc.

It ended with a threatened claim of damages for "said unlawful acts." Lew Platt, who claims in a reply dated July 19 that he speaks as Freed's "personal manager" (denied by defendant in the depositions and at the hearing) countercharged Moondog with the unauthorized use of his own name (WJW in Cleveland had a trademark, registered at the Patent and Copyright Office in Washington, D.C., for "Moondog" on radio programs) and advised Mr. Greenberg that his client's comments to the press had better be retracted. No further dialogue between Ohio and New York occurred before the case went to court, so probably neither of the two Moondogs retracted anything or ceased calling himself "Moondog."

The pre-, mid- and post-trial logorrhea, even in small doses, requires indulgence and distance. First the plaintiff, Louis Hardin, AKA Moondog, gave his deposition on September 8, 1954, the day after Alan Freed opened on WINS. He was, he argued, a serious musician. Having studied at the Memphis Conservatory of Music ("counterpoint, orchestration and theory"), he came east, and soon was Moondog to the likes of Benny Goodman, Duke Ellington, and *Newsweek*. He had appeared on WNEW and cut records with Mars and Epic. He goes on:

> It appears that my music has a special appeal to colored listeners due to the odd "beat" which I call "snake rhythm", although it was not intended to have any class appeal. As a

matter of fact, I appeared twice with my orchestra at the YMHA on Lexington Avenue in this city at a seminar of instruction for percussion instruments (drums).

He then traces Freed's descent upon New York as it was covered by the press, quoting from the *Daily Mirror, Variety* and *Billboard*.

The Allan [sic] Freed show opened…with the playing of my "MOONDOG SYMPHONY" and the salutation this is "MOONDOG" and then the "KING OF THE MOON-DOGGERS"…Freed said that the "MOONLADY" was there but that the "MOONPUPPIES" were in bed.

He ends by noting how such disc jockeys command "fabulous fees" as well as "favors and adulation"; therefore, "deponent prays that a temporary injunction be granted."

On September 17, Abner Greenberg offered his account, assuring the court that the *Our World* article had been verified by the magazine's editor, John Davis, who had stated further that "every word" had come directly from either Alan Freed or Lew Platt. A transcription of the September 8 broadcast was evidence of plagiarism, and a full documentation of the history of "Moondog" established priority. One instance offered was the distribution of the SMC record in June of 1951, before the registration by WJW of its "Moondog House" trademark on April 29, 1952. On Sunday, September 12, to further salt the blind man's wounds, Freed had held the first of his legendary shindigs at the Brooklyn Paramount Theatre. Mr. Leder of WINS, the plaintiff told the court, had been warned before Freed ever went on the air that "if he permitted…said misrepresentation over his station…he would become involved." Among the fourteen cited transgressions of Freed is at least one surprise:

the remarks interspersed between the playing of records are of inferior quality in content and [consequently] the general esteem and reputation of the plaintiff has been injured greatly to the diminution of his prestige as a serious student of music and to the resultant loss in his profession or business.

The sentiments expressed, so obviously Moondog's, are due warning of strong stance, maintained even after his legal victory. Mr. Greenberg, finally, prays for three forms of relief: that the defendants be restrained from using "Moondog" and any of its gritty derivatives; that they give Moondog any of the profits they might have realized by exploiting his name; and that they give him $100,000 in damages, plus "further relief" and costs.

The defense, to no one's surprise, drew its guns. On September 11, Alan Freed, Robert J. Leder, and Frederic A. Johnson, the defense attorney, entered affidavits. Freed denied both the case against him and the article in *Our World* as "pure fabrication," and asserted that the SMC record was used on his program solely as "sound effects," since he arrived at the name of Moondog by his own invention. He named his program "Moondog" before hearing the record, from innocent astronomical inspirations.

> My reason for the choice of the name "MOONDOG" for my radio program came as the result of my acquaintance-ship with amateur astronomers. Amateur astronomy is a hobby of mine. Any professional or amateur astronomer will certify that the name "MOONDOG" is derived from the description by ancient mariners of the ring around the moon. It is this ring which supposedly foretells the coming of a storm.[....]
>
> The word "MOONDOG" will be found in dictionaries with one or more definitions. It is obviously a work [sic] in common use.

Mr. Robert J. Leder, next, indicates that WINS has nothing to do with this action because Mr. Freed is under contract to the parent Gotham Broadcasting Company, a Delaware corporation. A glance at the contract, however, reveals this to be a lie, since it is WINS to whom Mr. Freed is legally bound for seven pages, and Mr. Leder himself, as WINS's Vice President, who signed the document.

The presiding judge denied the motion to dismiss, scheduling the trial for November 15, 1954. Before the courtroom drama, though, a subplot developed. On October 26 and 27 Alan Freed, John M. Brantley (a producer at WINS), Frederic A. Johnson, Robert S. Smith (the program director), Susan Ottinger (secretary to Mr. Smith), and William Cooperman (production manager of Daniel Press, a neighbor of WINS) all filed another sheaf of affidavits. Louis T. Hardin, they said, was aggravating the "deception" he would foist on the management of Gotham Broadcasting by picketing the station's headquarters (a short walk from the Aristo). According to attorney Johnson, "this is not a labor dispute," and thus "permission for plaintiff to picket will...cause defendant as well as other persons, not party to this action, irreparable damages between now and the time of trial and likewise afterwards." Moreover, such "acts alone are making its approximate date a veritable uncertainty."

The depositions provide some interesting assessments: Freed himself calls Moondog's picketing "plainly an act of calculated harassment." Mr. Smith notes that he saw Louis Hardin, "in peculiar garb and beard," carrying a picket sign. Ms. Ottinger calls the invader a "strange figure," Mr. Brantley is amazed to see anyone picketing anything at 11:00 p.m., and Mr. Cooperman, the most prolix of the witnesses, says that the picketer "was attired in what may be termed classic or patriarchal fashion"—clearly a case of "adverse publicity" if he ever saw one.

By the time of the show cause hearing (November 1), two weeks before the trial proper, Moondog had stepped up the inventiveness and pungency of his attack. More depositions poured in. Pat Gammer, Mr. Leder's secretary, described Defendant's Exhibits A and B, photographs of Moondog carrying sign-boards that read, front and back:

"WINS" UNFAIR
This Radio Station
Employs a Disc Jockey
Who Plays My Record
"Moondog Symphony"
and calls himself
'Moondog'
I AM MOONDOG

On the very day of the hearing, moreover, Moondog had esca-
lated. On the front placard:

I Sue Freed
for
$100,000 for
Slander of Title.
Trial Nov. 15
Supreme Court

And on the back:

His Majesty,
The King of the
Prune Frogers Has
Suddenly Stopped
Playing My Record,
Which He Has Used
As A Theme
Without My OK
For 3 Years.

Robert Smith had advised Mr. Freed ("for artistic reasons") to
stop playing "the few bars" of the troublesome composition at about
the same time the picketing began, even though, in his twelve years

of experience in New York radio, Louis Hardin's "name" had "no significance" he could discover. Freed, on an etymological holiday, waxed more creative in his defense as the trial date neared:

> I am prepared to prove upon the trial from the 1935 and 1941 editions of the dictionary by Funk and Wagnalls that "MOONDOG" was defined as a weather manifestation and that it was, further, especially, a matter of my own and popular knowledge in Cleveland from a direct journalistic account thereof in connection with the parallel manifestations of "SUNDOG" in the *Cleveland Plain Dealer* for July 17, 1949.

How, he asked, can this New Yorker pretend to be able to "monopolize a generic word"? A ten-page manuscript elucidated all that Moondog would have hurled at him on November 15, eight "separate and complete" defenses and four "separate and partial" defenses, as well as four counterclaims. According to this document, Moondog is "not an unique and exceptional composer," yet he is trying to use "an ordinary word" and a "generic term" to make a legal case. For his "wicked misrepresentations" as well as his "parades" he was to be sued, in turn, for a quarter of a million dollars. Abner Greenberg probably rolled his eyes at this, but it is easy to imagine the risk-averse lawyer pleading with his defiant client. For whatever reasons, Moondog stopped picketing, and the two weeks before the trial went by without incident or comment.

The trial was three parts theatre, one part law. It began a week late, on Tuesday, November 23, officiated over by judge Carroll G. Walter. Testifying for the plaintiff were such notables as Marshall Stearns (later to write *Story of Jazz*) and Perez Prado (the composer and bandleader). Tony Schwartz, who had brought a still-vigorous Arturo Toscanini, explained to the court that Moondog was one of the finest natural musicians he had ever encountered. Benny Goodman, deposed, called Moondog's music "arresting." The court, with grudging respect, now addressed Mr. Hardin as "Mr. Moondog." The press gorged: "Moondogs in Suit Over Use of Name" (*Billboard,*

Nov. 6); "Moondog Wins in Court Fight" (*Downbeat*, Jan. 12, 1955); "Freed Enjoined from Use of 'Moondog' Label" (*Billboard*, Dec. 4); "Moondog Wins Air Suit; Would Rather Be Disc Jockey than Press Claim" (*Variety*, Dec. 1). The message varies little from piece to piece, with *Variety* stressing the assertive independence, even in triumph, of Moondog ("nom-de-street" of "Thomas Louis [sic] Hardin"), who is "interested in selecting platters for the Freed show," and who "would rather program" than seek a monetary settlement. The more sedate *New York Times*, on November 24 and 25, treated the hearing with tongue in cheek rather than with accuracy: when Justice Walter heard the "Moondog Symphony," for instance ("the musical melange of jungle sounds, plus harmonies that sounded like melodies from a Chinese mambo and clattering chopsticks"), he "buried his face behind a handkerchief." Nonetheless, he held unequivocally in favor of the composer, granting the injunction to restrain Freed from using Moondog's name or music without due credit, denying the counterclaim, and ordering a calculation of damages.

It must have been an enormous thrill for Moondog, his family, and his friends to tune into WINS on the evening of November 24 and hear the King announce to his subjects that they must dance under a new rubric: "rock 'n' roll" ascended from the ashes of a lost civil action. Freed went on to ever more hubristic triumphs before fading from fame and dying in obscurity and disgrace.

Moondog changed not at all. Victory confirmed and hardened his principles: money, so hard to come by for so long, couldn't seduce him. He wished to improve, not despoil, his rival. Against a tide that would swamp American music, Moondog tried to share his good taste with WINS, to regulate the quality of the programming by choosing the records played over the air by the king. WINS declined, but his insistence created some interesting wrinkles in the end-stage legal proceedings.

His account of the "talk of the town" affair concentrate on the moral victory:

Judge Walter made it clear in his decision, just how hard it was to make a name in music or in any other field of art, and for the sake of artists who have made a name, that name should be protected, even though an interloper had a registration.

Despite his cynicism about judges (if the presiding judge had not been about to retire, would he have had the courage to rule against so mighty an adversary?) and lawyers ("Abner Greenberg took the case. 'I want a hundred in advance, / plus twenty-five percent of damages.... The twenty-five percentage deal before the case was won, became the forty / percentage deal—thereafter"), he was able to collect on the twenty-to-one betting odds he heard some gamblers laying against his chances. The "bow-wow voice" of Freed, "so up-tight" on the air, converted the wager and chased the "black-and-blues," the sycophants, into silence.

On December 14, 1954, all parties assembled in the offices of referee Charles R. Barrett, Esq., for the first of two hearings to calculate damages. Mr. Freed was subpoenaed to appear in person and bring "all documents" relating to his professional income "as a disc jockey, announcer, promoter of dances, balls, entertainment, shows, etc." since 1951. The fifty-two pages of testimony consist mainly of Mr. Greenberg's financial inquisition of Mr. Freed. Moondog himself appears only once, and then only to testify that he was "self-employed." The referee awarded the plaintiff $5,000 in damages, of which the judge awarded the referee $750. An out-of-court settlement with WJW (Weejeewoo) in Cleveland for $1,500 completed financial matters. In February 1955, after all the papers had been filed and fees paid, Moondog walked away with roughly $3,500 in one of his well-concealed tunic pockets, a substantial sum for him and his family at that time, but a pittance when weighed against the profits he was excluded from. Moondog was not in the mainstream even when it came to raping the establishment.

Abner Greenberg, bless his heart, kept pursuing those elusive dollars, but the case petered out after February, 1956. Nor was

Moondog successful in pressing charges against Columbia Records, his once and future friend, which produced a popular single called "Moondog," dedicated to Freed by implication and aiming to capitalize on the trend while it lived. Moondog's umbrage, and his surprising success against Freed, convinced the company that it had little to gain or lose, so it offered to take the record off the market after all of the pressed copies were sold. Moondog, naturally, refused, and Columbia's spokesman told him to his face: "You're a hard man." This hearing was speedy: the judge was so "deferential" to the defense counsel that Moondog knew, as he put it, he "wasn't going to get another bite out of that apple." The record faded into oblivion, and the best news he got on the day of the decision was that he was excused from court fees. As he had learned in the past, and would learn with pain in the future, brushes with the law tended not to have happy endings.

Moondog was not bitter about the small settlement; he was victor where it mattered. But deeper within, his cynicism hardened a little more. Windfalls would not blow in his direction; nor could he convert being right into coin of the realm. Because he wished to stand apart and beyond conversion, to refuse to play the game by others' rules, the price tag would always be just dear enough to keep him out on the streets.

IN SPRING 1955 another fine opportunity appeared. Julie Laurence, a producer of children's records, called at the Aristo to ask Moondog if he was interested in writing the music for an album of English nursery rhymes. Ms. Laurence had achieved a reputation by lecturing at schools, appearing on television, and preparing the catalogue of circulating children's recordings for the New York Public Library. For Moondog this would be something new. Within days he had written down the rhymes in Braille from her dictation and begun to compose the music while at his Times Square stand; then he dictated it to Mary, who inked the sheets. Julie Laurence had researched authentic rhymes from as far back as 1570 ("Multiplication is Vexation") and 1606 ("Thirty Days Hath September," from a play, *The Return from Parnassus*), preferring the older, original versions to their later refinements and distortions. She finally settled on forty-five lyrics and added an opening poem and closing "prayer" of her own composition. As the producer, she would gather the principals, introduce them, rehearse them, and record them. She was, without question, even to those who disliked her method, the album's driving force and guardian angel.

Tell It Again is an interesting experiment but not necessarily a successful one. In its favor, newcomer Julie Andrews is one of its two singers, and her pure voice interpreting Moondog's rhythms and history's rhymes is delightful. Julius Baker, an old friend and then lead flutist of the New York Philharmonic, plays gracefully. But the production did not, as the jacket notes suggest, bubble with childlike froth or flow in a jocular mode. "'We all had fun making the record,' says Julie Laurence" in the notes. Not so, says Moondog. As in the finest of fairy tales, reality intrudes with its vital, inescapable events. Martyn Green, then a famous international performer, was the second singer, and he had trouble with the deceptively simple Moondog score. Finally, when it came time to edit the recordings, Moondog and Ms. Laurence disagreed severely, and two years passed after recording before the prestigious Angel label released the album. In the interim (1955–1957), however, Julie Andrews had become a big star. A color photograph of her posed regally on a throne, and her name printed larger than the title, dominates the album cover.

In summer 1955, though, it seemed for a time that five professionals, none a superstar, had come together to do something each had wanted separately to do before. According to the jacket, Ms. Andrews had wanted to record nursery rhymes ever since she had sung them to "her three younger brothers...at bedtime," especially with Martyn Green, "one of the figures of the English stage whom she greatly admired." He, in turn, loved to perform for children, having committed to memory "hundreds of nursery rhymes" while also composing "nonsense verses and songs for his friends' children." Coming out of the D'Oyly Carte Opera Company, a British stage institution with deep roots in Gilbert and Sullivan operetta, he rose, from his first performance in 1923, to assume "the comic role" before leaving in 1951 for Broadway, cinema, and television. Julius Baker had performed for four symphony orchestras before being appointed to the faculty of Juilliard, becoming a founder of the Bach Aria Group, and swiftly gaining the first flute chair of the New York Philharmonic. Thus there appeared to be a rich amalgam of popular and classical strains, such as sometimes produces memorable and original statements. The planning seemed sensitive and intelligent.

After the initial research, scoring, and negotiations, Moondog met Julie Andrews when he went, on "rehearsal day," to the apartment she was sharing with showgirls from the cast of *The Boy Friend*, the Broadway play in which she was appearing. As the "piping pot" of tea was brought out, she asked him how many sugars he took, and he answered, with bravado, "two and you." Martyn Green's first impression was somewhat more theatrical. He came with his dog, whom he had perform a trick for the assembled company: when he asked her to demonstrate what a showgirl has to do to get a mink coat, she rolled over and spread her legs. In the studio, however, with the moment of truth at hand, relationships grew more strained. Mr. Green had "much trouble with fives and sevens": Baker on flute, Moondog on drums (with Mary, unacknowledged once again, on "extra percussion," including "an occasional drone on guitar"), and Andrews had no trouble with the rhythms. Green was "condescending" and "grossly underestimated" his parts to such a degree that Baker finally blurted out, sotto voce, that Martyn was "strictly a two-four man." In response, the ex-prince of the D'Oyly Carte "exploded," swearing at the ensemble, and carving big red x-marks into the musical scores. So much for the fun. Moondog's only response was to think to himself how Martyn "doesn't sing a song, he shows you how it goes." Andrews, on the other hand, was "very friendly," "a wonder." Moondog was impressed: "To sing these words [the song "For every evil under the sun / There is a remedy / Or there is none."] in five-eight with my trimbas to accomp'ny was to make / me see how sound her training was—for her to do it at a single take." She had the kind of voice that would always appeal to him, the ideal instrument to interpret his carefully forged rounds: pure, sparing with vibrato, unerring in rhythm and pitch.

Moondog and Julie Laurence argued about editing. While he "fought her follies" she "pushed her featherweight around." Even at the recording sessions Baker had asked what she was doing, running in and out, assuming, as both men noted, "the role of Madam Clout." The cost of this battle of wills was that Moondog refused her permission to release the album. Only when Julie Andrews indicated disappointment, two years later, did he relent: "I won't release the rights because of Julie You, but I'll release the rights because of Julie Her." Julie Her, by then, was also known as Eliza Doolittle, for *My Fair Lady* had opened in March of 1956. Angel packaged *Tell It Again* to take advantage of her name, relegating the other four project members to the back of the cover. In addition to her being alone, regnant, on the front, her black-and-white picture on the back (showing her fondling a disquieting dog) is twice as large as the two of Martyn Green, and her biographical sketch makes three of his. In one of his modest photographs Mr. Green is holding up a spaniel (the talented bitch, one can assume) with a knowing smile on his face. Poor Moondog's likeness is compressed into a square inch, looking benign, aged, and sheepish in a fuzzy night shot; he gets one paragraph of standard material. Julius Baker's face does not even appear to illustrate his three-sentence biography. "Julie Her" might have been an ironic eponym in 1957, but by 1959, the last time Moondog heard from her, she had moved into another orbit altogether:

In 'fifty-nine I got a Christmas-Valentine from her,
and on the back
was Jesus Christ her Lord—aboard a bike.

Now having portrayed several famous persons, and living in opulent seclusion in Switzerland, where the hills were alive with the sound of music, she failed to mention the music, the record, or the composer in a radio biography Moondog heard two decades later. Apparently, she told it only once.

THE YEARS 1955–1956, in many ways transitional, were as active as any others, but they lacked drama. His first extended stay at the Aristo Hotel ended when he moved to the East Village in lower Manhattan. At 179 East 3rd Street he and Mary lived with their daughter from 1956 until 1960, when they separated permanently. The epicenter for his activities moved south a mile or so, and he became a frequent sight in the 20s and 30s as well as in his old haunt, the Times Square area. With $750 of the Freed settlement he bought the forty acres in Candor, New York that would become increasingly dear to him over the next two decades.

As he moved he grew. Ideas proliferated, projects were born, idioms evolved. Moondog was one for whom custom could never stifle variation. Because of his itinerancy and outsider stance, data came to him erratically and in unusual shapes. The lyricism innate in the musician, the romantic, grew apace with his streetwise cynicism and alongside the Dionysian frenzy of his percussion. In the crucible of his mind seethed numerous paradoxes. Later in life, as a counterculture figure of the 1960s, he would flaunt his daring syntheses. In the late 1950s he was supporting his wife and young daughter, a hard-working American pursuing happiness. He worked, however, as a blind beggar, living the life of an unrehabilitated drop-out. He had turned his handicap into an offensive weapon. As the decade advanced and he moved closer to assuming the identity of the Viking classical composer, his self-presentation and self-conception as an artist changed subtly. Dogma and ritual together danced a new and daring dance. On May 26, 1956, at about the time he and his family moved south-south-east, Moondog turned forty.

He had been committed to his vocation longer than he had been a skilled apprentice. His energies had never flagged, but they tended to spread themselves thin. At some uncertain time he began his dissociation from some of the surfaces he touched. But couldn't this quiet change be compared to other, ostensibly more traumatic, moments in his life? 1943, when he came to New York just after an intense period of adjustment and training in music? 1960, when he was alone again? 1965 or so, when he would become the Viking of Sixth Avenue? 1974, when he left for Europe, never to return? Perhaps the day he was blinded, or the day he heard *The First Violin*? Good lives are not necessarily illuminated with verifiable epiphanies. The finest often work, like Yeats' long-legged fly, in silence. Therefore, to single out 1956 for special treatment requires argument.

In that year he moved from Midtown Manhattan after living there, with the exception of trips and retreats, for thirteen years. More important, in 1956 he first began to compose his couplets, a form he remained loyal to for the rest of his career, just as with canons. Couplets became in language what the canon was to him in music, a manageable, miniature form, ordered but unlimited in possibility. He could write one or hundreds of couplets, produce an aphorism or an epic (as he would do in *Thor*, piling couplet upon couplet); he could also compose a brief round or create a sound panorama made up of inter-linking arrangements of rounds (as he would do in *The Creation*). He thus acquired from his study of recorded poetry the second major means of communicating his ideas to the world.

In addition to new surroundings and forms, Moondog was encountering at about this time theories of art and ethics that influenced him substantially. Two events are worthy of notice: first, he met Edgar Varese, the composer of what Moondog called "sound panoramas," one of the most influential of the avant-garde figures of his time; second, he read and absorbed Machiavelli's *The Prince*.

Edgar Varese's life and work are too famous and complex to suffer a summary, but his work and values both inspired and alienated the blind composer. Thus, as is often when two original minds come together, nothing came out of the meeting. Those who seemed to share much often have one or two small differences sufficient to keep them wary and apart. (Moondog never met John Cage again after 1950.) Varese pursued an ideal that music should be pure sound freed from its traditional associations, composed, as one commentator puts it, in a "dissonant, nonthematic, and rhythmically asymmetric" style. Throughout his long, influential career, he encouraged and took seriously recorded and electronic music. By the mid-1950s he was a fixture in New York, having lived there for forty years. For Moondog, Varese the innovator must have suggested the kind of creative force in music he wanted to become, with a career shaped by both theoretical rigor and experimental daring. Yet Varese also represented another kind of force Moondog opposed even more: the development toward atonality, in the hands of inferior composers a formless, sterile undertaking. Moondog's rejoining the mainstream in the early 1960s as a proponent of tonality recalled his rejection, a few years earlier, of another alternative. Even while his three (already anachronistic) Prestige albums were in planning, Moondog was turning his back on atonality.

When Moondog first encountered Machiavelli, it was a marriage of minds. Here, immersed in a vibrant but crooked past, spoke a sane, cynical voice that resonated with the present. With Machiavelli's Prince is born Moondog's Thor, the mythic hero of his later poetry, the emblem at the center of his "sound sagas." Machiavelli's brand of realism, for Moondog, converted negative experiences to positive, for he could now begin to see the glimmerings of a covert power operating beneath the modern Christian state and hastening its (deserved) demise. When Moondog examined his own underpinnings, he saw that they did not provide satisfying answers. His father's religion, the society of laws and not men, the impenetrable and arbitrary systems of his heritage, offered no solace. On a pragmatic foundation, Moondog's Machiavelli had taken a stance that others might consider amoral (all right: immoral). In the day-to-day ironies of life in New York, as well as in what he would come to call "historic myth," Moondog sought a cause. In Machiavelli he found a guide. With *The Prince* firmly attached to his tunic, a Virgil to his Dante, he took another step toward intellectual independence, through an alternate reading of history in a tradition he would have to discover by himself. Beneath the stoic exterior of the pilgrim and beggar there rumbled once again an early strain of the Viking.

1957 BROUGHT MORE EXPOSURE for Moondog, but not greater success or wider recognition. Day by day and year by year, he lodged more securely in the imaginations of New Yorkers, and became less likely to shatter misconceptions or adjust over-simplifications. If you do something well, and get credit for it, you become defined and limited by it. Using the media to present one's image in the age of technology is almost as natural for a composer as conducting his own music. Moondog appeared on television at least twice, recorded hours of his music, and then released much of it on three new albums during roughly June's fourth year. He sold his Jersey land, after giving a farewell concert in the neighborhood. By most standards it was a busy year, but hardly a ripple stirred his equable temperament or his family's delicate balance, for the moment.

His first appearance on WNBC's *Tonight Show* (the second was in 1969), when Steve Allen was the host, occurred in two segments. First they filmed him performing in front of the Warwick Hotel with Steve and his wife, Jayne Meadows, who seemed nervous to Moondog. He strove to assure her that they had, appearances to the contrary, a common ground, preacher fathers. Back in the studio, he played drums live with Skitch Henderson's band, collaborating on "Frost Flower" and "Heath on the Heather." ABC's *Wide Wide World* documentary series featured him as a prominent performer live on a block-long stage on the west side of Manhattan where Lincoln Center would soon stand. In August, at the Hunterdon Hills Playhouse in New Jersey, he put on his one-man show in the place he had seen ever less of for seven and a half years and would never visit again. The list of celebrities for whom he held court—musicians, literati, media luminaries, politicians—lengthened further to include Thomas L. Thomas (the famous Welsh singer), James Dean, and Jack Kerouac. Columnists continued to use him as an item.

He was still recording his music, at times on his own exotic labels. "Moondog and His Honking Geese" is a good example, with four rousing brass numbers, inspired by jazz and Latin motifs, played by a pickup band with himself, Mary, and Sam Ulano on percussion. This ten-piece ensemble opened for Louis Armstrong at the famed Basin Street East several times. It is the first of several Moondog Records: two of the four tracks appeared in a slightly different form on the third Prestige album (7099); two others he transcribed for organ three decades later in Europe. All of the material composed in the mid-1950s, like all of the SMC 78s, appeared on the three Prestige albums released through 1957 and 1958. His *Snaketime Series* LP, not to be confused with his earlier 78s, would become, to the last note, Prestige 1 (7042); a single produced somewhere around 1955 and privately sold on the streets on the Moondog label, containing "Caribea" and "Oo Debut," was transcribed onto Prestige 1; a ten-inch LP called simply *Crescent Snaketime Series* (with a green label marked 19318, 19319) became much of Prestige 2 (7069). As always, he re-orchestrated, expanded, modified, and transformed earlier thematic statements. The three Prestige albums, containing much of Moondog's first decade as a composer, tapping the library of Tony Schwartz and the memories of the Spanish Music Center, became, in effect, a retrospective. The selections on these three albums represent Moondog at his primitive, street-wise best. To some, this is Moondog at his most original; to those for whom he was a bold synthesizer of jazz and Latin idioms, something of an aboriginal talent in music, here is plenty. Given, however, his admission several years later in an interview that his only real ambition had been, from age eighteen, to be a symphonic composer, and that his 1950s recordings in New York were by and large "extracurricular," done "to get recognition" and to earn his daily bread, these winning pieces seem less important. But they help delineate a stage in his development, dramatize his posture then, and illustrate his resourcefulness. For some, who regard his later music as effete and derivative, the Prestige albums represent his last fling in his New York eclectic style.

That cannot be the whole story. For his last recorded statement of the decade (and his last album for eleven years) he chose to replay some of his earliest efforts. But Moondog was already developing in silence toward a grander synthesis and bolder signature. If he had looked back (not a habit of his), he would have discovered that the Prestige albums had become collector's items. Several of the selections aired frequently on programs as different as those broadcast by WNCN (Gordon Spencer) and by WNEW (Jazzbo Collins). He would have been unsurprised to learn that they made no money. When he finally recorded again in 1969, his music arrived in a more polished package and communicated what he saw as a more highly-evolved idiom. Moondog the "primitive" (of the streets, of "Wildwood," as Mr. Rhythm) would pass on, and the Viking that would come to replace him signified more than a change of dress. Something had to be rounded off, finished, before the next step could be taken.

BY 1958 MOONDOG FELT the lesser tremors that precede eruption. He and Mary spent more and more time apart. Just as presidents relieve domestic pressure by seizing upon crises overseas, Moondog spent more and more time on the streets and made lengthy visits alone to his newly acquired upstate property. During the predictable let-down period when no new recordings or appearances were being planned, the tension did not wear well. Here is Moondog as he was seen one drizzly evening by a surprised theatregoer:

> It was slightly misty, and I suddenly felt a presence; I looked to my left and started, as did my date. We looked and then ran quickly down the street. In a doorway we had seen a Christlike figure with long hair just standing, not moving. The night being so quiet and drizzly made us feel we had seen an apparition. When we finally stopped running, I realized the figure was Moondog: he was not playing his music, he was just getting in out of the rain.

He had to work evenings, because of the brisk business he could get from "show-goers." But despite the six or eight hours he spent on location around town, while married he always had a home to come to. Money was his primary concern whenever he dealt with his public; the beggar's lot, however, is unpredictable, and the world often inhospitable. During lulls he composed beneath his cloaks, and when things got really slow he napped, chin on his knees. In the cold and damp of winter, when rest was nearly impossible, his hours were erratic, and often he did not get to sleep until 1 a.m. The street-smart Moondog would have nodded in wry appreciation at Orwell's remarks about beggars in *Down and Out in Paris and London*: To most "normal" people, Orwell speculated, beggars don't really "work" or "earn" a living; they are parasites, to be avoided or patronized as curiosities. The real reason they are despised is that there is no essential difference between beggars and "honest" work-men. The only distinction between a beggar and, say, an accountant or a literary critic is that the beggar "has merely made the mistake of choosing a trade at which it is impossible to grow rich." Mary shared Moondog's life on the streets at times, but after eight years even solid relationships can groan beneath such a burden.

Moondog traveled still, wandered still, never stayed still. When he wasn't on the streets or in a studio, he was on the road; when he wasn't in the middle of a crowd or before an audience, he needed to be alone. His travel was always well thought-out and planned, like his street-work; even in escape Moondog was the brooding intellectual. He knew that thumbing a ride was dangerous and impracticable: his "traveling office," gear, instruments, and accoutrements made any transportation less reliable and more perilous. He took buses nearly everywhere he went. He did not roam in the 1950s over large stretches of open country, but he did go away a couple of times without his wife and child, and these instances point to an unspoken recognition.

After his marriage he did not go back to his Jersey land. Mary was never interested in Moondog's style of outdoor living, especially with June to care for. The property finally sold in 1957, but not before he had tilled another retreat, bought in 1956, as its successor, in Candor, New York. Moondog had enjoyed his "little wooded lot" in the early 1950s, composing in the wild under Spartan conditions if questionable privacy. The journey to and fro was always tedious, and the string of break-ins annoying, but the place served a great need. Even the local reputation he had acquired as the hermit of the moors faded benignly into the past. Uncultivated, the spread went fallow, and the money was better spent back in New York, keeping the home fires burning.

In February of 1958, with a nameless young man (he attracted lads with the same ease as he did ladies), he went up for the first time to explore "Logue Hill," south of Ithaca, "a thousand miles from anywhere." On the first and last nights of their one-week stay, snow storms dumped a foot onto the foot already there. They had to pull out, for they had no structure to live in, although well stocked, mainly because his companion was not dressed for winter. A sign of the deteriorating marriage is the fact that he returned in the spring, one season later, for "several months," building a log shack. In 1958, in his glorious solitude, he worked out his marvelous perpetual calendar, with which one can find the day of the week any historical event occurred or will occur for over 3000 years (published in 1969) [See Appendix E]. He returned to Candor after his separation, through the next decade and into the Seventies, when he settled there for several years to hide, think, and write.

When he finally stood still to take stock of his life in late 1959 and early 1960, Moondog found himself where he wanted least in the world to be again: in a courtroom. The rancorous separation culminated with Moondog serving a sentence of 101 days on Ward's Island, by far his longest stretch behind bars. For most of the rest of his life, he refused to talk about these months, unsurprisingly. Neither his utterances nor those of acquaintances indicate any productive activity emerging out of that long, dark night. Before he died, he explained what happened.

Mary returned home one day to find Moondog dressing his seven-year-old daughter. In her eyes, he was fondling a prepubescent girl; in his defense, he said he was simply "looking at" his daughter the only way he could. For both, it was the final indignity, and Moondog told his wife of eight years that it was time to separate, this being as good a pretext as any. Mary was not easily mollified; in court she demanded—and got—alimony and child support from a man classified by the New York City Police Department as a beggar. At the hearing a blind rabbi testified that there might be support in rabbinical tradition for Moondog's position that he had been "seeing," not fondling. Moondog, however, did not have the heart to prolong the agony, so he admitted guilt and took his punishment.

Although no formal divorce ever occurred, he and his wife of eight years and his daughter of seven parted ways. They did not meet again until 1971, eleven years later. When their one happy reconciliation of a few months had spent its energy, much of it in the production of the second Columbia album, they parted, more amicably to be sure, a second and final time. Later, after the doom had settled and the adversaries were no longer intimates, he admitted that he had felt "cramped" by the marriage—not by their quarters, for he was an ascetic, but by an encroachment on something more precious than space. He was, according to a later, more flippant account, just not suited to domesticity:

> Moondog's time was almost completely absorbed by the cares of his family. "I stopped my music. Everything stopped." He eventually came to the painful conclusion that it was a choice between family and art. He chose art. The marriage lasted eight years. They're still married but don't see each other. "Marriage with all the commitments and involvements is not for me because I never expect to find a woman who will accommodate herself to the artist's life." (Interview with William Stout, *Corpus*, 1968.)

A facile defense would be Yeats' choice of perfecting either the life or the work, colored by Bacon's cynical remarks about a married man being a hostage to fortune. But this would be unfair to Mary, who, in her unobtrusive way, did much to accommodate him; nor would it be generous to so large a spirit as his. This is probably why he pleaded guilty: he knew in some way that he was responsible. Also, Mary allowed (indeed encouraged) Moondog and June to be re-united in 1971, so she must have been aware that her husband was not a child-molester and that the marriage had been over long before the incident.

Life did not give Moondog a free ride into bachelorhood. Starting a new decade in jail is more than symbolic: it is hitting bottom. He had to move in new directions after his release, because his old sources of solace and respect were gone: no wife, no child, no record contracts, no royalties. The melancholy chant of his most famous round would resonate prophetically, like old Lindy howling at the moon, as he ended so generous a stretch of time on so low a note: all was loneliness.

Plymouth Church.

Moondog college yearbook photo.

Moondog at Carnegie Hall, late '40s.

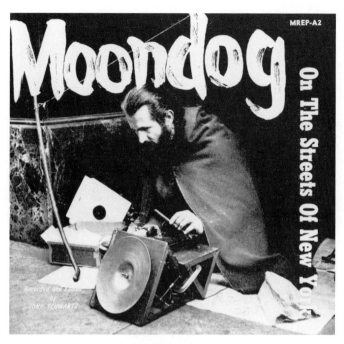

Moondog on the Streets of New York: Mars album, 1953.

Moondog with Mary and June, summer 1953.

Moondog in mid-'50s.

Moondog at a drum concert, May 1954.

Moondog with passerby, late '60s. Photo by Walter Karling.

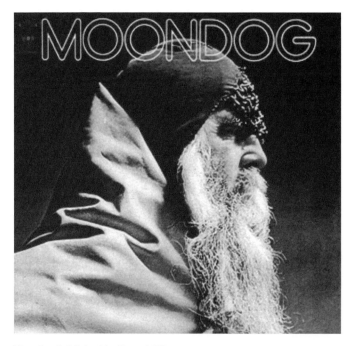

Moondog first Columbia album, 1969.

Moondog second Columbia album, 1971.

Moondog on the corner in Recklinghausen, 1975.

Moondog with the Queen of Sweden, 1981. Photo by Stefan Pedersen (Lakatos).

Moondog with newly-made trimbas.

Moondog in his last years. Photo by Ola Hjelm / SEBRA.

Moondog high on a windy hill.

Chapter Five

The Viking of Sixth Avenue

(1960–1969)

T he 1960s sometimes elevated the mere eccentric to the status of hero. Beneath the kinky glamour, the political vitality, and the shimmering variety lay a confusion that a hundred antiheroes could not dispel, and shaky underpinnings of a rebelliousness that was a symptom, not a cure. Today, free speech, free love, and peace before dishonor sound like charming artifacts of an adolescent sincerity. Some journalists of the 1960s have tidily covered their tracks, either subtly altering their previous positions or excusing themselves, with latter-day sobriety, for getting caught up in the moment. Skirts have come down and gone back up again, many times; entertainers still go into politics; rock stars are idolized in platinum with the same fervor (though their lyrics no longer seem to have biblical resonance). Those who lived through those bright, complex times, and who thought they confronted the issues honestly, may now wonder to what extent they were taken in. There was, in addition to a primal innocence and a radical response to social injustice, a great deal of mere surface glitter.

Other periods of history have seemed invigorating to those passing through and dubious to those looking back. Much good came out of the floods of energy playing over a nation plagued by dissension, generating a plethora of new ways of living, art forms, and ethical codes. To place Moondog accurately, one must remember the froth of the 1960s: the shiny patina, the nervous gesture, the dramatic over-response. In other words, while it brought forth much authentic, constructive activity, and generated an effective, muscular outrage at government arrogance, it also pandered as no period before it to the American teenager, fixing an unanchored idealism and skewed scale of significance into the national paranoia. One of the more predictable reactions by prosperous citizens to internal problems that dwarf exterior threats is to glorify self-awareness, to examine quirks and tics so closely that what in more tranquil times is background and trivial acquires gravitas and centrality. When many thought a revolution in consciousness was imminent, some of the energy for reform dissipated rather than crystallized: self-contemplation had slipped into solipsism. The Great Society died in the vise of the Nixon years. The Vietnam War ended through Kissinger's cynical shuttle diplomacy. Camelot turned into Watergate.

In this awesome, ironic decade Moondog was where he had been since he came to New York. With the exception of his few retreats to his upstate property, he spent the 1960s on the streets of Manhattan. After so many modest successes through the 1950s, no album appeared, no single event had the symbolic importance of the Freed case, and after the paralyzing loneliness of his separation from Mary and June, he formed no durable relationship for over ten years. There were concerts, appearances, readings, publicity, but little would have more than a brief and local impact. His old professional alliances gave way to new ones, and he was never without a wide circle of friends. But until the 1969 Columbia album, Moondog was, involved and outspoken as he always was, paradoxically quiet.

On the surface, this is surprising, for who was a more likely focus for the surge of counterculture happenings than Moondog, self-generated symbol of the anti-establishment and contemporary Diogenes? No explanation of how someone did not become a celebrity can pretend to make sense, but it would be interesting to try to understand why Moondog did not seize the day despite the loyalty and fervor of his fans, many themselves luminaries. The story of his obscurity illuminates the changes he underwent while the world changed all around him, for everything he was, all he stood for, made him appear other than he was.

To begin with, the Viking dress that became his trademark did not evolve until the mid-1960s, so while trends were born and died in rapid succession under the close scrutiny of the media, he was still struggling to achieve a new identity and philosophy. When he finally became recognizable as a rugged individualist, even a mythic figure, many of the ideas he won for himself in the process were against the grain. Scratch a rebel and you might get a reactionary: his myth was so far-out that it was too far to the right, and too old-fashioned, for those far-out times. Although he shared a horror of middle-class America with the young, the poor, and the outcast (he was one of the first and the most famous of the street people of our time), he did not lust after the lifestyles or ape the codes of these other outsiders. Moondog was sympathetic to the right causes, and gave them his time and support. He spoke out in public against the war and performed in civil rights concerts. Adding to his counter-cultural credibility, he had written music inspired by Indian rhythms, Latin rhythms, and black jazz. He preached about marching to a different drummer. But he was not, could not, become part of a "movement"; he fit none of the star-molds then current. The moment was never ripe for the man who matured at his own pace.

By far the greatest difference between himself and his erstwhile admirers was ideological. He acknowledged, with all of the critics of the technocracy, that civilization was diseased and in desperate need of regeneration. But his criticism was not born out of the struggle for equality by minorities, nor from the superimposition of Eastern dogmas. He held that our modern cancer was centuries old and stemmed from the loss of a culture that had been annihilated by the very forces still in power. When the "Christian state" wiped out the old Nordic infrastructure during the so-called "Middle Ages," a world-view disappeared, or went underground. Once there were benevolent dictatorships whose armies of loosely confederated bands struck terror into the inhabitants of southern, eastern and western Europe. After being converted and absorbed, the men of Thor lost their fire, became docile citizens of Christian Europe; the old beliefs became literary appendages. He would revive that ethos, if only in himself. In doing so, however, the Viking of Sixth Avenue could only give so much to the causes proliferating around him, for with his new system came a harsh reckoning of those who would call him their brother. To him, the new revolutionaries were often as much tinsel as the establishment they scorned, both committing the same fallacy. The new orders were as far removed from his concepts as the order they sought to replace. To return to a world-view only dimly recollected in Icelandic saga, after the oral tradition was finally written down, to ages and peoples untouched by the Christian state: this he would preach. He would write poetry that confused and embarrassed even his allies; he would compose building blocks of a Nordic sound saga; he would undermine his opponents by showing them how his gods would undermine theirs.

Aggressive, complex men with unpopular views almost never live comfortably. To make them into curiosities is easier than to take them seriously. Although Moondog was respected by some, few of those who heard him out could follow him to the limits of his engagement with the old order. In this sense, the 1960s could not absorb him. He was always "in," but he had far too many rough edges to be chic.

THE 1960S BEGAN for Moondog in olive drab, the dominant color of his clothes as well as the mood of his new daily life. By August 1960, after he left the House of Correction on Hart's Island, he was back at the Aristo Hotel, now paying child support (soon, alimony too). Ten years after his first stay at the creaky old building, his was hardly a triumphal return. Since the place no longer exists, we can only trust descriptions by visitors to 101 West 44th, and the consensus was not flattering. His home was, according to one caller in winter 1960–61, "a nasty little place of dreadful stench and dubious clientele. We made our way past a couple of passed-out drunks on the stairs and through dark halls to Moondog's door." Another visitor describes Moondog "huddled in a small, cockroach-infested room…with barely enough room to move after the mattress was propped against the wall." Another called it "depressing, a dump."

To those who remember Moondog as colorful, startling, and bizarre, the image of a blind beggar with the face of Christ, covered with dull, heavy garments made of army blankets, might seem surprising. For over twenty of the thirty years Moondog spent on the streets of New York, however, his garb was unspectacular (albeit unusual), and his life something less than a poor, suffering artist's romance. His unorthodox dress alienated him from Rodzinski and the Philharmonic, and figured in the Freed case as an ingredient of his public identity as an artist, but his ultimate sartorial statement was neither inevitable nor smooth. The progress of his life as he approached his fiftieth year, and his ideas as reflected in his clothing, were hard-won and sustained by devotion to his craft.

Now that he had left domesticity for solitude and had to manage his affairs with little aid from others, he resumed, with a renewed independence, his characteristic methods of remaking himself. In 1961 he showed a group of friends his new shoes, which were "splendid, made of squares of leather." Most of his garments were still made out of squares of materials hand-sewn together, and aside from "dress uniforms" would always be. The color scheme of choice at the time was "green, preferably olive drab," not only because it was cheap, but also because he was comfortable with the innocuous and meaningless then. In 1962 an out-of-town guest at the Warwick Hotel described his nocturnal encounter with Moondog near 54th Street and 6th Avenue:

> I stopped still and looked intently at that shadowy figure until I could make it out more clearly, though still dimly. I was startled as some of the features of a huge apparition came into focus: cowl, robe, strange footwear, alms-cup, beard, and, as I finally realized, unopen eyes. I took the person—if such it were indeed—for a Russian monk of some sort.

Weeks later, his courage bolstered by daylight, the man approached Moondog at 52nd and 6th to speak with the apparition: "He described the various articles that made up his garb, each of which was a square, even to the heavy cloth footwear." Moondog was now in his element: "He was himself, he said, a square, and all the music he composed was square."

Life at the Aristo was difficult for quite some time. Moondog recalled:

> It was hard for me to make enough money to pay rent, copyist and traveling expenses up to my place in Candor. There were times when I couldn't go up for over a year at a time. It was a case of either/or. Sometimes I would check out, putting my things in the hotel's storage room, so that I could spend a few weeks upstate. This was not so good, for when I came back, it was not always possible to get the same room, or any room, for a while. This went on until 1967.

Through the hard times people tended to be good to him. One instance of supererogation came about when Moondog, to make a little more room, tried several times to dispose of a foot-high stack of audio tapes. The New York City sanitation men kept returning them to him in spite of his expressed wish to be unencumbered. It turned out that they were the master tapes of his 1950s recordings. Although the tapes managed to get lost once more, others were watching out for his interests. Whenever he got a little more elbow room he spread out the papers for the more ambitious works he was composing, and much important music came out of this "Aristo period." He wrote the *Grosse Kanon* for piano and orchestra and some large symphonic works indoors. Most of his other new compositions were written, as they had been in the 1940s and 1950s, on the street: "Good for Goodie," "Ode to Venus," "Theme." For seven years, until he moved out of the Aristo in 1967 (shortly before its destruction), this was his life: a cycle of street scenes, occasional trips, infrequent appearances, and diligent work. During one feverish month, February of 1961, for instance, he wrote Book I of his *Art of the Canon*. "I set myself the task of doing a piece a day, through all the keys and ending in C, where I began: a total of 25 pieces. I did it in 28 days, including writing, editing and proofing." Each piece fills a page, with the exception of number 24, which is two pages long. Through this long and arduous period his work evolved, he became less occupied with public issues and more with his music, and his outfits began to take on some color.

Because Moondog found it hard (financially and logistically) to leave the city, any outing, any engagement with the wilderness, was welcome. One opportunity came in 1961, when two married couples invited him to go camping at Stokes State Forest in New Jersey. The junket began when Moondog was picked up at his spot, but had to enter the Dodge station wagon from the driver's side, parking being awkward in mid-Manhattan. A bus pulled up alongside, and the driver yelled: "Hey, Moondog, are you going to drive that thing?" Tranquil as always, he struggled in with his homemade canvas pack, and they were off. During this weekend in the high hills of the Appalachian Trail Moondog impressed his hosts both with his excellent survival instincts and his calm. Not aware that he was at home in the woods, thinking that he had not been out of the city for over a decade, they were somewhat amazed when a map sketched onto his palm relating the campsite to the road and stream was all he needed to settle comfortably in. They were even more surprised when he began to break up dead wood for a fire: he would smack a limb, listen for its impact on the ground, and unerringly track it down. After they had eaten dinner, he sewed a shirt out of six handkerchiefs, something he could do by then in ten minutes. The campers noted how he appeared to be bestowing a blessing when he pulled out the thread with an upraised hand, but he answered that there was a fat chance of him blessing anyone. On the next day, Moondog easily paced the hikers up an enormous hill, listening for "The Holly and the Ivy" sung out from ahead. A rattlesnake was encountered and killed in a furious mêlée, through which Moondog sat serenely, pointing out the names of the various birds cheeping and twittering in the trees. The frontiersman insisted that they cook it. When he proposed adding another entrée—a newborn porcupine retrieved by one of the party's dogs, with umbilical cord still attached—other sensitivities prevailed. One of the men, a Swedish reporter who considered Moondog "a living work of art," took numerous photographs of the trip. He also took several at the Aristo that ran in a Swedish magazine two decades later, in 1982. Moondog was one of the most photographed New Yorkers of his time.

A friend, Willa Percival, also a professional photographer, spent much time with him in the city and on the road in the early 1960s. She recorded a rooftop scene with the Empire State in the background during a cookout with a woman and child, Moondog by the fire; Moondog with a tourist on the top deck of the *S.S. Essex* in harbor; standing under the statue of George Washington with arm upraised, on the steps of the Federal Reserve Bank (a line of Hell's Angels motorcycles in the foreground); close-ups of Louis' profile framed by George's. There were many others: at the Cloisters, with the Hudson River in the background; on Fire Island; on the Avenue of the Americas; and even a few with "a family in Cornwall at a New Year's Day dinner (white table cloth)" as he sat on a sofa, chatting.

On Moondog's ideas the activity around him had little effect, and even the causes he embraced and the campaigns he waged tended to be personal and solitary. For a few Thursdays (rain date: Friday) during February and March 1961, for instance, he took his attack on the concealed church-state (what he now called "panchristianity") right to the power brokers on Wall Street, an action he had been mulling over for fifteen years. His theme and his charge were specific: the immorality of the Federal Reserve System, the grand legalized trust of all trusts in a nation that publicly prosecuted conglomerates and cartels. His plea was for monetary reform and a thorough revision of the existing antitrust laws. As in 1955, when he confronted his "opponent" (WINS) squarely and dramatically, the gestures were deliberately theatrical. He handed out one thousand little green slips of paper, printed up at his own expense. Thus, during the lunch hour of the business capital of the world, this eccentric from uptown appeared to be distributing cash. The passers-by snapped them up quickly and walked away with seven Moondog couplets on "The Monetary Issue."

One week he would attack the Federal Reserve, wielding Jefferson's warning ("a central bank is more of a menace to the liberties of men than a standing army"). The next week he would try to undermine what he considered the hypocritical "civil" code he saw as "bristling with Christian morality" (anticipating his Thor by a few years). Even though he made many new acquaintances during these weeks, among them some staunch bulls from the Stock Exchange, he did not maintain the pilgrimage for very long. As events in the age of petitions and marches and sit-ins began to accelerate in intensity and frequency, Moondog began to disengage, seeking seclusion with greater conviction. He predicted his retirement to Candor in 1968, four years before it actually came about; yearning to see his "root" culture at first hand, he longed to go to Europe for more than a decade before he did. As he turned inward and became more serious about composing, his attachment to the net of subcultures that tried to display him as a splendid catch loosened, and he and his age began to go different ways.

The Viking took his time emerging, as did the reclusive composer, since both were wrestling with the soul of the performer and activist, and Moondog had not, as far as is known, planned or contemplated a change in direction in the early 1960s. When the highlights of a decade are compressed into a couple of pages, the pace seems feverish, but noteworthy events might have gaps between them of months, seemingly uneventful stretches in which the work gets done. These quiet moments of increasing momentum elude biography. Many artists work best in peace, not when they must grapple with words in a crowd. Moondog had chosen the latter.

He was an engaging speaker who thought little of conversation as craft. (Probably with good reason: recorded conversations often fall flat as literature. What had seemed to be brilliant spontaneity reads as coarse or vapid, especially when compared with the writings of those conversing.) The "art" of conversation today seems little more than a social skill, inferior to its illustrious sire, the oral tradition, in which each trustee refines and polishes the myth, legend, and history he transmits. Moondog worshipped the oral tradition, be it of American Indians or of Norse scops, and knew that he was not a part of it. His public utterances may seem contradictory or banal, then, as most do. He conversed, often for hours a day. It went with the job, usually enjoyably. He learned new ideas and ways; the blind man's education centers around the spoken word. Yet however much he embraced the public, he always worked alone. The haunting realization that visits Elijah (I Kings) comes to mind: the real presence of God (the best part of ourselves) is not found in the fire or in the wind, but in the still, small voice.

Like Moondog the recording artist, Moondog the performer had bad luck. Timing, life kept reminding him, is the chief god in the pantheon of the celebrity. One of the most urgent reasons for abandoning his stage career was his cynicism about making it in show business; another was the time and energy (best spent composing) it took to mount even the slenderest of acts. Finally, he was deeply pained when he was typecast, even though every performer shares with his public the responsibility for his persona. Moondog's "costumes" were not part of an act, but living emblems of his convictions. Yet he had to earn money, begging being undercompensated, and many of his professional friends were anxious to make the right connection for him or to give him the proper exposure. But most, like Bob Dylan, still saw him as the paradigmatic drop-out and pariah. In his poem "Blowin' in the Wind" (not to be confused with the later song), published in the December 1963 *Hootenanny*, he writes:

> an Moondog beatin' his drum and
> sayin' his lines —
> an Lord Buckley's memory still movin'...

(Moondog never met Lord Buckley, but the juxtaposition is instructive: Dylan sees both as satirists of the middle class, and Moondog's oddity therefore coincides with his emerging world-view. What Moondog was sayin' is never specified—another example of his admirers seeing in him what they wanted him to represent.)

Others made him out to be even weirder than he was. A bizarre coincidence occurred on stage in Greenwich Village. On a few evenings (in 1961 and 1963 at the Big Fat Black Pussy Cat, in 1962 at the Long Theatre, and in 1963 in a midnight revue at the Living Theatre, for instance) Moondog shared the bill with an obscure and freakish act. This countertenor who strummed a ukulele and wore a tuxedo that stressed his pot belly and hermaphroditic shapelessness was soon to rise as a star, albeit meteorically. A review in *The Village Voice* by J.R. Goddard (July 25, 1963) starring "TT, Hugh [Hugh Romney] and Moon" captures the moment perfectly. The picture alone was worth the ten cents, with Tiny Tim beaming and Moondog, looking gaunt and spectral, gazing off to the side, abstracted. The article concludes:

> And then there's Moondog, resplendent in his long grey hair [not yet 50!] and beard, his hermetic monk's garb and even more hermetic voice. Usually seen around 53rd and Sixth...he reads couplets while a lovely young woman with strawberry blond hair named Suzanne Frenon (a Juilliard graduate who's just started working with him) plays his Bach-like canons on the piano. Just watching them is a delight—Moondog's peripatetic hands "playing" his couplets on a Braille sheet while Suzanne energetically plays at the decrepit upright. Aphorisms come out, some of them only corny doggerel, some of almost Haiku precision, some with a shocking aptness for our time.... Neo-Baroque and very Humanist, in spite of his aridity, Moondog leaves us close to reality, weird costume or not.

Lenny Bruce once joined TT and Moon, an ungodly trinity.

Moondog struggled through the early 1960s, poorer than he liked. Royalties had dried up, and his meager savings had drained

into the reclamation of his wilderness retreat. The occasional commercial or soundtrack adapted from his scores funded at most a
brief holiday alone upstate. Most of his appearances served as
showcases for his varied talents, but until 1966 none of his more
ambitious orchestral works had been performed. A typical program
included some verse recitation and some percussion pieces, usually
solo. He made several appearances at Town Hall, throughout the
1960s, with many of the jazz originals of his era. He was on stage
several times at the Village Theatre, once doing an early rendition
of *Thor the Nordoom*, another time with a sextet, reading antiwar
poetry while Allen Ginsberg held the microphone. He read *Thor* at
Steinway Hall and at Queens College, both with small ensembles.
At Alfred College he rehearsed some singers to perform a selection
of his madrigals and arranged a dance contest in which couples
stepped to his five-four waltzes. (The first, second, and third prizes,
$15, $10, and $5, came out of his fee.) In 1965, in the basement of
a Lutheran Church, he performed "a medley of strange sounding
musical canons" with "a couple of assistants." (Phil Tracy, "A Happy
Story," *National Catholic Reporter*, December 10, 1969) He was
front and center at this amateur night benefit for the grape strikers,
as for so many other worthy causes. In spring 1966, aided by the
director of Spectrum Gallery on 57th Street, he staged a "Moondog
Concert." (Charles Giuliano, "A Recollection of a Sidewalk Viking,"
Boston After Dark, October, 15 1969) A contract, witnessed by Mack
at the desk of the Aristo, provided for four musicians, "symphony
men," at $25 each. The quartet finally booked were members of the
New York Philharmonic. The specificity of his demands underscores
the rarity of the opportunity. After "hollering" in the hall to test the
acoustics, and after appearing for three hours on WBAI in what
amounted to an extended media notice, he "delighted" the gallery on
May 20 with the following program: his *Symphonique No. 9*,
arranged for string quartet; an interpretive dance by Linda Gudde;
and Moondog reading canons and couplets "to fill out the skimpy
program." (In his *Moondog Yearbook I*, earliest printings, he notes:
"I call [the *Symphonique No. 9*] 'Bird's Lament,' in memory of

Charlie Parker. We were to have cut a duet together. I wrote it after his death. Bernstein has been sitting on the score since 1960." It appeared on the 1969 Columbia album, rescored for reeds with alto sax lead.) Later, in summer 1966, Moondog gathered enough money together to hire actors and musicians for "an evening at the Cinematheque." There, with the help of Maggie Dominick, at 44th Street between Broadway and 6th Avenue, before what one observer described as "a dazzled psychedelic audience from New York's underground," he acted in and had enacted his most elaborate mounting of *Thor the Nordoom, A Norse Saga*. This anticipated his later work on the Columbia album and beyond. In keeping with his new image as the Viking of the avant-garde, he has a small part in the film *Chappaqua*, also featuring William Burroughs, Allen Ginsberg, and Ravi Shankar, who wrote the music. On October 15, 1967, with the help of his new agent, Al Brown (who was with him through the Columbia albums), he had an even more rewarding experience. As he put it in the *Moondog Yearbook*:

> My greatest ambition is to conduct my own work from memory. That ambition was realized...at the Village Theatre, thanks to Ron Wolin, who had me appear, but especially to Al Brown, violist, who gathered a group of fine players together to form my Mini Sym....

Once again, they first performed earlier scorings of several of his Columbia album selections. A few times during 1968, Jack Kalish had Moondog appear at the Folk Dance Center, 69 West 14th Street. Under the title "Moondog at Midnight: Poetry and Dance," with or without a recording of Beethoven's piano sonatas as accompaniment, Moondog read his poems, played his drums, and sold his music. He could not afford musicians at this time. Also at midnight, again in 1968, he appeared at the Vicki Hayes Theatre Workshop, 1741 Broadway, on Saturday evenings. A photograph of Ms. Hayes, "accepting reservations at 212-JUdson 2-3058," appeared in the earliest Yearbooks.

Others also performed Moondog's music. Elliot Finkel (a long-time admirer and internationally noted pianist) played the *Grosse Kanon* and selections from *The Art of the Canon*, Book I, several times and did a recital with his brother of Book I complete at Little Carnegie Hall. (*American Music Digest* and *Music Journal* printed good reviews—1970.) Moondog's ballet, *Nocturne* (originally *Suite No. 2* on the Epic album), was conducted in Central Park by John Draper, a longtime professional friend, and performed by the Donald McKayle Dance Company at the City Center, May 22 and May 25, 1969. (A contract from 1965 signed by Bethsabee de Rothschild of the Batsheva Foundation for Art and Learning in Tel Aviv promised Moondog $10 for every paid performance and $5 for every free performance of "Nocturne" mounted by their dance company.) Tony Schwartz paid to use "Theme" in a twenty-second television commercial for Hubert Humphrey's presidential campaign of 1968. There were others, less known, with little or no compensation.

Towards the end of the 1960s Moondog entered a new relationship toward himself on stage, along with the emergence of newer idioms. The seemingly impressive tally of appearances was spread over nine years and confined mainly to small venues. During that time his ideas on Norse mythology, history, and culture were beginning to coalesce. In turn, a fresh aesthetic and cultural mission guided his passion for expression. He lost interest in performing his work in fits and starts.

In 1964, in the second of three appearances (the others were in 1953 and 1969), Moondog filled a major time-slot on NBC's *Today Show*. An extravagant crew of technicians flew up with him to Candor to film him at his primitive best, reading his poetry and playing his drums in the woods near his shack, casting him again in a role he had to his chagrin repeatedly accepted. He bore a stigma that he was desperate to erase: the public saw and wanted him only as a street musician, based mostly "on the strength of the record I did fifteen years ago when I was playing on the street." This image was hard to change:

"They're just as content to let you stay in that category. If you are a street musician they'll assume you are nothing else. They would never dream you could write a symphony or a quartet."
(*Corpus*, 1960)

His belated realization that the glitter of his reputation as a performer had sidetracked his composing came with powerful undertows. His resolve to write rather than to give himself to an audience solidified when he became the Viking of Sixth Avenue. It is a paradox that he was more colorful then than at any other time, but it is not a coincidence.

I'm not really an entertainer; I don't know how to sell myself and I don't try. I can't put myself over like Jolson. I don't have stage presence; I think that one of the things that is a disadvantage to a performer is not to be able to see his audience. I don't know how to beat down that fifth wall—the wall between myself and the audience. I can't beat it down; I'm much happier writing.

The habit of composing became more natural as his commitment hardened. He had lived, now he wanted to write. Driven to solitude, not by it, his idioms shaped by new myths, he used the years without new recording projects to test himself as a composer.

THE VIKING'S EMERGENCE from the near past to a more distant one was a splendid metamorphosis: in dress, from drab squares to color and costume; in philosophy, from cause consciousness to poetic myth; in music, from the percussive and the primitive to canonic form and sound saga. Private yet garrulous, open yet firm, soft-spoken yet unshakeable, he danced between extremes. Some of his ideas were outrageous in their implications; some of his verse was chillingly effective, for those who knew no poetry at all as well as for those who thought his poems in the main amateurish and trendy;

some of his music intimidated the uninitiated traditionalist and impressed the open-minded, flexible professional. His activities, like his creations, cut across boundaries, castes, and cultures. The sophisticated admired the complex expressions of primal experience, and the undemanding enjoyed the familiar if slightly unusual tonalities so comfortingly close to what they knew and felt.

But what did it feel like to create, with so many obstacles to overcome? What was a typical day like for a man whose life was so enigmatic and strange? He had to live, whatever occupied his mind, in physical time and place. The images he cloaked himself with created distance through violent distortion, making a statement as they shielded him. Blind Tiresias, prophet of doom, a benevolent instrument of the gods; Father Time, with Olympian serenity reading the pulse of a decadent, nervous culture; Viking foot-soldier and bard, reasserting archaic values in the most cosmopolitan and urbanized of civilizations. However, most of his days passed by without special revelations, impressive discoveries, or grave setbacks. Even pariahs live in clock-time and meet the tax man. The life of a public man is measured by the impressions he leaves on those he touches, on the illuminations he transmits through his works and his deeds, seldom by the manner in which the work and the image is produced. While the exterior may be glitter and gloss, the long hours spent in lonely labor are barely worth mentioning.

And yet, working during spare moments on the streets, and through the night while the sighted slept, Moondog, step by step, garment by garment, note by note, remade himself. His ideas, which previously he had let his life or music speak for, or spread like fertilizer on the public with irregular pronouncements, tightened around several mythic concepts. The seeds of *Thor the Nordoom* and *The Creation* took root. The second half of the 1960s (unlike his first twenty years in New York and unlike the anarchy erupting all around) seems in retrospect a steady and orderly flow of music (orchestral suites, canons, rounds) and print (couplets, calendars, linguistic and numerical inventions).

Moondog was used to indulging his talents in a variety of fields, and his research, as arcane as his style, was fruitfully eclectic. It would be easy to dismiss his unconventional theories for all the conventional reasons (that autodidacts are prone to advance sweeping and hole-ridden theories, or that blind people have limited access to specialized sources, for instance). But this would be to say that, if their ideas make us uncomfortable, eccentrics live in a universe of extremes and have nothing instructive to say to normal people. Any of these arguments, like the facile *ad hominem* that Moondog merely tried to be a gadfly, are evasive answers for complex questions.

The periodicals Moondog produced in the late 1960s articulated his positions more thoroughly than any of his previous writings had. In order to leave behind several time-worn images (the street singer, the fey crusader, and the unfocused anarchist) and shape some new ones, he published the conspicuous and ambitious *Moondog Yearbooks* of 1967–1970, all puzzlingly called *Moondog Yearbook I*: Number II, though frequently promised, never appeared.

The five or more editions varied in minor details, but the core of each, four fifths of the whole, was always the long sequence of couplets arranged "in a strict mathematical formation" (according to Susan Lee Merrill, who wrote the 1967 introduction, replaced in 1970 by Moondog's foreword). The "root" is nine, "a sacred number to the Goths." Each couplet, though, represents a day in a year "based on the pre-Julian 10-month Roman calendar" (Martius, Aprilis, Maius, Junius, Quintilis, Sextilis, followed by September, October, November and December). Nine couplets make one "canto"; forty cantos, or weeks (of nine days each), with a five-day "year-end," (the Saturnalia) complete the cycle of 365. Soon he would eliminate all reliance on the inherited and hated Roman artifacts, but not yet. These are discursive, bizarre, and bold productions, varied in content and uneven in form. Nearly every "day" (couplet) of the year deals with a new item, and rarely does an idea last more than a "week" (stanza). From 1967: "Nothing is unimportant to a poet...I like to juxtapose the most irrelevant things to get violent contrasts. My poetry is a kaleidoscopic view of my mind." Three years later: "Most couplets are self-contained, having nothing to do with the one preceding or following." The meter is as free-wheeling as the matter it fleetingly regulates: the lines are long, enjambments abound, and the rhymes are virtually indescribable. Of his couplets he goes on to say that they are "in seven iambic feet per line, or iambic septameter or heptameter." This is the form of *Thor the Nordoom* in its earliest versions, comfortable for Moondog despite its inherent problems and peculiarities. To some extent his interest in the long, highly alliterative line came from reading Anglo-Saxon and Icelandic poetry. The major stumbling block to poets writing fourteen-syllable lines in English has invariably been the unavoidable sing-song of the iambs and the breathless length. Ms. Merrill, by implication, seems to offer one explanation for the evolution of his verse form: "Moondog is first a musician and it shows in his poetry." Vague slogans will not explain what he did, however, or say whether he did it well. The couplets are juvenilia, but are fascinating nonetheless. Later, in the program notes to his 1969 Columbia album and in interviews around that time, he said more simply that he liked regularity of form in his verse as well as in his music.

The peculiar and unusual subjects of these verses merit attention. Poems are about something, however strong the aesthete's argument that ideas do not make poetry. Moondog's couplets in the Yearbooks are formally impure and wander freely, uninhibited despite the numerical architecture, touching upon standard 1960s themes. His biases leap jauntily about, alluding to sources and programs but seldom developing any. Although both Ms. Merrill and Moondog insist that recurrent themes, as in a musical round, form a framework, these are really threads on which to hang moods, emotions, and concepts otherwise related only by free association. For instance, if "The Voice of the Cosmos" is heard "chiding man about his pretentions [sic] and fantasies," it doesn't sound all that different from the author's own chiding. The folk wisdom of the old street poet, regardless of his disclaimers, appears throughout, but it is idiosyncratic. Like his earlier music, some of his views were inspired by American

Indian lore; like his later music, others reflect the Eddas. Probably, however, many drew upon the streets of New York City. The marked cynicism is underscored by a strong, masculine rhyme. In the couplets that follow, spelling and punctuation are uncorrected. Arabic numerals indicate couplets, and Roman numerals, stanzas.

> In retrospect, he sees a pond and on that pond he sees
> two fleets of warring centipedes whose decks are
> lined with fleas. (XIV, 118)
> If children look like mortar, surely, parents look
> like bricks,
> that sandwich in a bit of soft mortality that
> sticks. (XXIII, 207)
> Menace and doom are prevalent:
> A sharpened whalebone coiled inside a frozen hunk of
> meat,
> Is laying for the Artic wolf who's fool enough to
> eat. (XII, 102)
> The Gods are riding herd, and we who constitute the
> herd,
> are on our way to slaughter pens, to die without
> a word. (XXXIX, 344)

Many of Moondog's old pet peeves resurface, but without the same bite. He sneers at the hypocrisy of the Christian state, for instance, as well as one of his nastiest villains, the Federal Reserve System, but in these instances the rhymes are feminine. The old angers seem somewhat tamed, not freshly rekindled. The couplets seem to make obligatory criticisms rather than vital attacks, and tend to vagueness:

> Through prosecuting other trusts, the Government
> protects
> the Money Trust. This glaring inconsistency
> reflects. (XXIX, 258)

Or to simple statement with less than alluring rhyme:

Called "the covenant with death," and also "an
   agreement
with Hell," the Constitution should be called a
   disagreement
with Heaven," for the Church, as Heaven's agent, must
   concede
her "anticonstitutionality" since Runnymede. (XXX,
   275–76)

Clearest in them is Moondog's new and vital identity with his
Nordic past. He devotes more narrative space, and the most consistently entertaining, original, and polished couplets, to two themes:
ethnicity and religion in general, and the Nordic adventure and
genealogy in particular. He tries to rise above the stereotypical Jere-
miad, and to begin to "re-write history," though through touches
and glances rather than with a new program. So, on the subject of
Western religion and race relations, some of his earlier views that
had alienated potential allies are softened, sensitized, and politically
corrected. The juvenile and derivative anti-Semitism of his *Millen-
niad*, for instance, becomes:

Jews and Arabs both are semites; therefore, antisemitism
   is a contradiction in Jerusalem. (XX, 176)

But he is still an autodidact whose biased readings of history
can be disquieting.

I agreed with Malcolm X concerning "separation
   of blacks and whites," as I agreed with his
   "repatriation
to Africa" alternative, as Malcolm X agreed with Lincoln.
   You who do not know what Lincoln
   wrote, should read. (XXII, 195–96)

In light of his previous broadsides these are quiet sentiments, expressed delicately. Only when he addresses his Nordic past does his poetry begin to breathe. In the 1968 *Corpus* interview, published during the height of *Yearbook* fervor, he makes his position clear:

> I was heading in the direction of Norse religion because I was tired of being called a Biblical character; not being a Christian and at the same time [sic] I was delving into my own ethnic past and I came up with what I really was and with what I really wanted to identify myself as, which is a Gothic. That is my background and I'm as proud of it as anyone should be of what they are....my idea of salvation is a modern one, not of being saved from sin but of being identified with my past. It's very much like a tree that is pulled up by the roots: it dies; but as long as those roots are in the ground it lives and that is very much the same situation with people. When they are uprooted from their own ethnic and religious past, they die culturally. If they don't know what their ethnic past is, and if there is no inner urge to find out, they will float around without any ties.

Reverend Hardin had been a forerunner of the new northman in his own inimitable style. Although a Christian, he was a marauder who could not be subdued by the pan-Christian west. Moondog, by becoming the Viking, completed the rebellion his father had started, rejecting Christian dogma and assuming pre-Christian rituals.

No longer drifting and criticizing, Moondog put down roots. Few of his data were new, but their assured, jaunty presentation was. His five-billion-year calendar, included in the 1970 version of the Yearbook under the rubric "Universal Reckoning," lists five names and dates in the last two millennia. The first is Jesus Christ, the middle Mohammad, and the last the "atomic age." What revaluations are implied by the remaining two! The second is the Battle of Teuterberger Wald (9 A.D.), when two of Augustus' finest legions under the command of Varus were annihilated in the Black Forest of Germania (a victory Moondog celebrated elsewhere, in verse and song). The fourth is Leif Eriksson's discovery of America. In canto ("week") XVI, there is an account of Columbus' apprenticeship to the explorers of Iceland, from whom he learned the route to the Americas.

> Columbus rediscovered Iceland fifteen years before
> he rediscovered North America, and nothing more. (139)

Columbus knew his voyage was not "a way to India," but toward "a place to stay," and he sold "the greed of royalty" on the idea of a "promised land" in order to open up as a mystery what he already knew was there.

> Why, in Odin's name, would Christopher have made a trip
> to Iceland fifteen years before, unless he had a tip? (141)

Pushing even further into the past, he tells how southern Europe was not only behind the northman in discovery and exploration, but also genealogically an offshoot of conquerors in the prehistoric past.

> Some nineteen years before the common era, Goths
>   would conquer Hatti, setting up the kingdom of
>   the Ghafs.
> They introduced the wheel of half a dozen spokes for
>   light
> and speedy chariots of war they drove in ev'ry fight.
> These Men of Iron introduced an iron which was nearly
>   steel, which taught all towns, as far as Babylon,
>   to fear. (XXV, 217–19)

Language, as well as warfare, traveled south:

> English, German, Swedish, Danish, Dutch, Norwegian,
>   Ghafik,

Italian, Spanish, Frankish, Czech and Greek are
    merely GoÞik
dialects all emanating from a Sanskrit source,
    Central Europe North, referring to the GoÞ, of
    course. (XXVI, 230–31)

He goes even further back, lightheartedly:

I smile each time I see and hear the phrase, "In God
    We Trust,"
because I know, as Noah knew, it means, "In GoÞ
    We Trust." (XXXI, 272)

Hyperbole, maybe, or poetic license, but nonetheless a refreshingly weird angle on prehistory. There is as of yet no poetic myth strong enough to pull all of the information together, but his immersion in things Gothic was still new in its fact-gathering stage. The first, now lost, version of *Thor* was on stage at roughly the same time the yearbook was being produced. The concept and design of reordering history through myth played over his sensibilities, Machiavellian and otherwise, as he searched for a fitting vehicle. *Thor* resurfaced, a more mature vision, when he reconstructed it after settling into his new German home more than a decade later.

THE *MOONDOG YEARBOOKS* WERE a compendium of wild and zany material, worth every penny of the dollar he sold them for. In the earlier editions he mentions his mid-decade concerts and prints the score for "Bird's Lament," *Symphonique No. 9*, arranged for string quartet, a mainstay on these dates. There is also a photograph of him reading poetry with the quartet on the last page. In the 1970 printing, a photograph of Moondog conducting his Columbia album at the 30th Street studio he loved replaces the other; beneath is a press release about the "New York legend" whose "original compositions, which were written in Braille and subsequently transcribed," are "now available at your local record store." On the inside back and front covers of most of the editions are scores for various selections from *The Art of the Canon*, Books I and II. The front cover, designed by Sharon Seftel, announces the title in Gothic lettering; the back cover is an etching by S. Einhorn of Moondog wearing his sloping square hat, holding his spear in his left hand and a drum stick in his right, with his trimba. Additional photographs show him leaving the Aristo ("Its manager, Jack Brooks, was my host for seven years") and holding up his moose foot: "Mr. Moose, the use to which / I've put your foot was up / to me alone: I own I've used / it for a beggar's cup." Snippets and biographical notes fill small gaps: he celebrates his twenty-fifth anniversary in New York; he notes, with pride, that he has added a thorn Þ to his typewriter; he apologizes for printing the thorn upside-down in the first edition. In 1970, his new signature, an "eight-legged M" derived from Odin's octopede Chleipnir, takes up a whole page.

Moondog had always been fascinated by numbers and symbols. The years 1968 and 1969 saw many old conflicts come to a head, and the fusion of ideas shed new light on conventional wisdom and history. Big changes in his musical idiom and in his appearance accompanied an explosion of other activities typified by his idiosyncratic reconsideration of dating, numerology, and linguistics. Although his theories seem like quirky excurses from his historic myth, in his mind they were central. Because of Moondog's peculiar way of tying arcana into new schemas, these exercises are part of his revised world-view, his attempts to superimpose his readings of the past on our present.

To accompany his couplets and their panorama of the year (365 couplets, 730 lines), Moondog provided in all of the Yearbook printings his "comparative calendar" with a restructuring of the past ten thousand years and a fresh look at the earth's five billion. He proclaimed: "To Science and Religion: Geocentric Reckoning is offered in exchange for Theocentric Reckoning," and established the Committee on Universal Reckoning in 1966 (9966, new time) at the Aristo. For example, in 1967, he proposed that the dates from 8000 B.C. through 2000 A.D. be renumbered 1 through 10,000. By the 1970 edition of the yearbook, 0 has been pushed back five billion years.

Alluring as this is, only its formulation is original. More impressively, he issued in a separate booklet in 1969 (and again in 1972, enlarged) his "Perpetual Calendar." Conceived in 1958, the first product of his Candor retreat, it is an ingenious chart for locating the day of the week for any date from 44 B.C. to 3200 A.D. For any independent amateur to see a project of this scope through would be a triumph; that a blind man living alone in poverty, immersed in several careers, could follow its conception into publication, at his own expense, is astonishing. This booklet was so ergonomic and thorough that information librarians at the famous New York City Public Reference Room preferred it for many years. The whole scheme encompasses eight pages: two for the Julian Calendar (44 B.C. to 1581 A.D.), two for the Gregorian Calendar (1583 to 3200 A.D.) (the "Chronologues"), two for the seven year tables (leap and non-leap years, days, weeks, months), and two for complete directions. The user who wants to know what day of the week he was born on, or the Declaration of Independence was signed on, can locate it in seconds. Unlike the more outrageous proposals for numerical and linguistic reform he published in the late 1960s, the perpetual calendar is a model of utility.

There were always two Moondogs: the struggling artist whose explorations led him down strange paths, and the down-to-earth, practical outdoorsman who sought, when he left Manhattan, quiet harmony with his surroundings. It is not surprising; his childhood was torn between two parents, torn from many homes, torn between conflicting patterns of belief, and torn apart by tragedy. His push into the world of adults followed no well-marked roads; he went ever further from the mainstream without ever leaving the good earth. As he grew older the paradox he lived expanded at both extremes. His appearance seemed calculated to put off; teenagers were frightened by (yet fascinated with) the wild man who danced in the streets and talked to himself. Yet his warmth and humor, often at his own expense, dominate the recollections of his acquaintances. His theories could be elitist, estranging weaklings, waverers, and parasites, yet among his closest friends were society's lowest. The same man who would attempt a new myth for his time could also harness a leather strap around his head and haul a two-hundred-pound stump out of the woods. Scratch a rebel tied to the past and (because sightless) even more tenaciously to his roots, and you'll get a survivor. Calendars are necessary, so why not have one that does it all, in one handy, compact package? This is imagination at the service of the real world, not escapism.

MOONDOG LIVED WITH PHILIP GLASS at 366 West 23rd Street for a little over a year, from the summer of 1968 until the early winter of 1969. We are left to speculate about how these two formidable personalities affected each other's work, since neither has a great deal to say about this time, though both are polite and affectionate in their recollections. It was, according to Glass, a time that was both stimulating and a bit off-putting. Moondog's musical talents are described in glowing terms in the preface: his ability to play all of his music, his facility in duplicating the sounds of others, and, of particular note, his interesting way of working lyrically with odd rhythms. Both men were respectfully aware that they were trying something new. Moondog was clearly modifying his idioms and styles as he evolved from a predominantly jazz-oriented to classical composer, and Glass was discovering and refining his own voice. Since Moondog was older, and had been writing in "minimal" forms for two decades by then, it would be natural to assume that the compression and repetition of his rounds, for instance, must have appealed to the younger man, and, indeed, stories abound. One evening (June 4, 1969) they and two other friends (Jon Gibson and the 31-year-old Steve Reich, who thought Moondog's rounds "good, solid music," and would appear at BAM when Moondog returned to the U.S. in 1989) had great fun recording some of the "old" madrigals ("All Is Loneliness," "Be A Hobo," "My Tiny Butterfly," among others) as well as a rash of "new" ones. A little later, downtown on Duane Street, Martin Scorsese, not yet a famous film director, taped Moondog, Glass, Reich and several others singing rounds on the sidewalks of New York. But these moments are the exception: once again, Moondog insisted that his proximity to other creative people seems to have left much less of an impact on his career and ruling passions than we might have anticipated. Of course, ego can never be dismissed, and few artists consider themselves members of "schools," and rightly so, yet it is also impossible to dismiss the inevitable cross-pollination that had to have taken place. Although Moondog would later aver that their outlooks on music were "as different as oil is to water," similarities and correspondences do exist. One day, when all archives are finally open and all reminiscences recorded, the inevitable interplay of creative minds can be more fully evaluated. Until then, we just have to listen to the music written in Moondog's "middle" period and Philip Glass' earliest compositions and note the echoes, citations, resemblances (as well as the differences, of course). The mesmerizing repetitions, in which short phrases are expanded into much longer statements, for instance, would seem to originate in (to mix a metaphor) water drunk from the same well.

It could not have been easy to cohabitate with such an eccentric, and Mr. Glass gives several indications in his introduction of Moondog's startling eccentricities. But his cavalier treatment of women's bodies and his garbage disposal habits were probably less offensive than some of his arcane ideas about race. Although not overtly anti-Semitic, for instance, a difficult position to sustain in the entertainment industry of New York City, he was asserting a new kind of "Aryan" identity that may have been myth to him, but which could easily be offensive to those who remember how easily such ideas became lethal historically. Despite philosophical differences, however, Philip Glass did help Moondog mount several bizarre and peculiar booklets, and they parted amicably just before the Columbia album restructured his public life.

UNLIKE HIS PERPETUAL CALENDAR, his new system of numbering and his modern version of runics did not catch on. Although too esoteric to be absorbed by their intended audiences (businessmen and purists "in the modern world"), they reveal the limits of his passion for imagining alternate ways of reading history, right up to the present. The proposals, too, are more condescending than was Moondog himself, and another manifestation of his paradoxical nature emerges in them, that of a man who thought himself superior but cherished all human contact. Consumed by his visions, he offered them whether they pleased, befuddled, or angered. Like any original, prolific, and versatile mind, his was uneven in its output, but everything he touched somehow seems as interesting as the energy of his excursions seems prodigious.

"Monumeriks" appeared several times in slightly modified and enlarged versions during 1968, the fullest dated September 18; all were signed by "Mondhunt," Moondog in German. (One of the clearest signs of a rapid, radical change in his opinions and ideas is his changing signature. In similar documents published in 1968 and 1969 alone, his nom de plume had at least three refinements.) A picture of Moondog in time present at his spot dominates the cover: Braille binders on his lap, canvas wrap over his shoulders, legs crossed and bare, head uncovered, his long gray hair in a ponytail, hands quietly at work, face contemplative. He is alone, and behind his right shoulder, tied to his resting spear, some booklets are displayed; above them, in a separate holder, a cup sits, inviting donations. Beneath the photograph is this legend:

The System of the One Number and the System of the Number One

Announcing the Third Numerical Break-Through in
the History of Numbering
Attention, Business Community: If Time is Money, so
are Space and Weight
Where Numbers are Concerned, Cut Your Costs in
Half with Monumeriks.

The back cover of the booklet depicts him and a Mrs. Eliot at
the Warwick Hotel, "He and [sic] Outside, and She an Inside,"
ending, in part, thus:

"With the Creation of Inglish, and Monumeriks, the Numerical Division of English, Moondog Finishes his Twenty-Fifth
Year in New York, Come This November Sixth."

"Monumeriks" is difficult to translate without confusion, even
with its explanatory apparatus at hand: like many esoteric new systems of communication, its theory is plausible and simple, but its
applications are harder than its creator intended. Perhaps to make up
for his hard line on the business community as an accomplice of the
Federal Reserve, he offered this pre-computer-age mathematics. As he
promised, he proceeded rapidly, one paper after another, to "go the
limit." The "nupiks," his coinage for the symbolic element in his system of numbering, "in Monumerik House," however, led Moondog
nowhere, and the venture remains today only a footnote to a fertile
period. The effort in conception, transcribing in Braille, translating to
type, proofing, printing, and distributing had to be substantial, and
the consequent dead-end disappointing. But, as his track record by
now clearly predicted, failure never slowed him down. New ideas
always came; new directions opened up. Moondog had seen his work
shelved, his music plagiarized, his credits dropped. The energy he was
drawing from his new posture in the world made him even more
resilient in 1969 than he had been. He had greater worlds to conquer.

Language reform came next. In several of his "street sheets" in
late 1968 Moondog shared his interest in Nordic with the public.

The first one, from December 14, 1968, was illuminated and lettered by the same Sharon who had designed the Yearbook cover. She also, along with Phil Glass, found him an apartment at 449 West 56th Street after he left the Aristo for good in 1967. There he remained until summer 1968. (While there he never knew that an old friend, Tony Schwartz, lived a few doors down. Because he was so productive and so mobile, this example makes it easy to forget how hard it is to be blind.) With Sharon's help Moondog conceived a grand new program. The leaflet promises a fuller development of the theme: "Moondog is working on a modern runic alphabet which will be out shortly." A brief history provides a background for Inglish. The runic alphabet "was a gift of the god Odin to the Gothic people"; from the Rhine valley, "the cultural cradle," the Germanic language "radiated." (Recall that his couplets also claimed a stupendous range and impact for the Goths.) "Rune" means "mystery, secret," as a passage translated from the old English of Beowulf illustrates.

> On the hilt of glistening gold
> Was carefully carved in runic letters
> Especially for the one whom the good blade,
> The spiraling sword, serpent stamped,
> Had first been fired.

He then prints the runic alphabets with their equivalent sound values and stave ("futhark") formation: the Germanic ("24 letters, divided into three groups of eight each"), the Scandinavian (sixteen letters, with simplifications, as different sounds were represented by the same rune), the Anglo-Saxon ("28 letters, later increased to 33") and finally the Completed Pointed (twenty-five letters, a "blend of all runic alphabets producing a systematic representation of all sounds in the language," used in Scandinavia during the Middle Ages by "cultured laymen").

Several four-page booklets announcing "Inglish, or Modern Gothic" appeared in early 1969, signed once again by good old

"Moondog," found still "by the Warwick," and produced this time with the acknowledged support of Philip Glass. (Glass has consistently taken on challenging and alien subjects for his more ambitious works over the intervening years: opera in ancient Egypt, music for a film about the Dalai Lama of Tibet, music for three films with titles in the Hopi language, for instance. One can visualize his "runic" collaboration with Moondog serving as some kind of seedling from which future grand conceptions could sprout. They must have at least talked about American Indian music and culture.) Other than the program notes for his Columbia album, this was Moondog's last publishing venture of the 1960s. Excluding the albums of 1969 and 1971, Moondog wrote very little that saw print until he reconstructed Thor in Germany, over five years later. Discouragement might be a reason, since so little came of his discoveries, but that is not all. A more immediate cause was his exclusive devotion to music, for he returned always to what he did best and wanted to do most whenever other ventures proved troublesome. Two major albums were imminent.

But now that all of the juvenilia had been exposed and the personal investigations brought to light, to grow in stature and sustain his originality required a different kind of struggle. Moondog was famous in New York by 1969, but he no longer chose to remain merely a street person. He would seldom again stride down the avenue of outrageous behavior and popular wit or patronize those whom he wished to convert. He took on a quieter humility to accompany his deepened commitment, and grew as a man and as a composer. In his last five years in America he was on the streets less and less; he devoted himself more selflessly to music and came to dislike the elaborate appearances he had to make to publicize albums.

LOOKING BACK FROM 1969, even Moondog would have to have been impressed by the music he composed in the decade before his Columbia albums. The volume is impressive, considering his blindness and comfortless working conditions. More significant, however, was the definition he gave to his early eclectic styles. He wrote many of his seminal works during the 1960s. His devotion to rounds and canons, first offered in his "Prelude and Fugue No. 1 in A Minor," 1961 ("from *The Well-Tempered Pianoforte*), was realized both in the *Grosse Kanon* (1961–62) and in the two books of the *Art of the Canon* (1968). His career-long devotion to rhythm, percussion, and song culminated in his madrigals, especially the schema for "Around the World of Sound" in his 1971 album. Just as he began constructing a new myth, so he expanded his oeuvre to more and larger orchestral pieces, his earliest soundings for *The Creation*. He coined "minisym" and "maxisym" to denote the way a piece of music can be scored, either for full orchestra or for a handful of musicians. Moondog was a realist: since he did not have the good fortune to conduct a sizeable ensemble until late in 1969, whenever and wherever the opportunity occurred to perform his work, he was ready.

> This is called stock arranging. The least number of musicians I can get by with is six, but that same piece is scored for one hundred or fifty or twenty or whatever I can get hold of. Stock arranging has never been used in classical music to my knowledge.

In addition, occasional pieces, program music for special events, songs all poured out through his Braille stylus and transliterators into final scores. He managed all this while surviving in good health and mostly in good spirits. The fleeting moments of glory that lay ahead could not repay him for what he gave to his craft. He carved out what many consider important music on the pavements of New York, in the wilderness of his acres, or in the "overheated" flats of his friends. Despite the hardships, his music was serene and disciplined, orderly and unstrained. He labored to transmute his darkness and the decay surrounding him with his own brand of sweetness and light.

Other serious musicians found his music. Artur Rodzinski looked at his early pieces; Bird Parker and Pete Seeger sought him out and wanted to collaborate with him; Duke Ellington and Benny Goodman praised his work; Philip Glass offered him lodging and support. There was, however, no consensus about him; different people liked different things. His eclectic music, like his eccentric publications, is as a whole unclassifiable. In an age of specialization this is limbo. Each of the many things Moondog did has found a small audience, but few will commit themselves to the whole corpus. Those who like the canons may dislike the madrigals; those who admire the unusual tonalities and subtleties of his early percussion pieces sometimes find the orchestral works predictable and academic. To some he is too far out; to others he isn't even avant-garde. But then by now he was accustomed to straddling two worlds (past and present, reactionary and counterculture), suspected by all, comfortable in no known school.

Nonetheless, he was a musician from the start. Excluding parts of his 1969 Columbia album, Moondog recorded none of his 1960s music during the time he wrote it, but his rate of composition accelerated. Those who performed his music knew it well enough to defend it staunchly. Susan Block called the selections in Book I of *The Art of the Canon* "little gems." Eliot Finkel and Susan Fremon were so devoted to the canons that for decades afterwards, on stage, in clubs, in New York, in New Haven, on *The Today Show*, on Morningside Radio, all over the Americas and overseas, they held recitals. Paul Jordan, who has performed Moondog's works for organ throughout the United States and Europe, has often praised the elegant and powerful compositions of the 1960s: the "hypnotic quality" of the madrigals and later organ pieces written in Germany (gathered into the Lögründr); the "lightness, transparency, clarity and wittiness" of the canons.

MOONDOG TURNED 53 in 1969, having lived in New York City for nearly half his life. In those years he changed his ideas and his dress, but the cynic might say that beneath some superficial changes in affectation he was still a boy performing on street corners for attention (psychoanalyzing: for his mother's or father's). To Moondog, however, the evolution was real. Poses might extract a momentary thrill, and outrageous utterances might attract a crowd, but in the long haul play-acting with Moondog's burdens would prove smothering, and he always seemed fresh.

There is another side to the lonely, sanguine eccentric who (critics of his attention-seeking might argue) brought upon himself much of his grief. Moondog had a host of friends, collaborators, and aides. He could not, despite his pride and independence, handle the details of publishing a pamphlet or musical score by himself, for example. Unsurprisingly, he had affairs with several of his female helpmates. He was a New York cult figure, after all, single and magnetic.

He almost married a second time, and lived at 449 West 56th Street with the young woman from Queens who bore him his second daughter, Lisa, on September 22, 1967. Her family objected to Moondog personally and forced mother and infant to leave him. Concluding that the sixteen-year-old girl could not take care of a child on her own, a social worker placed Lisa into a foster home. Twenty-two years later, when Moondog returned briefly and for the last time to the U.S., he again met his second child, and remained happily in touch with her during the final decade of his life.

It is easy to overlook the necessity of Moondog's closeness to those who helped him, just as it is easy to forget how fraught with peril his everyday life was, or what an undertaking it was for him to travel, whether to a concert down the street or to the country. Recall that one of the major reasons for his heavy headgear was to protect himself from the many metal parking signs at head level. The tedium involved in doing what others take for granted might have discouraged Moondog, had he not had many loving hands in support and many creative solutions.

Copying is an excellent example. Few can transcribe Braille or score music from dictation. Moondog in the 1960s, after being spoiled by Mary for eight years, found several he could work with. John Draper, who conducted "Nocturne" in Central Park, stands out. For $2.50 per hour (far below union scale), this patient and thorough professional inked the masters for the two books of *The Art of the Canon* as well as the *Great Canon*, gorgeously. When John Draper became too busy, Mark Unger took over. Pam Gross transcribed the four books of madrigals that in 1971 became the basic text for "Around the World of Sound," another lovely booklet. She was "a whiz when it comes to dictation, proofing, inking and paste-up. In proofing I can hardly keep up with her. She took down Book I in pencil and proofed it in one sitting, and inked it up in another." This includes reading each note back to him, of course. In the Spring of 1968 she did Book I; in the fall of 1969 Books II, III and IV. Moondog tried hard to hold on to such good help: "I take a cross-town bus to get to her house at 443 West 48th Street." The elaborate, repetitive process, equally demanding for each pamphlet as well, was a mutual labor of love.

Moondog had to leave the Aristo in 1967 when it finally closed. Although soiled and Spartan, the hotel had been for seventeen years (with several hiatuses) his home. He worked there, was photographed and interviewed there, played music in its lobby, and used it as a business address. For the next five years he stayed nowhere longer than a few months, sleeping on the streets more to afford bus fare up to Candor, where he would finally "settle down" in 1972. His madrigal on country life and city life sums it up. He hurried from one to the other because he "needs them both," having his cake and eating it too. But "going some, in going to and from" exacted a high price:

> [I]t was hard to maintain a hotel room, food, copying, plus transportation costs, all at once. So, I couldn't have a room when I kept going up there: either one or the other. So I got to the point of sleeping on the street.

There he was until *The Village Voice* printed a "plea" in its "Scenes" column: "On April 1, was forced to leave his apartment [on West 56th Street]. Since then he has not left his corner between the Warwick Hotel and the MGM building, sleeping upright, attached to his seat. Where are his friends?" Swiftly, "hippies" took him in. Their digs on West 82nd Street ("Hippie House") was a maelstrom of arrivals and departures. The drugs and loud rock music were too intrusive for Moondog's sober work habits, but he still composed a host of madrigals during the months he "crashed" there. After his year with Phil Glass he was again on the streets (in February 1969) until an offer from Ms. Ronnie Keath convinced him to stay on her barge, the *S.S. Clyde*, docked at Port Richmond, Staten Island, and there he remained until May of 1969 when work on the first Columbia album was beginning. In a life as bizarre as his, one of the lighter intermissions was this three months when Moondog, in costume, commuted to Manhattan on the Staten Island Ferry and thence north, via subway, to 54th and 6th. How many sets of eyes fixed this voyager? What legends did his fellow passengers concoct? To some, this would be an odyssey. To Moondog, it was going to work.

Moondog worked everywhere he settled—when he was lucky, in the long lulls of his rustications up north. He was through the 1950s mostly an occasional visitor, however, and his experiences with the curious noisemakers and the vandals had soured him on the place somewhat. Blind and alone, he could not exploit the possibilities in separation from his "father and mother," among the sounds he had incorporated so successfully into his early short pieces. During the 1960s Candor attracted him more and more strongly. From 1961 until 1974 he worked to make a home that was a respite from the city. His spread evolved into a permanent home by 1972.

Moondog did not get back to Candor to begin a permanent structure until 1961. His first effort, a little log cabin, the inevitable intruders all but leveled. "Most every time I returned to my shack it would be broken into....I could have spared myself a lot of worry if I had left nothing...without a lock on the door, thinking: nothing to steal, nothing stolen." Faced with starting over each time he went back, Moondog rose to the challenge by going one step further, with a new refinement each time.

The original shack was made of huge logs, many weighing several hundred pounds, dragged out of the woods nearby by tying them with ropes and then securing the ties to a leather band around his forehead. The work was so grueling that he could only do it in good weather and at night, to the astonishment of local friends. However difficult the pull, his sense of hearing was so acute that he knew someone was approaching, and he always stopped to offer a hearty greeting.

But it was for several years merely a primitive retreat from the city, shelter against the elements, barely a cut above his Jersey pine box. Gradually he improved it. First, to the awe of the utility, he requested a telephone (to stay in touch with his New York "office"). The installer found what amounted to a raised cave, with a nest of snakes living over the roof, unknown to the nocturnal and blind resident. He got his phone.

Beside his lintel he constructed a stone pyramidal altar to Thor. As he noted in a later interview:

> Yes. Yes, I do believe in the Norse gods....The way I go about worshipping the Norse gods is very much like a Moslem who would worship Allah: he can do it in a desert or anywhere, it doesn't have to be in a mosque. If you want to think up when you think of the deity you raise up your head, you just salute the invisible; it can happen any time; if you feel like communicating with something beyond humanity, you just do it.

Only at Candor did he build a permanent altar. Despite (or because of) what he had to overcome, there was a certain magic in the place for him. Willa Percival, who had traveled by his side to photograph him at his work, described him "building an addition to his cabin where he wintered—howling wind down the mountain, lighting a fire on top of the monument he erected, and with heavy clothes on inside the cabin by a wood fire—his only heat." Moondog liked to cook on this open fire: the first pit was near "Moondog rock" under "Moondog tree." Eventually he acquired a potbelly stove which he cooked inside of, reportedly with great success. After the fire started, he would rest a coffeepot or a large soup can on a ledge above the open flame and fish out the victuals with his hands, sometimes enduring nasty burns. His stews became famous (fresh meat and vegetables only), his strong coffee (brewed by boiling water in a can with the beans) a necessity everywhere he went. His spirit of adventure never flagged. One Thanksgiving, for himself and Bobby Ayers, a young boy "up the road" who remained Moondog's friend and companion through 1974, he roasted a large turkey, with stuffing and vegetables.

Bucky Moon, from "over the hill," became Moondog's closest Candor friend, and stayed so until Moondog finally left for Europe. Bucky, a farmer, was a great help. Along with Bob Dutton, another neighbor, he helped Moondog finance and construct his first permanent building in 1962, a 16-by-8 tarpaper shack that later became the bedroom of the larger house that evolved in the Seventies. There was a lone window opposite. In one of the two full corners was a built-in bunk bed and a table, and in the other was his stove. For Moondog this was opulence. Yet the journey (eight hours by bus to Owego, eight miles uphill to the place) and the life there were not without peril. One winter he almost died when he trekked up in a blizzard (cabs being unavailable) and missed the final turn. He got hopelessly lost in huge snow drifts, but Bucky Moon rescued him. Another winter Bucky found him nearly dead with pneumonia in his cabin after he had been too weak to start a fire. This time he was taken in by his good neighbor and nursed back to health by Bucky's mother, an octogenarian whose energy amazed the bed-ridden Viking. Another time a car hit him on the eight-mile strip of Route 96 north from Owego, leaving him "lame for a month." This "bad show" of June 6, 1969 lingered as a cautionary example, working some reverse magic. He wrote one of his most opulent and optimistic madrigals (Book I, 3) the day after the accident. "What's the most exciting thing about life?" it asks, and answers: "Love."

Some of his fondest Indian memories, no longer ambiguous and unresolved, colored his "stamping ground." He hunted (with an arrow tied by string to the bow) and fished. But when he built, "Thor's hammer" drove the nails. Friends helped, rewarded with good music and the stuff of memorable anecdotes.

After the new place was finished, Moondog went up more often to work. In a 1970 article in the *Rochester Democrat*, when he had become more famous and started to attract regional interest, he showed his visitor around what had evolved over ten years into a modest retreat:

> On a little wooden table near the bed is an old skillet, a fork lies in the middle of the pan, left over from Moondog's last meal, whenever it was. A few empty and a few unopened cans are stacked and piled up together behind the frying pan.
>
> At the front edge of the table a one-foot square space has been cleared away and it's here that he sits and writes…. For Moondog, that one square foot is about it for work space because that's all there is in the shack.

Hardly "spreading out," but more comfortable than a lap in the middle of a city sidewalk: it was his own space, at last. Of course, things could be better:

> Tending the stove is all right, but it's awfully time-consuming when it's really cold and I can't concentrate on my composing. An electric heater would be nice.

But things had been much worse.

So Moondog faced the last year of the decade in which "the man with the face of Christ" (an image he had come to abhor so intensely that he began to look like Thor) dissolved into the Nordic apostle to New York. He was about to become a mysterious sort of media happening. Moondog's "quieter" 1960s, the Aristo, Candor, and the rest, gave way to a strenuous burst of publicity. What he did in these nine years, though, shaped the grander visions of the rest of his life. To many, for whatever reasons (respect, nostalgia, whimsy, incredulousness, ...) and regardless of whatever else he did, he will always be the Viking of Sixth Avenue.

Chapter Six

Wunderjahr

(1969–1970)

On October 1, 1969, and for several months thereafter, Moondog moved one block south from his usual spot at 54th and
6th. This was more than a symbolic gesture, but had concrete and
specific causes. Columbia was soon to release his first prestigious
and nationally successful record album, his most famous American
production by far, and the people at the CBS building (51 West
52nd Street) thought it fitting that he stand by his latest associates.
After a quarter-century in New York, now at fifty-three, Moondog
seemed to be heading for fame as a serious composer and person of
substance, not a streetside noodler and theatrical curiosity. Many
public relations workers, performers, and producers were soon to
help his cause, and he had his moment in the spotlight at last.

James William Guercio, an influential producer of popular
recordings (his enterprises, Poseidon Productions and Archimedes
Music, listed Blood, Sweat and Tears and Chicago among their
credits) had simply "met Moondog down the block" and admired
the work sufficiently enough to persuade Columbia "Masterworks"
to produce the first of two albums. According to Moondog, in his
program notes for the second (1971):

> One September [in 1968] evening a young man fell by the
> Warwick and started rapping. He said, "I guess you don't
> remember me. I talked to you last year when I was with a

group. Since then I have gone into producing." It was Jim Guercio. I laid a copy of Book I [of the rounds recorded in 1971] on him, never expecting anything would come of it. A year later he came by with a man from Columbia Records.

Moondog agreed to the terms, provided that Columbia executives did not hear the album before it was recorded, a situation that "doesn't happen much in this day and age." The contract, signed March 6, 1969, was for two albums. James William Guercio and Al Brown, Moondog's "manager," would coproduce. The composer's address that spring was still c/o *SS Clyde*, Bayonne Ferry Slip, Port Richmond, Staten Island. He was excited: he felt he had grown so in his music that any opportunity to reveal his latest idiom was a special dispensation. He was, and had been for decades, his own best advertisement, yet for all the music he had sold through the years, and despite the plethora of interviews, articles, and appearances, no other offer he had ever received could match the potential of this one. There is no mistaking the big time.

Work began quickly. Al Brown, who had made the 1967 "Minisym" possible, assembled fifty first-rate musicians and turned over artistic control: "I never would have had a chance to have such an orchestra," commented Moondog, "if it had not been for Al Brown, a prince of a man, who put the whole thing together." Throughout the hubbub around the production, however, Moondog remained, if elated, serene:

> One of the biggest thrills of my life was to stand before the cream of New York musicians and give them the down-beat on June 3, 1969, at the Old Church, Columbia's main studio on East 33rd Street. On the podium on which so many famous conductors had stood, I was on Cloud Nine. Most of the players went along with my unorthodox style of conducting, and we did a good job in spite of the fact that we had no rehearsals before the session itself.

Moondog was released on October 1, 1969, an elaborate and lavish production. The publicity was ample. Two articles are emblematic of the excitement in the air from June through October: one, a prerelease review by Alan Rich in *New York Magazine*, appeared on July 21; the second, an interview taped "a few days before the initial [sic] session," was printed in the December *Penthouse*. Rich, first, praises the music of "one of America's great originals," which is "simple" but "subtle," with "long, spontaneous-sounding melodic lines," and, when written for the voice, "full of reverence for words." Extraordinarily, he calls Moondog's poetry "extraordinarily beautiful." Like some purists who feared that the new, "classical" Moondog would somehow betray his early inspirations ("what was so good about his music was that it was short and totally free of pretense"), or those fond of the rhythmic force of his 1950s recordings, Mr. Rich went with "some trepidation" to see and hear Moondog conduct at the Columbia studios, hoping that the "idea of going symphonic" was more than a "gimmick." He emerged, however, more convinced about Moondog's talent.

> He still works with canons, for the most part—big, fluent communicative tunes that work their way through the orchestra...with a fine sense of sonority and shape. Stylistically, his music seems rather old-fashioned; his harmonies are right out of Brahms or Mendelssohn, and his scoring is a lot like Ravel. But there is great skill in his writing, a marvelous sense for voice-leading that keeps his textures airy, a buoyant rhythmic organization.

Moondog, he concludes, is a "primitive," but one whose "horizons are vast" and whose presence on the artistic scene is "gentlemanly, aware...and beautiful."

The general conclusions of this first and probably most important notice are articulated by Moondog himself in the *Penthouse* interview. Paul Nelson taped Moondog in the presence of Mr.

Guercio and Robert Altshuler (who worked over a decade earlier on the Prestige albums), and it is clear that the "awesome figure," as Mr. Rich called him, "knew what he was doing." Allowed to range freely, Moondog always returns to his unshakeable convictions: "I'm a dyed-in-the-wool classicist, and I'm tonal"; "I would rather listen to rock 'n' roll than to Schoenberg because rock music is tonal and simple harmonically, as is mine." He speaks out (this is 1969, remember) against electronic music and illegal drugs ("I get my highs with tobacco and coffee") and speaks up for his canons, rounds, and couplets. The program notes for the album, which Moondog composed, in his own style, say the same thing, a pattern of thinking now taking final form. When Moondog pursued an idea, theme, motif, or form, he pursued it tirelessly, and as diligently in one medium as in another, often repeating himself. He would tell the passer-by what he printed in his broadsides, yearbooks, and poetry; he would say the same thing in the media. It was a cycle of creative obsession co-extensive with his life in New York, but in 1969 two factors distinguished the dissemination of his concepts: first, his syntheses were far more organized and systematic than his stances of the past; second, his audience was broader and more discriminating.

Moondog, on Columbia Masterworks, had a lush and colorful fold-out cover. Front and back together form a 24-by-12 poster of the composer in his Viking regalia; the only text is the unobtrusive title above his head and the list of tracks in one corner. Beneath the chain mail resting on his forehead, sewn on to the head wrap of burgundy and green wool, his distinctive nose and flowing white beard dominate the profile. Of the two inside pages, the right contains four color shots of Moondog conducting, one a close-up of his face in concentration, three with baton. Elegantly produced program notes present his latest defense of classicism, the "constant" that subsumes originality in tradition: "I deny that there is such a thing as originality," he states, only "personality." A near-tautology from twenty years earlier gets a fresh translation: "I do not strive to be different for the sake of being different, but do not mind being different if my difference is a result of my being myself." But his previous stridency has mellowed, in part because of his acute awareness of his place within a tradition. "Though I was born in the United States, I consider myself 'a European in exile,' for my heart and soul are in Europe." Further: "I feel like I have one foot planted in America and one in Europe, or one in the present and one in the past."

From the new image and refined beliefs followed an adjustment, maybe a concession, to tradition in the performance of the music. Fewer of his original instruments were used, in large part out of deference to the principle that experimentation was defined as that which enhanced and enriched tonality rather than undid it. "My heart is not in jazz," he admits, although its improvisational and spontaneous roots had interested him for twenty years.

> I just wanted to try my hand at it to prove to myself, if to no one else, that I could accomplish the difficult—that of using classical means to arrive at an unclassical end, that of making a carefully written-out piece sound like off-hand improvisation.

Although he might be considered "rhythmically" as "avant-garde," he is really, "melodically and harmonically," of the past. "I am much happier walking humbly in the footsteps of the great masters…upholding the values they upheld." Only the trimba, hearty veteran of two decades of campaigns, newly polished up of Honduran mahogany and soft leather heads, and the hus (Norwegian for house), a newly designed bowed stringed instrument, augment the orchestra of strings, reeds, horns, and percussion. The sound is bigger and more substantive, the control tighter. His theories of voice-leading, contra-tempi, and phrasing, strengthened after years of study, are purist: "I never deviate from modal rules." Many of the selections were composed in the 1950s and early 1960s, rescored on this occasion for "maxisym" (roughly, full symphony orchestra). At last he could develop some of the more elaborate structures he had been nurturing for years. They were in his head, but he usually wrote out only the parts to halve copying time. He still uses this method of scoring in 1969, with further refinements: "Anyhow, if my pieces were ever in demand, a score to each could be made from the parts."

Moondog plays in half an hour. In one bold gesture Moondog had redefined his career, recapitulated and expanded his old agendas, and, consciously or not, reimagined his future. The impact was immediate.

JUDITH BERGER, WHO HELPED Al Brown redesign and run "Moondog Management" and moved the business address from the defunct Aristo to the more respectable 39 West 55th, also planned a taxing but thrilling publicity campaign. Moondog had never minded repeating himself, a skill any performer working the media must master, but now every retelling would reach larger numbers. Within a week of the official release date, August 14–22, Moondog gave interviews to *Book Magazine*, *Newsday*, the Canadian Broadcast System, and several of the underground publications that had for so long been among his staunchest supporters (*The Village Voice, Rolling Stone, Changes, Fusion, Newspaper*). During another fortnight just after the October 1 release, he appeared on "Gabe Pressman's New York" spot on NBC-TV news, NBC's *Today Show*, *Cousin Brucie* on WOR-TV, and *The Merv Griffin Show* on WNEW-TV. In November he was on NBC's *Tonight Show*, and among his several radio spots was a long interview with Father O'Connor of Riverside Church in December. The Viking saturated the airwaves.

At an interview for an appearance with Johnny Carson on the "Tonight" Show his horns scraped the dropped ceiling in the office as he entered, but the embarrassment was more than compensated for when Skitch Henderson (for the second time in fifteen years) turned over the baton to Moondog and the band played "Bird's Lament." He got mostly good press. Gabe Pressman used Moondog for the opening installment of a series of "Human Interest Stories" for NBC news. This advertisement appeared in the *Daily News* for October 13 under the caption "Will Success Spoil Moondog":

Poet. Musician. Beggar. Chances are you've seen Moondog yourself, standing on his favorite corner, Sixth and 54th. But like everyone else in New York, there's a story behind him. And this one may even be a success story.

Advertisements that winter played on the exposure. The one most frequently used had bold headlines fronting a head shot ("Listen to this man's music; he'll never look the same to you again") preceding a racy bio and a shot of the album cover. Interviews with trendy responses to the music ("a blending of classical form and harmony with occasional jazz syncopations and spiced with recurring intimations of the folk music of the American west" appeared in *Newsday*), inaccurate gossip by old friends on the wrong track (Earl Wilson mentioned the "melodies inspired by vibrations from the rumbling of the subways" in *The Daily News*), and wrongheaded and erroneous profiles (one has his Candor plot on 150 acres near Syracuse; another calls him "a unique exponent of consciousness expansion") cropped up. But the occasional Moondog bon mot can relieve the monotony of hype. To the charge of looking "menacing," for instance, he replies:

Actually, I'm a peaceful warrior surrounded by warlike pacifists. I just wear this costume to remind people that the government doesn't have a monopoly on violence. I'm a great traditionalist. This harkens back to the day when every man had to be his own army, navy and air force.

The subtitle of the piece was "Blind Pacifist Has Songs to Sell."
Into December the articles continued, and Moondog appeared in the oddest places—in *The National Catholic Reporter*, for example, and *Coffee Newsletter*:

Moondog brews his coffee in a large juice can. He cuts away half of the top, puts in a handful of roasted beans and water and boils the mixture.... "It's strong, but that's the way I like it. To write I need a good heavy table, a cigar and my coffee. Many times coffee has been the source of my creativity.

This could be interpreted as expanding the consciousness.

Within a month the word was out that *Moondog* had sold 25,000 copies, but this was as inflated as some of the rhetoric surrounding the whole project. Still, it seemed to be going well, and nearly every initial response seemed to corroborate the high hopes. Reviews from as far away as Coral Gables, Florida ("Highly recommended") and Indianapolis, Indiana ("Very imposing") are typical. The St. Louis Symphony performed *Minisym #1* on November 16. *Cashbox* and *Billboard* predicted triumphs: the "sophisticated orchestration in stunning packaging" of Moondog's "first classical gas" might "pick up an underground following," said the former; "one of the most unusual albums in years," "exquisite," "sublimely melodious, rich in subtle rhythms and harmony," noted the latter: "Excellent album that could do quite well."

1969, therefore, ended on a strong upbeat. *Variety* (October 1) opined that Moondog so "demonstrates his serious composing skills" that "the disk thoroughly deserves its classification in Columbia Masterworks series." *Entertainment Today* noted, weirdly, that Moondog was no longer "tripping" as "a freak attraction," but instead was now "a fine rich-sounding composer in his first time at bat." *Downbeat* recommended the album, which, each time it is heard, "becomes a richer pleasure" and "an adventurous musical experience" with "a sound for all seasons." Not every review was a rave, but none was wholly negative. The worst said about the album was by Stephen Smoliar in *Boston After Dark*, and even that is more sober than destructive. The "contemporary classicism" of Moondog, he writes, the attempt to realize "traditional techniques through contemporary materials," although well-intentioned, does not quite come off; especially disappointing was the failure to develop the fullest potential of the minisym: "Either the musicians never got into the spirit of the minisym or the recording engineer upset the balance of the performances. But too many important facets are almost totally drowned out." In spite of these reservations, which strike at the heart of one of Moondog's radical forms, and also accurately locates one of the recurrent problems he faced when his ambitious music was performed, the review closes by praising "one of the more stimulating musical oddities of the twentieth century."

Initially, therefore, came the good news. The *Billboard* weekly survey of the best-selling classical LPs reveals that during the week ending October 25, within four weeks of release, *Moondog* entered the chart at number 39. It then climbed steadily to number 24, number 17, number 13 by November 22. Then, good news for Moondog, who had long and dearly hoped to pass Leonard Bernstein on the charts: by December 12 the album held at number 6, slightly behind *2001: A Space Odyssey*, two synthesized Bach recordings, Leontyne Price, and a selection of arias from French opera. *Bernstein's Greatest Hits*, after 130 weeks in the top ten, had dropped to 12th. The new decade seemed to promise a Moondog renaissance; with one success on hand and another album contracted for, he was riding high.

BY EARLY 1970, HOWEVER, the album's position on the charts dropped steadily, and Moondog had not yet received a royalty check. Life had begun to slow nearly to a normal pace, though it was never the same again. From May 1969 until early 1970, Moondog once again lived on the streets; in other words, while the album was produced, recorded, and released, and through all of the interviews and appearances, he had no permanent roof over his head. In fairness to the unwillingly homeless, Moondog was on the street by choice, saving money for something else. Also, besides money, Moondog always had invitations. A woman named Joyce, for instance, gave him a set of keys to her apartment in the East 70s, where he could sleep in the daytime and dictate his music to Mark Unger before returning to his spot "to make a little money for food." Similarly, one cold morning, while he was having breakfast (al fresco as usual) a man named Rick made an offer hard to refuse: Moondog could stay overnight, after business hours, at the offices of Ice Leather at 105 West 55th Street. "I did, from the winter of '70 until November of that year, at which time the company closed. [But not before designing a line of clothing, discussed later.] After that the apartment was taken up by a madam and her girls. The new name I called Nice Leather." So, despite all, the same cycle repeated: he visited friends, used their rooms for naps (or dictating, copying, and proofing), performed some evenings, slept at night wherever he could, and retreated to Candor whenever he could afford it. It would take another Columbia album, a little more than two years down the road, to hasten his alienation from New York, as it had taken the loss of his faith and his mighty ego to sever his ties from his original family in 1943. First, he would leave Gotham for Candor, then Candor for Europe, and his need for an authenticity that required expatriation began to become clearer just as his restlessness seemed to be winding down into success. It was not to be—not because he would never have another chance, and not because he refused to be bought, but because the exile had to go home. As a child he had had many homes, all lost or abandoned. As a young adult he foundered in blindness until he found his music. He came to New York and made music on the streets, but that, too, had to end because, despite its grip on his soul, he wanted to grow beyond his environment. The cycle had to be broken before he could find peace in his work.

In the meantime, though abating slightly, the publicity flowed on. Articles generated by central casting appeared in such unlikely conservative organs as the *Daily News* and the *Long Island Press*. Old "friends" such as the columnist Bob Considine quoted him (in *Signature Magazine*), as usual, making him seem more off-center than he was. When he talked like a "philosopher" (as Mr. Considine condescendingly portrayed him), however, he could repel the attempt to make him look foolish by his hard-won common sense. (Moondog later said: "He was very polite, even respectful to my face, but in his column he made me sound a bit comic or even ridiculous. A bit two-faced, I thought.") From the article:

> "The war in Vietnam will continue through 1970 and years beyond," he confided to me recently, in accents mournful and grey. "The advisers around the president will say this must be, or else great calamity will befall the economy. So we must look beyond the advisers. Who are the advisers of the advisers? Wall Street and the great industrial complexes, that's who."

There is a clarity and a directness here, if he is being quoted accurately, despite some of the old posing ("So we must look beyond"), that cannot be garbled in translation even by someone looking for "material." When Mr. Considine turns to the music, however, sound and sense begin to part company. Moondog, we are told, "tends toward hypnotic rhythms, simplistic melodies given elaborate treatment, and rather colorful orchestration," and there is "a fascination to his music that transcends the question of quality." It is easy to wonder at moments like this whether the appeal of an ice cream could transcend the question of how it tastes. Such evasive rhetoric may have masked the reviewer's bafflement: Is this guy serious? Is the music pretentious or deep, gimmicky or artful? Is the project introducing a neglected composer to a larger world or yet another object of Madison Avenue hype dressed up in a Masterworks label? Of course, Moondog himself both aided and impeded any serious discussion of his work: charming, if fey, challenging if not dangerous, he required a hardy sort of admiration.

But he was taken seriously, then as earlier, by serious musicians. As one of his ten-cent broadsides put it, Robert Sherman of WQXR was playing the record: "When you are played on WQXR you have arrived." Some of his old friends and colleagues reclaimed him. Sam Ulano praised him in an unsigned article in his publication

What's Happening in Music (January 1970). He wrote that he had known Moondog since 1948 and had performed with him many times for over a decade, the most memorable being the 1952 Percussion Society concert at the YMHA. (He also appeared on two of the Prestige albums, most prominently in the duet "Drum Suite.") Moondog, he goes on, is an innovator who "knows his music well," and his relationship to an orchestra "relies on a perfect ear.... If asked what a certain instrument played at a certain bar in the piece, he could not tell; but when the orchestra is playing and something is wrong, he knows it immediately." (Sam was Moondog's first choice as second drummer on 1971's *Moondog 2*, but that did not work out.)

Another influential admirer was Gordon Spencer. Twice in the 1960s he aired radio interviews with Moondog, including comments from people on the street. On his show for WNCN he played selections from the first two Prestige albums over the years. In the July 1970 *WNCN Program Guide* he wrote a brief celebration of some of the dimly remembered achievements of Moondog, especially since the 1950s recordings were now out of print and Mr. Spencer greatly admired the earlier music. For instance, when this "serious" composer went to live among the Indians in 1948, he revisited "a childhood environment that has colored...much of his writing." "Stamping Ground" was born there: "the music was simple, as his always is." Moondog, additionally, confided to Mr. Spencer more about his planned "sound saga" than he had in his program notes ten months earlier, a clear indication that *The Creation* was still brewing in the less active summer of 1970. This was not to be an opera, as he had been misquoted as explaining, but "opera without scenery"—sound creating space. Moondog notes: "I believe the popularity of opera on radio is proof scenery is not needed. You can create it in your mind." He was "hopeful" that his symphonic works would be taken seriously by the serious musical world: "new recordings and concert bookings are strong possibilities." Wistfulness muted pronouncements that had rung with self-confidence a few months earlier.

Some of the couplets in his dime broadsides at this time reveal his state of mind in 1970. On New York City, for example, his "parents" for so long: "Considered independently, the city is a curse, / and only seems a blessing when compared with something worse." On his independence, now invested with a certain wryness, as if the frisson has mellowed and the romance cooled, he says: "The Leaning Tower leaned a little farther south and said, / I wouldn't be so famous if I had a level head." Yet despite an incipient disillusionment, Moondog worked on. During one two-week period he gave a lecture on *Beowulf* at the Borough of Manhattan Community College (critiquing what he considered one of history's greatest anonymous artistic abuses, the Christianization of pure Gothic legend) and took part in a concert of his works, as "reciter and drummer," at the Whitney Museum. The program, "A Moondog-Charles Mingus Concert," featured, in his segment of the evening, selections from *The Art of the Canon*, Books I and II, performed by the Aeolian Chamber Players. Since the "Composer's Showcase" series in which it appeared was a prestigious outlet ("devoted to the encouragement and advancement of contemporary music of merit") sponsored by the National Endowment for the Arts among others, and included on its advisory committee Leonard Bernstein, the evening was a triumph of Moondog the musician over the cult figure.

Yet an image that took a quarter of a century to evolve was not easy to change, let alone erase. Indeed, one of the major tactical errors Moondog and his publicists may have made (although it may have been unavoidable) was to present two different images to the public. The man and his music may have been inseparable to Moondog and his close admirers, but for most, in the media kaleidoscope of new faces and sounds, he would always be the Viking. The man on the street, if such a creature really exists, unlike Moondog and Janus, is not necessarily at ease with paradox. Columbia made decisions that were to change the direction of the "Masterworks" track for *Moondog*, long before *Moondog 2* was under development. In June 1970 "Stamping Ground" became the theme music of the three-day Holland Pop Festival. Among the performers listed were Al Stewart, Neil Young, Jefferson Airplane, Santana, Hot Tuna, The Byrds, and Pink Floyd. Bunny Freidus, Manager of Promotion and Information Services for CBS International, in an October 9, 1970 letter to Judith Berger, now approaching her second year of sustaining Moondog Management, noted how the single ("Theme" was the B-side), under the guidance of CBS Holland, "had considerable airplay in the Benelux countries." The *Rotterdamsch Nieuwsblad* (June 12, 1970) reproduced the cover of the record in its article on the happening. The drift is clear: Moondog is to remain a "pop" figure, a folk hero. It was no surprise, therefore, that in 1971 *Moondog 2* appeared as a popular recording. Although a very different effort from *Moondog*, it is no less demanding on the listener, and that is part of the problem.

The events created ironies as well as press releases. An elaborate scheme to produce a boutique show of Moondog fashions in July 1970 by none other than Ice Leather Company, where Moondog had been spending his evenings for six months, had some interesting design premises. To be featured were items, all cut in squares, such as a hat, cape, short shirt, shorts, and pants (with codpiece). Moondog polo shirts were also on the drawing board. Unfortunately, none of this ever got beyond the planning stage. Had even a few Moondog originals reached the public, it would have been a marvelous, if ironic, triumph for the man who refused to dress like anyone else, who refused to put on manufactured goods, and who steadfastly costumed himself as a labor of love.

By the end of summer 1970, Moondog was back at his old spot on the corner of 54th and 6th. The New York Hilton now had competition for its proximate landmark: full-page ads in the newspapers announced the opening of the Mill at Burlington House "up the street from Radio City, down the street from Central Park, and across the street from Moondog." No money had arrived from Columbia, but by now, he admitted, he was "not overly optimistic," even if his plans were many and big.

Despite the opportunities and contracts, Moondog was at no other time so alone as in the winter of 1970. For years he had had no family:

> The not knowing where his mother is—"somewhere in Missouri, I think." [She died in 1976.] The brother who's a doctor somewhere who never answered Moondog's last letter three or four years ago. [He would never again communicate with Creighton.] The note from his stepmother saying his father "is dead and buried."..."They didn't invite me to the funeral. Even in death, they wouldn't forget appearances."
> (*Rochester Democrat*, Feb. 22, 1970)

One could add his sister, Ruth (closest to him of all after his blindness, missing for years and presumed dead), two failed marriages, and two estranged daughters. Moondog's "complexes" arguably arose from parental rejection and the inevitable, restless need for a home, for requited intimacy. No bravado or surrogate could compensate.

Yet another kind of logic was pulling Moondog away from the vortex of his own creations. The city as "curse" as opposed to parent (nurturer of idiosyncrasies, disparate creative impulses, and the homeless artist) created a tension he could no longer hide. He chose to embrace fully what he had in part adopted earlier. Soon passers-by saw less and less of Moondog at his "station." But as 1970 ended, a year after Moondog's Columbia release, when it was clear that he would not "take off," he was wandering still, vacillating between New York and Candor, between careers and images, solidifying his myth and idioms, always restless. He was fifty-four years old.

Making the Rounds

(1971–1974)

A blind man on the streets of New York is vulnerable, and Moondog was fortunate to survive intact for so long. Only minor pilfering and occasional brushes with the law blemished his performances around town; the day-to-day events of his life changed little, sometimes for years. Within the chaos around him he could hear the ephemeral melody when it came, and he often had to stop whatever he was doing to capture it in Braille, or it was "almost impossible to retrieve it without its sounding strained." Back on the streets during winter 1970–71, with irregular stints in friends' apartments, he was still the Viking, and the famous and the obscure engaged him at his station. Yet the same aura that made him nearly invulnerable to illness or gratuitous violence also gave his readings of people a charming disingenuousness. As customers passed, Moondog greeted warmly and argued heatedly, but all were equal to his ears: in his blindness he did not distinguish the importance of a voice, only its quality.

Through the two years between Columbia albums Moondog slept where he worked. A marvel of fortitude to his friends, he endured his last two winters in New York without a cold. Whenever he was not at Candor, or indoors, he would curl up after the theatres were dark at the well-lit bank on the ground floor of the MGM building on the corner of 55th and 6th, under the circumstances a most secure spot. A continual stream of customers visited the all-night depository, and concerned friends including a nearby doorman kept a vigilant eye on him. He always woke up whole in the morning. Sometimes the staff at the Warwick Hotel brought him coffee and a danish. At 5:00 a.m. he would go into the Joy Deli, 105 West 55th, as he had regularly for years, to get his rousing breakfast of a quarter-pound of pastrami, rolls, coffee, cruller, orange, and more. He remembered the "friendly Greeks" there with the "fondest regards."

One evening in April of 1971, at his station, two familiar voices greeted him: Mary and June. It had been over a decade since they had spoken, and June was now almost eighteen. They could not have predicted that their coming together that spring would culminate in their collaboration on an LP. Mary performed on his first and last American albums, and June had been serenaded as an infant on the first and sang with her father on the last. Nor could they have predicted that, after May 1972, when Moondog toured the Midwest and then moved up to Candor, they would never see each other again, or even keep in touch after a few more letters. Their relationship, so strange, so strained, so compellingly creative, is a chapter in Moondog's life that reads like bad fiction. For him, however, so used to the bizarre, it was another unexpected illumination. The moment burned brightly, briefly.

But that spring day was a reunion in the fullest sense of the word, extinguishing the buried rancor of years. First they had a long talk over coffee and sandwiches. June, who was attending the New York School for Performing Arts (in the days before *Fame*), told her father that her fellow students were "raving about that man Moondog and his music." (An analogous moment: when his mother heard from his brother's daughter—whom he never met—that her uncle had just released an album on Columbia, she said that the family had always considered Louis "an early bloomer," an observation they had never shared with Louis. He heard the story in the letter informing him of his mother's death, shortly afterwards.)

Although June did not admit that he was her father, she did ask her mother to re-establish a relationship. Mary agreed, having recently broken up with the man she had lived with since the separation in 1960, and the old nuclear bond formed again. They invited him to visit, perhaps even to stay with them, and he did, off and on during the spring, after they moved into the Viking House (of course) on the upper west side, not far from Columbia University. Perhaps because he always felt as if he were "roasting" in their overheated apartment, he invited them up for a May weekend at Candor, but they still didn't like roughing it (the flies, the wood smoke, outdoor cooking, primitive facilities without running water…). They would always be, he said wryly, "city girls." By summer, after completion of the recording of *Moondog 2*, he was sharing an apartment on the ninth floor of the Viking House with a young man, a fellow traveler who offered daily sacrifices to the Norse gods on an altar like Moondog's in Candor. Here he stayed until May 1972, when he left the city for good.

The family's initial weeks together were busy and fruitful, for the timing of their newly defined relationship was lucky. Even though it did not appear until December of 1971, the second album for Columbia was recorded in May. Immediately June and Mary were included; Moondog taught them to play percussion parts, mostly eight-bar patterns. June also learned the vocal parts in a mere two weeks: Moondog was not only pleased by her sense of timing ("she had me standing on my toes") but also by the quality of her voice ("so full, without vibrato, and in tune"). In light of some hitches they encountered, and some strong disagreements, the sessions went quickly. The "madrigal album," as it is sometimes called, was performed largely in the Columbia east side studios at 50th Street, though parts were done at the Old Church where *Moondog* had been recorded, and which he loved for its excellent acoustics.

In retrospect, the delightful album finally released as *Moondog 2* had a poor chance, despite its favorable reception. Just before the recording session, Al Brown and Moondog had several skirmishes. Moondog had hired his old friend Sam Ulano as second drummer. Sam, who had played duets with him on the Prestige albums and in concert, was able to read his rhythms. Al fired Sam without informing anyone about it, and Moondog walked in to find another drummer in the studio who couldn't read the rhythms. What had been painstakingly worked out note by note had to be "improvised." The cheery program notes euphemistically call this procedure "super-imposed ad lib percussion." Moondog was no stranger to performers who struggled with his music, of course, and Sam complained to the union and to Columbia, but the only result was that he got paid several thousand dollars for his rehearsal time out of Moondog's expense account. Though "put out by this," Moondog went along with the change once the pressure point was passed. But then Al made a pass at June, who snubbed him, and he was put out by that. In retaliation, it seems, Mr. Brown, who was black, returned after the incident with two white girls, one on either arm (for years he had promoted black-white combinations in the acts he sponsored and booked). Through their association in the late 1960s, through concerts and recordings, this "prince of a man" did more for Moondog than any other professional musician in his entire career. But when Moondog's material merely suggested possibilities for Al's unique interest in mixed groups, the two men had to go their separate ways. Mr. Brown wanted two black girls and two white men (to sing the four proposed parts of the madrigals) on the cover of the album. Imagine his shock when he discovered father and daughter were to be the only singers. Imagine his even greater surprise when some of Moondog's earlier unconventional views on "ethnic purity" filtered back to him. It seems his (white) girlfriend interviewed Moondog and got direct answers. We do not know what he was asked nor what he answered, but what seems with hindsight to have been the inevitable breakup accelerated. On the whole affair Moondog commented, "Although he puts miscegenation before art, I am beholden to him for all he did for me, before and after the recording."

In addition to the bickering about the performances, there was a major rift between principles of production: Mr. Guercio, certain that this album was a far more modest package than the first, knew that it would not be "classical" in any sense. He suggested electronically amplified instruments. (Since Mr. Guercio later refused to discuss the Columbia Moondog records, his intentions remain obscure. Did he intend to bring Moondog closer to the mainstream all along? Did he really care about the nature of Moondog's music or only about its potential audience?) Moondog adamantly refused, writing in the program notes that "all the instruments used in the record are acoustical." The most "modern" instruments were the piano, celesta, and guitar; with them appeared an early prototype of Moondog's troubadour harp, pipe organ, virginal (harpsichord), recorder, and viola da gamba. Electronics, he observes, are "disquieting." He was moving in other directions: "With this recording of Book I it is hoped a new trend may be set in motion, and it is hoped that many will be turned on listening to, and then performing, rounds." Further, he practically admitted that this music was unclassifiable, a departure not only from his first Columbia album but also from anything popular: "If this music has anything to do with rock, you might say that this is what became of rock, rock gone classical or rock come of age." It is not easy to forge new categories, however, and like so many fine innovations that simply do not catch on, his concept of a hybrid form was not successful despite the effort and the praise.

Not all the news was bad, and the creative vision and the fine performances lifted hopes high. His main player, Kay Jaffee (recorder, harpsichord, and organ) was "tops." "I never had a better player." Gillian Stephens played a composition on the troubadour harp that he composed for her. (Moondog was so impressed by her performance that he dedicated a booklet of pieces for troubadour harp to her.) June and Mary were with him. But more important than the activity was that this recording of the madrigals freed him from lingering unfulfilled expectations. He had written his first rounds in 1950 ("In late winter or early spring, in a doorway on Fifty-first Street, between Seventh Avenue and Broadway") but had all but abandoned them after "nothing much happened." Later that year he completed Book I and was selling it on the streets. His twenty-year devotion to the form would finally get its due: its test and its exposure.

The program notes to *Moondog 2* are less formal (script rather than print) and more conversational than those produced for the Mastererworks album. Interwoven with biographical snippets he discusses his plans (Book I is the first of "a series of nine," each having twenty-five rounds), his ideas, his ruling passions. The clarity comes from his obedience, general rebelliousness notwithstanding, of the rules of voice leading and passing notes. "It well may be that I pay more attention to modal contrapuntal rules...than any other composer from Palestrina on." The round, "the strictest of canonic forms," is ancient, tried and trusted; its tradition "goes back hundreds of years in European musical history." The madrigal, strictly speaking a love song, now ranges "far afield in subject matter"; and accompanying the album was an eight-page songbook called "Round the World of Sound," which he describes this way:

> ...starting in C major and going around the chain of fifths through the flat keys into the sharp keys, ending in C major again. By way of each major and relative minor...pieces are pegged, varying in subject matter, mood, meter, number of parts, though the number is arbitrary, and can be arranged at will.

Pam Gross, that "whiz" at dictation, gets credit for inking the manuscript. The subtitle (on the booklet only), "A Cycle of Rounds in a Double Chain of Fifths, Gotham and Hinterland," is jocularly carried over into the observations printed between the madrigals:

> "Round the World of Sound" is a take-off on "Around the World in Eighty Days" which will be eighty minutes, more or less, if these 25 rounds were sung or played, back to back, or back to Bach.

Moondog had published his music before, but this was the most opulent booklet of his material ever printed in America. He had never had the space to explore in such technical yet playful detail one of his most cherished forms, or the opportunity to record so many madrigals.

The public life of *Moondog 2* was briefer and, aesthetics aside, less spectacular. The problems encountered in its release and distribution followed it to its failure. Unsure of what to do with it, those who made the decisions did far too little for an album like this to get a grip on the public. The ambiguity and, perhaps, neglect (the contract for two albums had been honored) carries over to the cover: above a headshot less colorful than the spectacular photograph gracing the Masterworks album was the title *Moondog 2: 26 Songs by New York's Great Street Poet*. In the second pressing the subtitle quietly vanished. There was an additional difficulty: it was one of Columbia's first albums in quadrophonic, which did not play well on most of the stereo sets of the time. Some of the channels were not audible, and occasionally half the voices did not come across. Although quad was dropped soon after, *Moondog 2*'s sound and sales were not helped: few had the equipment to appreciate it, so few did. It was soon out of print.

A few advertisements appeared. Typical were those in *The Village Voice* (December 23, 1971) and *Rolling Stone* (January 20, 1972), old friends of the amorphous, unspecified Moondog audience. Under a heading in black, superimposed upon a blazing sun between two skyscrapers, "Miracle on 53rd Street," Moondog is viewed in full regalia from a ground-level camera, a mountain of a man amidst concrete and glass. The inevitable biographical hype is there as well as the predictable fluff: "*Moondog 2* is a simple and beautiful album: Much like the man who stands on 53rd and 6th selling his poems to the world." (In retrospect, it is amusing that Columbia did not give up its geographical claim even after Moondog had moved that one block north again.)

But this time around, two years after the first whirl through the spotlight on Columbia, there were no TV appearances, no special magazine or newspaper features, and generally little ado. No one pushed the album. The reviews, though good, were sparser. *The New York Times* (December 11, 1971), which did not review the

Masterworks album, praised the "versatile, schooled composer" who sustains the listener's interest "to a surprising degree," especially with the "sprightly rhythms" of the rounds. Here is the conclusion:

> The combining of a fairly strict classical form with a surging jazz feeling, and the unusual mixture of Moondog's home-made percussion instruments with harpsichord, recorders, viola da gamba, etc. results in music which is, for my taste, far more interesting than the academic sounding orchestral works on his last recording.

Other voices offered different accolades. The *Sunday Record* (December 11), for instance, observed that the music sounds like "12th Century Burgundian," though "more complex." Moondog was to the reviewer, however, unequivocally

> a man ahead of his time. The 20th Century may be catching up with him at last, but I doubt that it will pass him by. And just because these pieces are of a few measures' duration each—brief, in the way a Japanese haiku is brief—is no reason to deny that Moondog is one of the truly creative men of our time.

Chris Van Ness, in the *Los Angeles Free Press* (November 12), wrote a review so panegyrical that advertisements for the album well into 1972 carried his taglines. "This is a magic album," he begins, that will "lull you into a kind of peacefulness to the point where you would hope that the music would go on forever. There is no way to put into words the beauty contained in these grooves." The vocals are "perfectly and delicately handled," the instrumentation is "authentic Renaissance," and the whole is "augmented by Hardin's own peculiar percussion." The design of the madrigals, though "simple in concept," becomes "a very intricate piece of music in the hands of a skillful musical technician" who "has blended technical wizardry with the soul of a human magician."

Not only has Moondog "taken the simplest of melodic lines and…formed his own language that can communicate on both the most basic and grandest of human levels," he has also "distinguished himself as a very fine poet."

Despite the good notices, sales started slight and fell fast. Twenty-five madrigals and a harp pastorale were not likely to galvanize the popular record-buying, radio-listening public, yet that must have been the intent. *Moondog 2* foundered in confusion, with no strong publicity campaign or vigorous distribution to save it. Moondog was not then or ever a composer for a mass audience. *Moondog* (1969) had succeeded in its own fashion because the special, if unclassifiable, nature of the music had been a premise. Because Moondog refused to bend his design into pop, but preferred to maintain an integrity of clear lines, delicate harmonies, and meaningful lyrics, his admirers diminished through attrition. Too intricate for the idle, too specialized for the fan, and too much like popular song for the classicist, this delightful statement wound up pleasing only a few.

Whether or not Columbia let it die when it did not inflame the underground is unknowable, but many changes were imminent for Moondog, at least in part as reactions to another deferral of his dream. His relationship with Guercio and Brown dissolved. By the end of May, after performing several concerts, he would move out of Viking House; by summer he would make his second cross-country tour. As had happened so often in the past—in the 1950s, when his recordings and his performances stayed obscure, and in the 1960s, when his rebellious antiheroism kept him on the streets—a new Moondog emerged from the crucible of disappointment: a more serene and confident composer, more devoted to his craft than ever, having passed yet another test on his own terms.

Deeper down, Moondog had wearied of life on the streets. A quarter of a century is a long time, and he was still poor. More frustrating, however, was his failure to make the mark he had wanted on the world of music. He had lived the life of an artist, at times suffering deprivations while working long hours in the service of his craft, but in 1972 he was no longer getting out of it what he needed. Not only did he turn another degree inward, but he was now ready to leave.

PAUL JORDAN WAS MOST INSTRUMENTAL in getting Moondog to Europe in 1974, and was one of Moondog's most consistent and serious supporters thereafter. Some time after 1950, when Mr. Jordan was studying recorder as a child in New York City, his instructor, the composer Tui St. George Tucker, used one of Moondog's 78 RPM organ rounds in ensemble sight-reading sessions otherwise devoted to pre-Baroque music. Paul was so moved by the music that he resolved to seek out the composer. Arriving at the Port Authority Bus Terminal one day, he got into a taxi and told the driver: "Take me to Moondog." Because Moondog was "so much a fixture," the driver knew exactly where he was. Although Paul stopped by several times in the intervening years, occasionally chatting, he never had a chance to bond with the blind symbol out of his past. In 1971, however, after he had established himself both as a music teacher and organist, he decided to try to make productive contact.

As music director of the historic United Church on the Green in New Haven, Connecticut, he conceived a service centered on Moondog's music. It took him a while to locate his quarry from the evidence on the first Columbia album, but he finally accosted the Viking on 54th and 6th with his proposal. Moondog accepted eagerly (it was around the time of the second Columbia album's release) and met with Mr. Jordan, Mary, and June at the Viking House several times to establish and begin rehearsing the program. Moondog had to leave before Mary to get the New Haven train at Grand Central Station because it took her too long to put on her make-up, but that was the only hitch in an otherwise splendid day. Thus "Moondog Goes To Church" (as the headline for the feature article in the *New Haven Register* on January 23, 1972 phrased it) became a reality: the Sunday service was the fullest house of the year, including Easter.

The program, performed by Mr. Jordan (piano, harpsichord, recorder, organ), Elliot Finkel (piano), Gillian Stephens (harp), Jeannine Dovell (soprano), Lois Lounsbery (piano, organ), Mary (percussion), June (voice), and Moondog (voice, percussion), consisted of the following: *Der Grosse Kanon* (which some parishioners especially liked, even though it was too long to be in the program proper, serving instead as the prelude to the service as people took their seats); several two-part canons transcribed for organ; the "Pastorale" for troubadour harp; and, as the musical centerpiece of the service, several madrigals. The Reverend Mansfield Kaseman's sermon, "The Paradox of Inequality," took inspiration from the madrigal lyrics and from Moondog's gentleness and fearlessness. The article describing the event concluded thus:

> His creative work has become known to an astounding number of musicians and laymen both here and abroad for the special classic lucidity and vigor of his compositional craftsmanship—drawing heavily on modal counterpoint, together with Moondog's personal synthesis of harmonic and rhythmic dimensions—blending elements of the "primitive" and jazz with the traditions of Bach, Beethoven and Brahms in a unique manner.

There were other concerts. He performed at the Parsons School, and his "Witch of Endor," originally written for Martha Graham, appeared on a dance program at Barnard College. After the performance, the choreographer, Karlynn Lander, stopped by at Moondog's spot, as she did for eight of the ten years she spent in New York. "It was truly gratifying to realize," she notes, that Moondog had a real knowledge of different kinds of dancing, "that he knew 'modern dance' did not mean jazz." Also, his Madrigal No. 8 was performed as a round for four tubas (one F, one E flat, two B flats) at the William Patterson College of New Jersey as part of a special concert entitled "A Recital of Music for Multiple Tuba Ensemble," produced by Don Butterfield (who had performed on the *Moondog* album) on March 16, 1972.

For a host of reasons old and new, by May Moondog had decided to leave the city permanently for his upstate New York home. As he had said often about his feelings for America and Europe, he loved the former no less than before, but he had come to love the latter more. After nearly thirty years of big city living he wanted to "settle down"—not to be idle, but to compose, at least for a while. Often during the sixteen years he had owned the property he had been unable to afford the bus fare up, once for over a year. But now, with a few dollars in his pocket and his music better known than ever before, the moment for making the break came at last. It was a decision saddened somewhat by his parting from Mary and June, who almost immediately moved out of his life, to Los Angeles when he last heard from them, where they had joined a Buddhist community. (Mary died shortly after Moondog; there was no contact between him and the two women after 1972.) But he had waiting for him some old friends (Bucky Moon) and some new (Thelma Burlar), a secure, peaceful retreat, a new season. First, however, he had one more visit to make to his roots, one more "round" trip.

SHORTLY AFTER ADOPTING the name "Moondog," in 1948, he had marked the occasion by taking his Portland-to-Portland trip. In 1972, Moondog headed west once again to market his recordings. He planned to visit some old friends and some familiar places, to play some concerts and to lead some intimate "Evenings with Moondog," mainly on college campuses. One of Jack Kerouac's heroes was back on the road. Why, right after his fifty-sixth birthday, did he decide on this onerous journey? As he noted in an interview given on the trip:

> I've never been satisfied with the sales. So much good work goes unknown. I want to have the first classical album to sell a million copies. I'm convinced that there are that many people who understand and want such music. (*Plymouth [Wisconsin] Review*, August 19, 1972)

He would travel from town to town, meeting with the young audiences always most congenial to him and responsive to the challenges he embodied; he would distribute flyers about ordering his records. He was, as ever, convincing. He played to large audiences and attracted responsive press notices. One article notes in closing:

> Perhaps through these very personal 'evenings,'…the record companies will realize what a rare and precious jewel they have in this extraordinary man. (University of Wisconsin *Daily Cardinal*, August 31, 1972)

It was the last time he played to the American heartland, where he was born and grew to manhood, lost his sight and the faith of his father, and discovered his talents and vocation. He paraded the full range of his abilities: orator, composer, musician, spokesman for the world's disenchanted artists. He returned to Candor two months later with pleasant memories, albeit without profits. In his knapsack he brought back a new custom-made instrument.

The journey began on July 12, 1972. His first stop was an overnighter at Paul Jordan's home in New Haven, and from there he went to Boston, where local fans greeted him as he stepped off the bus. Within a couple of days he gave an outdoor concert (part of the summer festival series in Cambridge Common) of madrigals and "Bird's Lament" with saxophone solo. Then he went to Buffalo and Niagara Falls. When he refused to pay six dollars for a seat in a private car to the national park, strangers picked up the tab. However impressed he was by the sound, the tourists were clearly as taken with the Viking as with the natural wonder behind him. He was told that more people took pictures of him than of the falls.

By August 19 he was in Plymouth, Wisconsin, where he had spent 1919–1922 at St. Paul's. Barry Johanson, the assistant editor of *The Plymouth Review*, took him in for a while and recorded an interview, interspersed with Moondog couplets, which he printed in the newspaper immediately.

Phone calls from the watchful had warned of his return to Plymouth's present....There he was, after all, 6'5" (in horns) of 57-year-old [sic] Viking standing in front of Adams Rexall drug store across from the Dairy State Bank.

"Plymouth itself," of course, had brought him: "His mother, Bertha Alves, was brought up near Chilton. Grandparents Herman Alves and Bertha Meyer came from the town of Meeme on the Sheboygan-Manitowoc county line." Settling into the sheepskin on an old leather chair which Mr. Johanson felt good about, for it was "once owned by my Norwegian relatives," Moondog produced his two Columbia albums for his impressed audience of four adults and two children and played them.

"Moondog," whispered my two-year-old son. I am in awe at the blind Viking, at the red and green capes, the five-foot wood staff and the floppy leather boots with chain mail toes.

In that living room, fifty years after he had last been in Plymouth, he traced the history of his life and beliefs. On his costume: "It's part of a time when there was no mass-produced clothing. Each man designed and made his own. There could be a lot of difference that still fell within the regional or tribal cultures." On his quest for his Nordic past: "I was bitter at our educational system which ignored the ethnic past of most Americans and concentrated on the Greeks and Romans." He visited his old home, the rectory, where he had played on the lawn, and found a young lad playing on the same green. In the church, where he had crawled into his father's arms while the pastor preached one Sunday morning, and where he remembered the sound of his mother playing, he tested the same organ and recited couplets from the pulpit.

But he did not stay very long, even in Plymouth. Within a week he was headed southwest, to Madison, where he had scheduled several "evenings with Moondog." They were, reports the *Daily Cardinal*, a complete success:

Within his voice there is an unforgettable gentleness and his presence pervades an entire room with a white aura. Listening to Moondog recite his poems is perhaps like consulting the ancient Greek blind seer, Tiresias.

The praise is high, even if the prose is purple and the allusion ominous. But this is the way Moondog had always been able to gather superlatives: we are overwhelmed by so gentle a man holding such combative ideas and living such a severe life. Even more dazzling is the contrast between the martial costume and the remarkable lyricism of his music, as the review of the other half of the evening confirms:

As a tonal composer it has been difficult for Moondog to convince record companies that music which is both pleasing to the ear and written during this century should be recorded in this age of industrialization and atonality. It is unfortunate that music as beautiful as this should be denied the American public.

The reporter took good notes: the earnest naïveté is the impression Moondog gave, but (to be fair) few atonal composers have had two albums on Columbia. Quibbles aside, Moondog was definitely in his element.

While he was sitting under a crabapple tree in Madison, two of his fans approached, classical guitar teachers and instrument makers (*Madison Wisconsin Times*, September 20, 1972). Moondog confided to them that he had been "nursing a dream" for two years about building a troubadour harp, and they invited him to their commune so they could develop a prototype for him. He stayed at the seven-member household for a week, enjoying the company of young people, their energy, their sanguine world-view, their inventiveness: Moondog qualities all. "They have the right attitude," he noted: "never to become cynical or bitter, always to retain high ideals, always to be creative." There, in that large farmhouse with its yoga meditation room, a hay loft which doubled as a dance floor and a boxing ring, "amid a constant coming-and-going," Dan Hecht and Glen Johnson worked on the front porch, making a "smaller and lighter" harp which Moondog tried in vain for months afterward to market.

> It is played on the knees instead of standing on the floor, and has 27 strings as opposed to 33 on the standard model. Other innovations include changed wood grain direction on the sounding board, and easily available guitar strings replacing harp strings. The instrument, made of oak and top-quality imported aged spruce, weighs about 20 pounds.

Southeast he went, his baggage somewhat heavier, to Evanston, Illinois, at Northwestern University, where he stayed in the home of the local Columbia representative. Fine musicians, students with the Chicago Symphony, performed with him there. The twenty horn players made the unveiling of his Heimdall Fanfare a great success. This piece, one of the earliest building blocks of *The Creation*, so impressed the members of the orchestra that they stamped their feet in approval at the completion of rehearsal.

His last stop was the campus at Bloomington, Indiana. There he renewed an old friendship with Professor Harvey Phillips, whom he had known since 1950 in New York, when both were freelancing into the world of music. Moondog described Mr. Phillips as "the greatest tuba player in the world," one who handled the huge instrument "like a French horn." (In January of 1986, at the Carnegie Recital Hall in New York, he gave a concert exploring the "many facets of the solo tuba.") Moondog had dedicated a musical composition to his fellow traveler, who organized a large brass chorus to play the Heimdall Fanfare. With only two days of preparation and publicity, he gave the concert to a capacity audience, which also heard Moondog read "Thor," introduced by a processional and followed by a postlude.

As the fall of 1972 set in, Moondog set out for Candor. His grass-roots promotional tour could not rescue *Moondog 2*, but, as the trail of headlines following his progress proclaimed, he left "Moondog territory" with "a very warm feeling," trailing a skein of good memories. He stopped briefly in Erie, PA, where thirty-five years later the first full-length recital of his music in the U.S. after his death would be performed. Back he came, east and north, to linger for a little over a year after his fifty-sixth birthday before embarking on another journey which, in a lifetime of giant steps, was the longest of all.

MOONDOG LIVED ON his Candor land for about sixteen months, a period intimately connected with Thelma Burlar, known to one and all as "Teddy." The two had met years earlier, when she was still married. As a painter she was drawn by Moondog's life and work; to Moondog Teddy was an attractive and intelligent kindred spirit. After her marriage ended and her four children grew up, she and Moondog shared more and more time together until she finally moved into the "spread." The transition for her was not without trauma, however; she had had an affair, and her husband had become violent. He beat her, and Moondog provided sanctuary. When the husband appeared at Moondog's door the police had to be called in. Teddy, before she died in 1982, described the artist's paradise "Logue Hill" had become, especially in the magical year 1973, and the quiet, enriched happiness she believed the two of them had shared. In the publication of the Tioga Council on the Arts (*Focus*, January, 1983) she described their relationship in this way: "Joining forces" with Moondog had been "a mutually gainful experience in learning and self-expression" which produced "a platonic professional" union and "a wonderfully deep friendship." She made no mention of the proposed marriage, which never materialized. This pastoral setting, however, may have had a snake or two in its grass. According to Moondog, she complained of the groupies who assaulted the delicately balanced peace. (One lady, according to Teddy a jilted fiancée, cornered her faithless swain in a noisy confrontation.) But for him the fragile serenity had more than one enemy. Yes, fans and admirers often appeared, but he had no truck with the idle and the curious, and when they showed up he put them to work, which deterred them. (Once, his daughter Lisa was brought up from New York by her mother to see him, though she, six years old, was not told who he was. It was the last time they met before 1989.) Thelma herself might have been part of the problem. She was, he admitted, "a very congenial companion, a marvelous cook, and very energetic, not only for herself, but for me." Yet it seems both came to resent the very isolation they had desired. "Gone were the days when I could sit and write for hours on end, only stopping to feed the fire or my mouth, or feed the dogs, or build on the house, or go on hikes with the dogs through the woods." She, it appears, had visitors of her own, "admiring males" making Moondog feel "a bit out of place, if not jealous." She often told him she had "bedroom eyes." They needed to and did keep some distance, but the feelings were strong. Years later, when he knew he was not going to return to America, he sold the parcel of land on which the structures stood to her for $1,000. (The remaining acreage had been sold a year earlier, in 1977, for $11,000.) Until her death it was her summer home, much of it, she said, "constructed with my own hands"; though "primitive," it "expresses a natural, simplistic [sic] way of life." Teddy was his companion even when he went to Europe, and she hoped for years afterward that they would be reunited.

This year was an aesthete's paradise. After the frenzy of the city and the fervor of the road, Candor was quiet and rewarding. His altar to Thor he consecrated with stones a friend sent from Thor's Nest in Iceland, along with some heavy woolen socks. He erected new dwellings but still most treasured the handcrafted "hemlock house," an elaborate lean-to. There he wrote and sometimes slept. He added a kitchen and laid the foundation for a stone house (with the help of students from SUNY Binghamton, where Paul Jordan had become a professor in the music department). With a Braille grocery list, he shopped at John's Fine Foods in Owego, near where his bus to and from New York stopped. At home, as always, he put creative wrinkles on life's pedestrian experiences: tilling a garden at night with strings as guidelines for the rows; swimming in a small pond carefully marked with ropes to indicate depths and points of access; pulling a sledge with a headband along wooded trails. German shepherds Thor and Freya (joined a little later by Saga) came to live there and soon produced a litter of seven, many of whom neighbors happily took home. One friend, Mike Gulachok, who wrote about Teddy and Moondog in several Tioga County publications over the years, recalled taking Moondog on a paddleboat in the Susquehanna River to Hiawatha Island, and how "enamored with the history and mythology" of the area he had become.

Candor was wonderfully isolated and highly protective of its famous eccentric. One visitor, Sid Mesibov, a columnist for the *Ithaca Journal*, went in search of Moondog in summer 1975. The residents, who felt "a proprietary guardianship" toward Moondog, steered him into "another world" that "sang of tranquility....a jealously guarded bastion to be entered only by those who come to feel and sense and enjoy; but not to change." At Moondog's old spread the reporter met "a woman who looked like the traditional pioneer" (Teddy probably), "rugged of face, strong of arm, determined in facing up to things." After telling him she had no idea when Moondog would be back she "turned and went back into the shack."

Into this charming retreat Moondog introduced his summer concerts. Candor would be, as Sandalwood in New Jersey was intended to be but never became, a cultural oasis. A bulldozer leveled a stage (now the floor of a barn) and cleared a meadow. Teddy's son, David, along with some local and college youths, helped carve a musical theatre: two outhouses, a stadium, and a parking lot. On three Sunday afternoons, the last in October, at "Moondog's Concert Shell," audiences heard innovative classical music. Twice string quartets performed original pieces while he read his poetry. Once, on September 23, at 3:00 p.m., Edward Brewer, "who has studied in Europe with the famous Helmut Walcha," gave a harpsichord recital of music by "the Baroque masters" and Moondog. Over one hundred paying guests attended. Some of Moondog's oldest dreams were coming true.

But one dream, older than most, lingered. From the earliest days of his musical longings, from *The First Violin* and from Wagner on the radio, Moondog had yearned for Europe. Although he could have chosen to live productively at Candor, perhaps even furthered his career, "Europe had too great a pull on me, historically, ethnically, artistically." It was the place a "European in exile" was meant to be: "Especially for *Thor* and *The Creation* I wanted to be where it all happened, as I was writing it." He had experienced disillusionment, anxiety, and impatience, though never despair. He could not wait to get to New York, could not wait to leave, could not wait to get back. He renounced the city only to find that the magic of the country wore thin. However many times he seemed to settle down, he never could settle in. The reason was simple: home eluded him because it always had, even as a child, even as a young man, even as a husband, a father, and a living legend. Home was waiting for him, at roughly age sixty, far away and long ago. He felt called, chosen.

After the New Haven concert of 1972 he and Paul Jordan had kept in touch, and the latter continued his active support for the composer whose work he admired, performed, and recorded. Mr. Jordan knew what Moondog wanted, and an opportunity came when a friend of Jordan's Europe-based family, Dr. Claus Schnorrenberger (a medical acupuncturist, author, director of the German Institute of Chinese Medicine, and former musician), encouraged Ernst Stiebler of Frankfurt Radio, an enthusiast for contemporary music, to invite Moondog to structure the concluding portion of a live broadcast concert of music by composers whose work would "not fit into any of the usual categories." Moondog would receive equal billing with the two other groups in the program, but unlike them he would not need to bring his own players; the station would provide an orchestra and a chorus from Berlin for the occasion.

This was it. Once Louis Hardin had left Memphis for New York, a "shot in the dark"; now he would leave New York for Germany.

Despite the intimidating logistical challenges for a blind and cumbrously attired and accoutred first-time flyer, Paul and Thelma managed to arrange the trip, passports, luggage, and all. To keep the costs low they would fly Icelandic Airlines into Luxembourg and finish the trip by train. Icelandic still flew prop planes and had a layover in Reykjavik: what could be more appropriate to the Viking en route to his roots?

Thus in January of 1974, almost fifty-eight, Moondog and Thelma left Candor for New York, where Paul met them and took them to Kennedy Airport. In the middle of the night Moondog walked the ground at Reykjavik while the plane refueled, something akin to a religious experience. He returned to "USA" only once, briefly, despite its strong pull. This trip was a bolder experiment in living than any he had ever taken: he was going to where he had wanted to be all along.

Part Three

The Viking Returns

(1974–1999)

Chapter Eight

Managagarm

(1974–1986)

Once he had finished with city life and cross-country tours, and after the comparatively quiet retirement at Candor, the old stirrings could not be soothed by activity; the missing center had no substitute. In the cold of January 1974, after it had long attracted his imagination, Moondog finally arrived in Europe. The next twenty-five years were his triumph and vindication, for he acquired, at last, international fame. Maybe more important than the new recordings, exhilarating concerts, or adulatory notices, however, is that he finally found serenity and peace there. But it did not happen right away.

Small successes followed his first immersion in things German. Before the big Frankfurt concert, Paul Jordan arranged a natural opportunity for the showman. In the small town of Weinheim, Paul performed a program on the church organ, half of Bach and half of Moondog. The advance publicity brought in a full house, including many counterculture types who clearly had not been in a church in a long time. Moondog, serene in his costume, was a big hit, as in the U.S., with the young. He also won over the more conservative burghers, appearing long afterward on the front cover of an advertising brochure for the local bank. (Paul Jordan, on a later one of his frequent visits to Germany, recorded twenty-eight canons from *The Art of the Canon, Books I–III*, in summer 1978, on the Hillebrand organ in St. Martin's Church, Dortmund. This recorded but unreleased performance interpreted Moondog's organ music with great sensitivity.) [Six tracks from the recording appear on the CD bound in this book.]

The Frankfurt radio concert, the pretext for the trip, went mostly as planned, although the wrath of Moondog exploded when his last-minute changes met resistance. (He won.) As he was conducting the brass ensemble, though, an unexpected problem came up. He had been indicating when the sixteen orchestral voices of the canonic "Procession of the Aesirs" were to come in by flipping over, one by one, printed numerals hung on his chest. In the excitement of the performance he accidentally turned over two cards at once. Enormous havoc would have ensued if Paul Jordan had not spotted the problem and swiftly and unobtrusively risen from his seat on the stage to correct it. Not surprisingly, Moondog's music was poorly received at first: in a concert of "unclassifiable music," the reviewers noted, at the center of postwar European atonalism, his was insufficiently avant-garde. The audience of about a thousand, however, was jubilant, and the concert tape, edited and with commentary, has been rebroadcast over the years.

Before Paul left to return to his teaching duties, he arranged a meeting between Moondog and the internationally famous Helmut Walcha, also blind, whose celebrated organ interpretations and arrangements of Bach and Handel Moondog admired, and whose student had played at one of the Candor concerts. Although Teddy insisted that Moondog take off his horns before entering the house of a devout Lutheran whose wife could see, no other sparks flew. They were kindred spirits of sorts: both had been blinded at about the same age (Walcha by complications from a smallpox vaccination), and each experienced a revelation about the nature of counterpoint through a Bach two-part invention (one in F major for Walcha, one in C minor for Moondog).

After Paul Jordan left, Teddy and Moondog spent the rest of their three weeks together on holiday. After visiting the Teutoburger Wald, sacred to the Viking who admired the Germanic resistance to Imperial Rome, they went to Hannover, where Moondog won over yet another young audience at an impromptu music school concert. A Russian prince with an unpronounceable name dedicated a poem, "Der Mondhund," to the American pilgrim, another tribute in feverish verse to the now internationally ineffable figure. Some of it, in translation, reads:

> Where does your ship go?
> Some say:
> following the sun.
> Others:
> to unknown shores....
> Listen, he is singing.
> Is it yearning?
> Is it grief?
> Or is it the song of the Norns?
> The song of death
> and destruction.
> Nobody knows.
> Not even you.

Despite the fun, Teddy had to return to America. Their parting, as recalled by her five years after it happened, was touching, not least because Moondog was apparently unaware of what occurred at the last minute. As they approached the Luxembourg border by train, on their way to meet the flight to New York, he said suddenly that he could not go back, that he felt good about what was going to happen to him in Germany, and that he was getting out at the next station with nothing other than his traveling sack. The last time Teddy saw Moondog, he was facing straight ahead, sitting in one train, while across the platform Teddy, seated in another, headed in the opposite direction. Gone, in an instant, was the last love from America, the last vestige of the past. They never saw or spoke to each other again. Moondog had been alone before, in New York and in rural retreat, but here he was heading to tenuous contacts in a strange country, with little knowledge of the language, no longer a young man on the rise or on the make, but a mature, worldly composer still on the move.

Like a crawdaddy, traveling backwards to move ahead (his image of himself), Moondog took up old habits in his new, adopted country. He spent a year in Hamburg, living first in a home for rehabilitated drug addicts and then in the apartment of a furniture restorer. The Burgermeister of Hamburg did not care for the American Viking in his town, but Moondog managed, as always, despite resistance. He took part in a few benefits and publicity sessions before heading for the city of Recklinghausen in 1975, when a friend had written that there was a chance for work there. Not long after he had settled in, an offer came from Paris for a concert engagement; there also arrived from America a letter inquiring about recording some harpsichord pieces. Both communications were lost in the chaos of his new environment, the dank digs of some young motorcyclists who had taken him in.

By spring 1975 Moondog was unhappy; his life was beginning to seem merely a continuation of the New York scene he had given up in 1972, performing, selling, manufacturing for his portable office the artifacts of his unique and demanding profession. He had decided at last, ill and depressed, to return to America, and had even reserved a seat on Icelandic, when a box of Columbia albums he had ordered came in. It was kismet: after he had finished paying the C.O.D. charges, he could no longer afford the plane fare.

It is at this moment that Ilona Goebel, who would so radically transform his life through accommodation and talent, enters his life, and, until his death in 1999, their story together became an accretion of accomplishments. She was twenty-three when she first saw Moondog; he was fifty-nine. She was a student of geology planning a career, living at home in the nearby town of Oer-Erkenschwick. Often, with her mother, her younger brother, Frank, or friends, she would go shopping in Recklinghausen. There, on that spring day in 1975, probably within a week after Moondog had first arrived, she saw him. A month later she saw him again, this time sitting in a chair. In July she defended him and his way of living in a lively discussion with friends, who thought him either a nuisance or a fraud. Just before Christmas, she spoke with her family about this haunting stranger: how he must be lonely at holiday time, and whether to invite him over. This led to sympathy, but no action. In January 1976 she saw the Columbia album (from that fateful shipment) he had placed in a store, and she bought it. After the family listened in "stunned silence" (her mother was especially moved by the energetic affirmation of "Good for Goodie"), another, more concrete discussion took place, with Frank offering the most encouragement.

Admittedly, they were put off by his appearance, and for years afterward mother and daughter would think him a "stubborn child" about his costume. To Ilona it was obvious that Moondog was saying, to his dead parents and the surrogate world at large, "you rejected me, so now I'll give you reason to." But in 1976, compassion outweighed fear of the unknown and weirdly attired stranger.

Moondog had had an awful winter cold and had lived, in the stoic manner of old, with his illness in the "dump" he shared with "two young men" for weeks. Ilona sought him in vain at first, but she persisted, moved by a compelling goal: "everybody needs one fixed point." He did not seem to have one. Perhaps she could give him that.

Finally, one afternoon she found him and persuaded him to come home with her. The family all recall watching with awe the layers of homemade garments peel off as he made himself comfortable. After this first visit he returned to his inhospitable place, but not for long; a second severe cold made it easier to lure him back. He stayed on even after he was well. He stayed on through the spring and the summer and into the fall. He stayed on, in effect, even after Ilona got married, for the rest of his life.

Moondog, after resisting for most of his life, was "domesticated" at age sixty for several reasons. Ilona's assistance and creative input empowered him. Compared to the best days of his past, the apartment in Oer-Erkenschwick was a composer's paradise. He had to surrender a part of his freedom of self-expression (he did not dress Viking at home), but such small compromises went a long way. He was adopted almost immediately by an extraordinary though not affluent family, enriching their lives while they made his nearly completely his own. His partner was an attractive younger woman the same age as his daughters. (Mary Whiteing had successfully broken the sequence of older lovers.) New possibilities emerged rapidly. He soon realized previously infeasible projects and surmounted previously impassable barriers.

Within months Moondog formed a professional alliance with Ilona (to be called Managarm, Norse for Moondog) that grew steadily in variety and productivity, and began to enjoy steady, undisturbed stretches of work. For years, especially in the country, Moondog had preferred to work in the quiet and solitude of night. In New York he often could not, since he made money from walking, waking patrons, and in winter the cold was inhospitable and dangerous. In Oer-Erkenschwick Moondog happened on the ideal arrangement: while the world slept he would take a few hours to write, compose, create. During the less pleasant daytime hours he would sleep, rest, or engage in more passive pursuits; at other times it was business with Ilona, including copying, correspondence, and proofing. If it got noisy, he used filberts as earplugs. He had meals, creature comforts, and a room of his own. America celebrated its bicentennial; Moondog celebrated his sixtieth birthday. Europe finally came home to him, not as historic myth or only in its music, but with a family.

Within months, he was conducting in several countries, releasing more records, traveling often, receiving frequent media coverage, undertaking ambitious projects both alone and with other artists, reworking *Thor* and polishing *The Creation*. Wherever he was, he spent most of his time writing (*The Overtone Tree*, for example) and composing—the volume is staggering. Unfortunately, creation is itself seldom of dramatic interest: events, as noted in the chapters on the 1950s and the 1960s, delineate an observed life rather than the work accomplished in privacy and silence. On the one hand, most of Moondog's final twenty-five years passed uneventfully; on the other, some events equaled or surpassed anything before Europe. This chapter and the next sketch his major accomplishments of 1976–1999, concentrating on the development of his music. Ilona, more and more, became his eyes: superb copyist, careful editor, sensitive critic, intelligent companion. (She was not trained to be a copyist, businessperson, marketer, creative assistant, or manager. She learned on the job with astonishing speed.)

For Moondog, the really important thing, the quality of his music, was beyond life and time. All of the opinions about his monumental oeuvre are not yet in, nor will the question of his importance be resolved soon. As the world sees such things, Moondog was famous for a second time in his second home, certainly a satisfying accomplishment, considering how difficult it is to start from the beginning for anyone, let alone a blind foreigner of sixty. Few get to know the best of two worlds, yet he did that, too, a figure on center stage in two continents. It is as though life finally reached out to meet his enormous resources of willpower, self-confidence, industriousness, and vision.

In his "crummy" pre-Goebel room or on the streets of Recklinghausen, he worked continually on his large organ pieces and "The Creation," which grew ever more defined. Not long after he had settled in Oer-Erkenschwick, he made two deals, both as a result of finding letters misplaced in turmoil. The first came from Paris, an offer by Martin Meissonier, a young music critic and broadcaster, to conduct and perform his music on French state radio. After mislaying the offer and confusing a first letter with a second, more specific one, Moondog was rescued by Ilona, who helped respond, organize, and prepare: "Louis and his music consume my life."

And so in 1976 Moondog and Ilona were in Paris, where he conducted the premiere of a piece for seventy-six trombones written for the occasion. The concert received quiet but positive responses. Said one critic: "Moondog brings back the Golden Age in music." Said another: the music "is not rock or jazz, nor a variation of classical or folk; it is Moondog." Since that day, Paris radio, like some PBS programming in America, has played Moondog often, adopting him first in Europe not as a character in exile but as a distinctive musical voice.

The second letter precipitated events that took Moondog's music back to America shortly after he had left it. Gavin Black, a former student of Paul Jordan's, had requested permission to record some of the canons on harpsichord and put an album together. In

1976 Moondog met the organist who would perform on many of his German albums for over twenty years, Fritz Storfinger. The two were then recording selections from *Lögründr, Book I.* (In the program notes Moondog explains the term: "log" means law or canon, "grund" means ground. Thus he combined two forms, with canons in the manuals, and, after 1974, when he first started writing specifically for the pipe organ, with ground in the pedals. He dedicated the enterprise to Paul Jordan.) His *Heimdall Fanfare*, called here a "canon in the Dorian mode for 9 horns," a chaconne, and a romance for string quartet filled out the program. The Musical Heritage Society liked the idea, and with the effort and funds of Gavin Black (who played harpsichord and wrote the program notes), *Moondog: Instrumental Music by Louis Hardin*, MHS 3803, appeared in 1977.

Although *Le Monde* once said that Moondog was living "incognito" in Germany, he gradually assumed a more active part in carving out his fame and fortune. He was soon taken seriously, despite some snide remarks such as the one calling him "an amateur Odin," and the circle of his admirers widened, in little and big manifestations. On a trip to Bonn he was escorted to Beethoven House, where he signed the guest book and got permission, "not often granted," to play one of Beethoven's Hammerclaviers. The moment brought him, in his words, "full circle," for he flashed back to the day he first heard the *Moonlight Sonata* in Vinton, Iowa, at a crucial moment in his young manhood, when he moved from exile to composer in training. In a life of many strange wishes, this was a dream come true.

They remembered him at home. As soon as he was discovered once again to be alive and well, articles began to appear in newspapers as diverse as *The Batesville Daily Guard* of Arkansas (April 16, 1979 and afterward) and *The New York Times* (January 3, 1979). The latter, by Adele Riepe, was "caused" by Paul Jordan's brother, Don Franklin Jordan, a well-known American radio journalist in Bonn. This substantial report put to rest rumors that Moondog was dead, and it linked the old world with the new. A Berkeley, California-based comic strip by George Metzger called "Moondog" depicted a wayfarer who looked unmistakably like the original. *Tamarask* (Summer

1980), one of the small publications that featured pieces by and about Moondog, printed a longish poem in the beat mode called "For You, Moon Gaffney, and kindred spirits," which could be described as a sexual elegy for one in good standing with the underground, wherever and whatever it might be. It reads, in part:

> Better than the excited animation of nursery rimes,
> with Walt Disney goosing
> a happy cow right out of her pasture,
> egged on by a cat and fiddle, suicidally playing,
> non-union, most likely,...
> Yours, Moon, is a dark and sexually multiple persona.
> Jung has said so and it must be true,...
> and consider the androgynous chance
> of being got with child
> by an alien yet fertile moon inseminating Moon,
> Moon Dog descending in a flying saucer
> to cause the unorthodox havoc.

Surrounded by a magic space, charged by an energized, unorthodox glow, Moondog survived in memory in many guises, even though he no longer even remotely resembled the object depicted.

In 1979, in four weeks, Moondog reconstructed "Thor, the Nordoom" from memory out of the lost American version he had used in the late 1960s and early 1970s. Enriched, and published at last, it had been an obsession for more than a decade. In some ways it is a consolidation of many strands of poetic, mythic, and narrative modes Moondog had been refining for as long as he had written poetry; it was also something new and more daunting. It is his most ambitious poem, a verse epic of 900 long and dense lines. Arguably, since he is not primarily a poet, it ought to be treated as a curiosity, an auxiliary to his music, or an idiosyncratic source of images (like Yeats' *Vision*, for instance) that serves as a commentary on his Nordic tone poems. Because it was intended to stand on its own and is so printed, however, to dismiss it thus would not be honest. Moondog's earlier satires and couplets (the early and misguided *Milleniad*, for instance, or the desultory cycles in the Yearbook, among others) concentrated on his revisionism about the past and explanations of present ills. In "Thor," this idea is given a fuller dramatic context and a precise historical axis: centuries-old values, customs, and rituals (embodied in the Saxons) are threatened by the new (the Franks and the Catholic Church). What is at stake in this historic myth "tragibook" about the "dim and distant past" (in the book's words) is the sacredness of the Nordic religion and social fabric. What replaces it is the repressive institutions that mark in the poem the beginnings of Moondog's version of the decline of the West. [See the Appendix.]

The protagonist, Thor, not the god but a great man in the old sense of "hero," has the power to uphold his rule (doom) of the north (nor). He is the vessel that preserves the truth through ages of decay (in one of the legends attached to him, he sleeps in a cave until he awakens as Santa Claus). His resistance to the antagonist (Charlemagne) is forced underground after Widukind embraces Christianity in a betrayal of the past. Like Julian, the last of the "pagan" Roman emperors, Moondog could say through his characters: "Thou hast conquered, O Galilean." Like Nietzsche, Moondog felt that the Hebraic-Christian tradition was an oppressive and inevitably destructive burden dishonestly packaged as altruism. Having for years compiled symptoms, now, in Europe, he thought that he had arrived at the cause: the real enemy is not merely the king of the Franks (the Churl) or even his fanatical followers (the Charlemaniacs), but the emerging state religion that paralyzes individual expression and deliberately buries the wisdom of its predecessors. Thor adapts, deflects the new order away from his real power, works and waits patiently for his opportunity, and eventually triumphs.

His "religious retaliation" against the crusaders ("Join the Church or Die!") is to create an anti-society "under-operating" the machine of state. Like a good Machiavellian (which Moondog had been for twenty years), Thor comes to control world finance through a monopoly on gold. Although his victory takes over "a dozen centuries and sixty years" (the earliest date in the poem, the hero's birthday, is 721, and

721 + 1260 = 1981), it is not only satisfying but, because he has remained invisible, also unchallengeable and complete. The last date is 1987, when he is celebrating the one thousandth anniversary of "the nine- / eighty seven sailing to the Viking land of Wine."

Thor has two major sections, with one insertion into the second part. The Introduction, by a nameless author who disavows responsibility, as any bard or scop would naturally do, is composed of five eighteen-line "strophen." The remainder of the work is Thor's great monologue of 810 lines, of which 84 lines is Oza Votahn's (Odin's) "Song of Creation." The variety and the novelty of the rhymes and alliterations, its interesting numerical substructures, its many levels of puns, and its neologisms all make *Thor* intriguing beyond a subject that might be, to Americans at least, weird. Finally, *Thor* is, to borrow Moondog's pun, under-operated by history. The soliloquy is filled with historical incidents, characters, places, and dates. Nordic myth (especially in the sensitively evoked "Song of Creation," an atmospheric set-piece in homage to the poets of the *Eddas*) comes to life. The work grimly reconstructs the bitter and bloody Franco-Saxon wars and parodies the mechanization of the contemporary money-state. Thor himself is a character rather than a force, compounded of Odin and the original Thor—timeless rebel, contemporary existentialist, and Machiavellian manipulator.

Such revisionist history is also, in the tradition of romantic confession, disguised autobiography. Odin/Thor is his personal god. Moondog rediscovered himself in a vital persona, located his ideas in verse pulsing with the past, and wrote a panegyric that settles many an old score. Thor, one of history's oldest "kerrikters," urges his dogmas in the practice of his rituals: beneath his terrible (though far from swift) sword, injuries heal and justice prevails. To father, mother, the Christian God, and a society bristling with religious prejudice and hypocrisy, Moondog says: the Viking has returned.

MUSIKVERLAG, MANAGARM SOON increased its output by leaps. From 1978 to 1980 Moondog and Ilona published much besides music. "Hardin Cards," composed of ten canons each, were printed with words and music on a variety of celebratory occasions. Opus 47, Numbers 1–10, for instance, offers selections for holidays, birthdays, anniversaries, and so on. "Canons and Couplets," Opus 46, Numbers 1–10, attractively packages Moondog's devotion to the "two strictest forms." The yellow-covered booklet contains an introductory page on poetics and an end page devoted to "The Discovery of America," a poem honoring Leif Ericsson's voyage. (After all, A-M-Eric-A is named after him, isn't it?) More ambitious was the magazine-sized, blue-covered *Navigators of the World*, an extravaganza containing over forty canons, interspersed with couplets, devoted to the role of Nordic civilization in discovery, exploration, and cultural dispersion. All of these publications carry the copyright date of 1979.

Managarm was busy on another front also. From 1978 through 1980, with Roof (Kopf) Records, three Moondog albums were released. *Moondog in Europe* (RRF 33014) has much of the same material that appears on the Musical Heritage album, including a similar selection from *Lögründr, I*, played by Fritz Storfinger, two string pieces ("Romance," "Chaconne"), and the *Heimdall Fanfare*. *H'Art Songs* (RRF 33016), with Moondog performing again, came next. The songs, written and recorded in 1977, were, Moondog explains in the liner notes, "on a higher level than most popular music," but with "an appeal to a whole range of tastes." Six are two-part canons, four are more homophonic, "like a chaconne." They are sung without vibrato (as always) and without harmony, since "the harmony is exclusively in the piano parts, which are more complicated." On the album appears this couplet, similar to one from twenty years earlier satirizing Martyn Green's performance on the *Tell It Again* album: "Moondog singing Moondog? Really! Even goodness knows / That Moondog doesn't sing a song; he shows you how it goes." Aside from a few unusual effects reminiscent of his recordings in the 1950s (the trimba; fingertips beating out a rhythm over a hole in a gourd; an out-of-tune piano giving a honky-tonk texture to the autobiographical and nostalgic "John Wesley Hardin"; the striking of a grass mat with a steel brush; striking a fur-covered mallet on a wooden floor), the novelty is in the subject matter, eccentric yet lyrical, offbeat yet alluring: "I'm a Hop-Head," "Do Your Thing," and "I'm This, I'm That" present Moondog's philosophy of living at an earthy pitch; "Aska Me," "Pigmy Pig," and "Enough about Human Rights!" deal with mankind's abuse of natural resources. The verses are generally sportive, parodic, and more buoyant than those of the 1960s madrigals. Finally, *A New Sound of an Old Instrument* (RRF 33017) features Fritz Storfinger playing six organ solos (four of them logs) and, with Wolfgang Schwering, six organ duets. The duets have a distinctly near-Eastern flavor ("Oasis" comes down from the 1950s, "Mirage," "Crescent Moon March"), and one, "Single Foot," is unabashedly a Wyoming memory transformed. The "instrument," depicted on the cover with Moondog flanked by the two performers, is the same one used in all three albums, the Breil organ at Herz-Jesu-Kirche, Oberhausen. [See Appendix D.]

As America entered the Reagan years, Moondog was polishing *The Creation*, a work in progress for decades, made up of many complete parts, some recorded, others performed, still others existing only on paper. This grand "sound saga" was by far the most ambitious and problematic undertaking of his career. Now that he was no longer "cramped" by his environment or limited by the logistics of copying, his ambition grew to accommodate his vision of the northern sagas. In the conception of the whole rather than in the perfection of the parts Moondog took up his greatest challenge. For his mastery of many small forms, widely considered his most serious artistic accomplishment, is not necessarily a prelude to bigger compositions. A frequent criticism of his earlier orchestral pieces, as of those on the first Columbia album, is that they either are derivative or lack the tightness and concentration of his less ambitious and more idiosyncratic work. Some have accused him of slightness, based on an understanding that does not go beyond the sweet, innocent quality of his music, its naïveté. (How often he has been called a "naïf"!) Gordon Spencer, who played Moondog's earlier pieces on WNCN for years, said that his best work is "marginal," that his public image was essential to his exposure, and that many composers as gifted but less charismatic and forceful have languished neglected and forgotten. Thus, even if he did exhibit craft and an autodidact's mastery of canonic form, the output generally was immature, an insubstantial product propped up by a persona, a juvenile pose translated into music. Since "he never got out of his childhood," this position concludes, he remained "musically simple," as public fascination with the persona rewarded the infantilism and eliminated any incentive to develop as an artist. Paul Jordan, while praising the "pearls" that are Moondog's canons and madrigals, points to an analogous hurdle. Most long musical works cohere around a transmusical idea. Although Moondog does perceive vividly a cosmic order within which his small forms could be set, longer pieces of music in the West, most specifically those in the sonata form, are "rooted in competition and contrast." Moondog's serenity, his genial spirit and crystalline surfaces, may just be "on the other side of conflict." Thus, once more, his gifts could undercut his more ambitious orchestral works; paradoxically, the awful burdens he had to shoulder in order to write anything at all, practically dictating that he work at one-page scores, may have stunted his art. His optimism in the face of terrible odds, his decision to live the life of an artist when he could just as feasibly have chosen to pursue fame, may have guaranteed his survival but may have also made the inner tension arguably essential to great, large artworks difficult for him to experience, let alone translate into the language of music. To such arguments Moondog might have proposed two possible answers. The first is that brevity need not be a defect. Is Charlie Parker, for instance, less than he might have been because most of his music is composed of brief pieces? Conversely, would a composer like Wagner be more sublime if he had also managed to become more succinct? The second answer borrows Poe's idea that there are no long poems, only short poems strung together with bridges, fillers, prosaic transitions, and the like. Poems are made word by word, so that even what appears seamless is really a patchwork of disparate materials and recalcitrant images, Yeats' "rag and bone shop of the heart." Its perfection concludes a battle with the elements: the medium, the message, the materials, the artist's mind. Perhaps *The Creation*, if it is ever performed whole, will emerge, as Gavin Black felt, as one "mammoth melody," or perhaps the memorable segments within a problematical architectural design might be enough to win over some skeptics. (For how many listeners does every note in a four-hour opera really count?) It is foolish to predict, but not out of place to hope. Not only would a successful sound saga be a posthumous triumph for Moondog, but it might also be a rich contribution to modern music. Ambition so nobly motivated ought to be encouraged. *The Creation* opening to mixed reviews would be better than no *Creation* at all. It is what Moondog, the composer who did not live to see that day, sensitive about being typecast and programmed as he was, lived for.

By 1980 Moondog was fast becoming an industry. When he was taping portions of *The Creation*, "a blend of orchestral excerpts and incidental sound effects," many of which have never been released, he appeared on a Radio Deutsche Welle TV series, *Americans Working in Europe*. In a September program marking its twenty-fifth anniversary, the Westphalian Orchestra played the *Procession of the Aesir*. Meanwhile Moondog, ever ready for an adventure, was coining two terms to explain two new musical syntheses. At a church concert he unveiled his "tonata" for organ and viola, a work of twenty-five minutes. Tonata is "a form having certain features of the sonata though in canon form, the three movements thematically related. Even the developments are in canon form, with only occasional harmonic sections." As early as 1953 Moondog had worked with violas and cellos, which he felt made "the best combination for canons, because of inversion, as opposed to the traditional quartet of two violins, viola and cello." Thus, instead of the "homophonic" quartet, Moondog wrote for the "canonic" quartet of two violas and two cellos, calling the compositions *bratschelli* (*Bratsche* means viola in German). Members of the Westphalian Symphony performed a twenty-minute program of *bratschelli* at a castle, relieving an evening of speeches and other events.

Moondog knew that he had established himself as an institution in Europe when imitators began appearing, as they had many times during his New York years. One rock group out of Holland, named Moondog, was heard often on German radio in 1980, twenty-five years after the Freed case. Fortunately, like many of the trends through the years that had treated Moondog as public property, this affront faded into the ether.

At the age of sixty-five he enjoyed more acclaim and respect than at any other moment in his life. 1981 was the year, as he called it, of his "official recognition." The Historical Museum in Stockholm opened a summer-long exhibition of Viking artifacts. A film made to publicize the event used Moondog's *Creation* music, and the director, Olov Isaksson, was so struck with the composer that he promised future honoraria beginning with a live concert. First, on June 18, at the opening ceremony, Moondog met the king and queen of Sweden, the queen of Denmark, and the Minister of Education, among others, while in "half my Moondog outfit," replete with two tails representing Odin's two wolves, but without the horns, which the museum forbade as "inauthentic." (Ilona was pleased.) He neither bowed nor scraped, but shook hands "as if among equals." Two months later he gave his two-part concert, each segment containing nine selections from *The Creation*, to an enthusiastic, mainly youthful audience. The eighteen musicians came from the Stockholm Music School, and Moondog was pleased with them after the first rehearsal. Three hundred posters, five feet high, with a reproduction of Moondog's bust, were placed throughout the city by the Rikscon-cert people to announce the celebration. Managarm released an LP later in 1981 called *Facets*, side 1 being selections from the live concert and other small pieces and side two "movements" or sections of *The Creation* (Opus 81), mainly for organ. The titles are as alluring as the music: "Black Hole," "Magic Ring," "Midgard Serpent," "Ginnungagap," "Milky Way," and, of course, "Heimdal Fanfare."

For Moondog this was a triumph in the deed as well as in the word. Never had he felt closer to his ethnic past than when a pilgrim to the "holy hills of Uppsala," where, centuries ago, "the great temple in honor of the Norse Gods" had stood. There, on the first day of summer, he celebrated with piccolo (played by Kerstin Rydermark) and the "new hexagonal drum" he had constructed with Stefan Lakatos by playing "Horr the Heroe Hunter" dressed in "freshly-made clothes inspired by the styles of long ago." Here, on the first day of winter, the old new year's day, an ox was sacrificed to Odin with great festivities (the "juleblood," precursor of today's tamer yuletide). In Sweden, he noted, where he would live if he could afford to, "there is a growing interest in the old ways and beliefs. The Faith that was imposed by force is being deposed without force." The joy of such a spiritual arousal coincided with new fame. The numerous reviews in the Swedish and German presses praised the music's "poetic magic" and "suggestive power"; the *Creation Suite* is "timeless in tone, a sound-painting in a dark hue"; "one is overcome by the throbbing pulse of the percussion, a rhythmic flood"; it is like hearing "a cultic drama" in which one is "pulled by ritual and invocation." It is no wonder that Moondog predicted an even rosier future. *The Red Snake* was read to him, fiction that "sounds factual," about Sven, the son, defending the Norse gods Harold, his father, had given up. It reinforced what he had long inferred from the "bits and pieces" of his research, that a reorientation was due, away from the "Indo-European" tyranny to the "Eurindian" axis. Culture moved out in a diaspora from north-central Europe. On September 9, therefore, the day in 919 when Sven Forkbeard and his allies, "defenders of the Old Faith," defeated Olaf the Renegade, a "turncoat" later canonized as a saint, Fritz Storfinger (with Wolfgang Schwering on the duets, as on *A New Sound of an Old Instrument* in 1979) recorded the organ version of the *Creation Suite* in Stockholm heard on *Facets*. He even planned "Sagadag," a day for recounting the stories of the *Eddas*, preferably on June 21, and if not at Uppsala then at the great rock in Teutoburger Wald defiled by later Christian artists. There would be processions, recitations, musical interludes, folk music, and dancing, all amplified through the sacred hills by well-placed speakers. The Viking had come home ready for action.

EACH YEAR IN GERMANY brought forth new ideas or revisions of old ones. In 1982 Moondog was again giving a concert in Paris for Radio France, memorable for what it shows of his famous attention to detail.

He told Stefan Lakatos, one of the newest members of his growing team of loyal performers, that it was "very important" to beat the gong with a spear point during one of the pieces. Because doing so would ruin the gong, it was forbidden. When the normal mallet was used, Moondog was clearly disappointed, as was Stefan.

In other places, Moondog was working to explain himself by enlarging his literary output. From "snaketime" rhythms thirty years earlier to his latest "serpentine" sonnets, his exploration of life's slippery edges and form's elastic boundaries found its latest incarnation. The new creation, fourteen lines with nine iambic feet each, has, instead of traditional end rhyme, internal rhyme; it is, in his words, "two forms in one." There are some poems on personal ("On Love"; "The Apple") and speculative ("On God"; "On Form") themes, but there are also three sonnets from a projected epic sequence never finished, *The Thracians*, about one of Moondog's oldest historic myths:

I have the time to tell the story of the river basin where
The Thracians dwell, about the Danube which has played as
big a role as any other water-way, throughout the world,
and there are many.

Further:
There'll be a storm of controversy on the part of those who have
to do their homework over, in the light—of what is coming true,
to push the Age of Reason back another thousand years,
in Thracia, not in Egypt nor in Mesopotamia.

Moondog also turned his poetic, ironic, bemused eye upon himself, writing, again in nine-foot couplets, a verse autobiography about the first half of his life. It is the source of many of the spicy, witty turns of phrase sprinkled throughout this biography. Once he found his new poetic groove, the impulse was hard to resist.

Moondog was in Vienna for much of 1983 and there realized another long-postponed dream. With Ilona making the way smooth, he joined forces with the artist Ernst Fuchs, "one of the founders of the Viennese School of Fantastic Realism." Mr. Fuchs had admired Moondog from as long ago and as far away as New York in 1957, when he had sat beside the composer in a subway car. Now, twenty-six years later, the two became the principles of M.A.S., the Multimedia Art Synthesis. Their first program (Moondog called it a "musical happening") dealt with the story of *Creation* "from the atomic point of view," wherein "each of the 92 elements is represented by its own motif." This "total cosmic experience" involved poetry, paintings (set designed by Fuchs), video light shows (performed by a group of young artists called "Morgana Light Arts"), acting, ballet, mime, recitation and singing—the synaesthetic experience Moondog had hoped to achieve as the vehicle for his many-sided conceptualizations, something akin to creating a twentieth-century Wagnerian opera. The two men were brothers in spirit, their collaboration serendipitous. But Mr. Fuchs had not contacted the man he would come to call "Pythagoras" until a student noted the striking parallels in their works. (Fuchs, for instance, insists upon the "exhumination of the forefathers" in order to find the "lost style," thus keeping "the information of the timelessness timeless.") The bond lasted until Moondog died (and after: Mr. Fuchs designed his tomb in Munster). Now more and more a celebrity, Moondog enjoyed the professional adventure in "this highly cultivated town," another old vision he had lived to experience.

Nearby Salzburg was the scene of his next triumph. While in Vienna he visited the annual musical festival in the summer of 1983, reveling in the "atmosphere" there. While a guest of state at the Villa Schmederer he decided to write the first three "Salzburg Symphonies" (as Mozart had) in six weeks. He created such a sensation in 1983 that in 1984 he was invited back at the request of the government to attend their premiere. By then, August 9, he had finished twenty symphonies, most of which have never been performed. The concert was so successful, and the promise of future debuts so enticing, that Moondog went into a frenzy of composition. Soon the "Salzburg Symphony Series," Book I, twenty-five symphonies, one in each key, was behind him. On he went, planning nine books, a total of 225 symphonies (he did not finish the project before his death). As one advertisement noted: "What started as a Mozart-Moondog Marathon is continuing as a Haydn-Hardin Heat." He was amused to win a commission to write a string symphony with, as he puts it, "strings attached": the leading producer of instrumental strings was the patron. Moondog felt as if he were "in heaven," surrounded by the ambience and history his soul had craved, "in exile," for so long.

Ernst Fuchs called Moondog "Pythagoras" with several layers of meaning. On the horizon then was the culmination of the esoteric, exotic, and idiosyncratic literary development of Moondog, whose earliest manifestations were the newsletters, broadsides, and yearbooks printed over a period of twenty years in New York. *The Overtone Tree* appeared in 1985, and Mr. Fuchs said that Moondog "had the world by the tail" with it. This 120-page book is monumental, but, according to one of his oldest apologists, Paul Jordan, "it moves in a realm, a borderline area between music, music theory, mathematics and cosmology," that makes it challenging, puzzling, and unsettling. The diagrams, illustrations, and mandalas are lovely and elegant. As another admirer notes, it "makes enjoyable and fascinating reading," and, like the music, "it speaks of a spacious and visionary mind." It is so personal, however, that it is difficult to share. The same voice that praised its dynamics could also say that *The Overtone Tree* "should more appropriately be viewed as ideational resonance" from his music rather than read as having "independent theoretical context." (In other words, like his poetry, a source of transmusical ideas rather than a free-standing accomplishment.) Some have discovered inaccuracies, inconsistencies, and gaps, caused in part by proofreading error, and others question Moondog's theories of mathematics, history, and musicology. Nonetheless, here again is Moondog's plenty: from the Cosmiclock to Contraction Trees to the Instant Collective Present to the Rainbow Canon, there is something for everyone. With its puns, alliterations, music from *The Creation*, numbers of astronomical size ("M and the 60 Lions"—remember "nupiks"?), and touching childhood reminiscence, like all of his larger undertakings, *The Overtone*

Tree is many things, ambitious if flawed, stridently unwilling to fit, like the man, into an existing category.

Several innovations in orchestration and compositions exemplifying them occurred in 1986. In a book on the Ruhr region sponsored by Westphalia, Moondog was one of the few photographed; he appeared again on German TV and even appeared on stage at a local concert given by his old friend, Pete Seeger, on tour. Moondog had written works over the years that were discrete units as well as voices in a larger design. When several marching bands in the U.S. asked him to compose a piece for each of them (he wrote music for bands from 1978 until his death, a loyalty dating back to his earliest musical memories), he not only created one apiece, but so conceived them that, should they ever be played in one place at one time, they would together comprise an organic whole. Thus many bands could form one mammoth halftime entertainment in some ideal football stadium. (Although he did not write marches until the late 1970s, they were in his blood. Danny Thompson recalls him sitting in a darkened room listening raptly to recordings of Sousa in 1992.) It is his 1960s "stock arranging" further refined: from the days of the minisym and maxisym, when Moondog had scored his work for both small and large ensembles. "Tout Suite," a new series for "peaceful" saxophones (*Sax Pax*), with different playing combinations, was another extension of the same premise. Here is "an authentic 'American School' of music, a blending of many unique ethnic influences in the 'Roaring Twenties' to be elevated into...the 'Soaring Eighties.'" The suite was finally recorded and released in 1994. Many of these experiments evolved into recorded works.

Moondog's association with Stefan Lakatos deepened. Stefan had appeared in the Swedish concerts, on the *Facets* album, and in the Radio France concert, heir apparent to the title of master in the Moondog school of percussion. So close had they become that Moondog took Stefan into his confidence on one of his infrequent, child-like moments of rebellion. This was Moondog's playful, conspiratorial side, hidden to those who worked with him, for then he was all business and his presence intimidating.

On June 3, 1981, when Ilona had to go to New York on business, she had instructed Moondog: "No nonsense!" No sooner had she left than the teacher suggested to his pupil that they go shopping for some mahogany to construct a new six-sided drum. While they were out, how about getting material to make some new clothes for the upcoming tour? Soon Moondog was happily sewing up new pants and caps, threading the needle by putting both needle and thread in his mouth and feeling the one into one another. That was not enough: how about a new helmet? The old one, with horns, no longer pleased him, nor was it "authentic," so he was not allowed to wear it in the house ("The suggestive power of women," he would say by way of explanation) or on his visits to Sweden. After cutting out a pattern on newspaper, Moondog went on June 20 to the art school where Stefan's girlfriend, Lisbet Sand, helped him cut pieces of thick leather and drill holes for the stitches. Soon he had new headgear, finishing the job by himself, gleefully recreating and celebrating the days when he made all the decisions, bad as well as good, for himself.

In another illustrative incident between the two Swedish tours of 1986 and 1988, Stefan received in the mail three songs: "Hnossa," "Thor and the Midgard Serpent," and "Out of the Mouth." He naturally thought that Moondog was thanking him for his good work by personalizing some of his previous productions. Stefan did not consider then that the songs might have been written for him, since he was still somewhat in awe of Moondog, who had mailed similar songcards for years. When he visited Ilona in Munster after Moondog's death, he found the originals in a file named "Songs for Stefan L."

Moondog, with new friends, new connections, and a comfortable, supportive environment, might have sat back and relished the limelight; instead, as always, he sought the dark to work. He might have been proud of his accomplishments in his first decade in Europe, but he knew success to be fickle and evanescent, and comfort did not make him lazy. He felt as though he were beginning, not ending. He had ample strength and drive; he only wondered, twelve years after coming to the old world, if he had enough time left.

Chapter Nine

Heimdall Fanfare

(1986–1999)

As Moondog's reputation grew near his German home, he was more in demand as a conductor and performer of his own work, a situation he had become accustomed to over a lifetime in music. Even after Ilona married and the now smaller family moved north to Munster, his days consisted mostly of the luxury of creative activity, usually while others in his time zone slept. (Danny Thompson, in an interview for the BBC broadcast, *Howling at the Moon*, in 2001, remarked that he had heard his house guest in 1992 scratching with his Braille snatter all through the night, and was at first unnerved by the sound, which resembled the noises of mice.) But, as always, a serpent lurked in the composer's paradise.

Moondog had always enjoyed robust health and an even more robust appetite, despite his risk-taking. In 1986, though, he learned that he had diabetes and would have to be less casual about his diet. No more cupcake at midday! He underestimated the seriousness of his condition, which led to his decline and death. But energy drove him, not ego; it was not in his flight plan to land yet. He rarely cancelled engagements, even when travel became harder on him. His first reaction to the news was to cut his sugar intake (even in his beloved coffee) and get to work.

Even though he was involved with several multimedia experiments, usually in collaboration with Ernst Fuchs, the late 1980s and early 1990s were devoted almost exclusively to composing. Like many who hear Death's knock, he grew more eager to finish his life's work. He reconstructed older compositions (from as far back as the 1950s), transposed and rearranged, and wrote much new music, some in modes previously explored tentatively or not at all. The story of Moondog's final period, viewed from a comfortable distance, was a series of appearances. From close at hand, though, life went on as usual, serenely and (despite some upheaval and disturbance) successfully. As his physical condition deteriorated, even in the final months of his life, he hardly slowed down. For so long unable to get everything in his head into a form readable by others, because of the elaborate, expensive, and time-consuming process of transcribing from Braille, Moondog knew he would have to use every available moment to tap his ideas. His ebullience among colleagues and friends did not desert him, even in his final moments, when he flirted with an attractive nurse on his deathbed. Faced with the inevitable bad news, Moondog was able to make it into a cosmic joke or a memorable vignette.

When he came to New York in 1943, Louis Hardin was struggling to emerge as a new man from a damaged childhood and horrific tragedy. In the 1950s he assumed a new identity and began a career that lasted half a century. The 1960s started drably and despondently but ended in Technicolor triumph. The 1970s found Moondog, by now an established icon, restlessly starting over in new locations. By the early 1980s, he was fast becoming a European celebrity and cultural artifact, acclimating himself to his final home. What, then, was left other than more acclaim (if he was fortunate), more rewards, more comforts to support his final creative phase? Was Sweden to be, in retrospect, the high point of his life? Vienna? Which of the many recordings produced in Germany would last the longest? Which shows him at his most variegated and daring? Although it is too early to isolate all of the parameters for evaluating his career, or even a segment of it, one can measure what actually happened against two standards: was it what Moondog wanted to happen, and does it demonstrate a deeper command or wider scope?

At his death Moondog left an enormous legacy, much of it still unpublished, unreleased, unevaluated, all of it accomplished with dispatch and sparkling good humor. In his final years his difficult past no longer seemed to haunt him into obscure corners, and the bitter survival lessons he had learned only made his present ease more productive. The old spirits—his parents, his siblings, his childhood successes and traumas—still played around in his mind, but he managed to express them in compositions, like the haunting organ piece (*Lögründr XIX*) dedicated to his mother, the marches in homage to his father, and the witty, irreverent vision he inherited from both. Out of his blindness he created what few of the sighted have, an affirmative body of work. Out of his public identities emerged the building blocks of his further education, the tools of his trade, the elements of his syntheses. Some will accuse him of posturing, even in his final, more sober years, of still missing opportunities (out of stubborn pride), of deflecting his talents from more promising directions. But no one can say that his time was squandered. For the opportunities afforded him he gave back a multitude of gifts.

Even though the years 1986 through 1988 did not begin with good news, Moondog achieved some modest but important milestones then. Summoning old reserves, he turned away from his illness to projects long contemplated, with fresh and promising new performers. In June 1986, Moondog, Ilona, and Stefan Lakatos were back in Sweden, this time to do a series of concerts and to record for the first time the *bracelli* compositions. This album, not to be confused with the posthumously released (2004) version recorded in 1999, did not satisfy Moondog, though he would hear several pleasing renditions in concert. The recording session with the Flesh Quartet took place at the Bromma Church, the oldest structure in Stockholm. How Moondog and the performers came together is, like so many of his arrangements, foggy. An acquaintance, a saxophone player, knew them, and so there they were, the composer, his friend, and a group not especially moved by the music or (since the players apparently had other priorities and experiences) attuned to Moondog's rigorous demands. This recording, now out of print, does not have consistently satisfying intonation, but the percussion, trimbas, and dragon's teeth drums are excellent. Moondog, perhaps trying to salvage something from their first recording together, said to Stefan, "You are steady as a rock." Mr. Lakatos says he "grew two inches" immediately. On the liner notes, Moondog avows that Mr. Lakatos is "the leading exponent of the Moondog method of drum playing," something people who have heard him perform will affirm, especially those who have also heard Moondog. The *bracelli* were performed three times in Sweden in 1986.

Between these dates Moondog conducted the *bracelli* on June 27, 1986, but this time he led Position Alpha, an all-saxophone group that he also worked with two years later when he introduced his *Sax Pax Suite* to the world. After a relatively quiet and productive year in 1987, possibly convalescing, he was back in Stockholm by May 1988 to appear at the prestigious Kulturhuset with a complex and innovative program. He and several others rehearsed twice at a local coffeehouse with a small stage. There, with Stefan and Tina Kjebon on percussion, and the accomplished pianists Torbjorn Langborn and Arne Forsen, Moondog read some of his poems, and all celebrated his seventy-second birthday (May 26) with madrigals, H'Art songs, and canons. Although the producer of the main event was not thrilled by these modest unscheduled evenings, and even threatened to cancel, Moondog, serene as ever, managed to calm the waters. *Sax Pax*, a staple of his last ten years of life, finally became public. The suite was lavishly recorded five years later in England. Also included on the eclectic program at the Kulturhuset were songs and dances, one featuring the percussionist Ms. Kjebon, in 5/4 time, with bells on her ankles, and a computerized version of "Hardin's Hundreds," celebrated by a poem: "I duly dedicate the Hardin's Hundreds to the Scandinavians, / above all the Swedes of Stockholm, / on the twenty-seventh day of May on turning two and seventy, / myself a dragon in the Dragon year." Many of Moondog's works were first performed in Sweden during 1981–1988, including the marches, and large selections from *The Creation, Bracelli*,

Sax Pax, Tout Suites. They loved him so much, and bestowed their hospitality and respect so openly and often, that he repaid them with his latest and best.

The 1988 "Transmusicales" annual festival in Rennes invited Moondog to take part in a program of his compositions featuring the Orchestre de Bretagne. This festival had presented mostly music that was both popular and cutting-edge, "inventive, open and sparkling," according to its publicity. The musicians, however, though classically trained and more comfortable with Beethoven than with Moondog's styles and forms, disliked the long rehearsal schedule (ten days, a luxury for such a modestly-budgeted event) and the composer's demands; they were probably accustomed to a more easygoing repertoire. Since Moondog did not speak French, he had to work through a translator. His request that the orchestra play without vibrato (one of his decades-long crusades) was met skepticism and trepidation. With such impediments only twenty or so of the simplest pieces were ready by the day of the performance.

Another stranger hurdle lay ahead. For financial reasons, the orchestra had not signed its approval for the concert to be filmed. On opening night, however, clandestine cameras entered. In the middle of a piece (*Vercingetorix*), the lead violinist and most of the musicians simply stood up and left the stage after they caught sight of a red camera eye in the darkened hall of the Italian Theatre. This "lamentable and sordid moment," according to the liner notes of the CD issued in 2003, not only led to the cancellation of the second planned concert the next day but also to pandemonium in the hall that evening. The audience was indignant. The loudest voice, that of the noted actress Clementine Celanie, lambasted the players for their lack of professional dignity and for the implied insult to so important an artist. When Moondog took over as conductor, the audience was ecstatic and the remaining players finished the concert as best they could. Through it all Moondog was imperturbable, "entirely absorbed in the music," despite all the agony and anguish. A journalist, "RFI" on the liner notes, had recorded the entire performance, warts and all, "discreetly." This strange and "magic" evening, along with an interview with Moondog the next day, is on *Moondog in Rennes* (Pas-Cher Records, 2003). His serene and measured response and his explanation of his compositional theories are charming articulations. Now he had the comfort of looking at potential disaster as a momentary glitch and possibly a blessing in disguise: several of his pieces are unavailable anywhere else, for instance *Napoleon's Retreat* and *Vercingetorix*. Other benefits of the experience in Rennes became apparent a couple of years later. By meeting Stephan Eicher, who was instrumental in getting him to France, Moondog met Danny Thompson, a longtime fan and soon-to-be friend. With the help of John Harle, who organized ensembles for later concerts and recordings, Thompson got Moondog to London, and another chapter in his European adventure began.

1989 WAS A WUNDERJAHR of a new kind, a triumphal re-return of a homegrown exile. In November of 1989 the Viking returned to New York for two weeks as a featured composer in the Brooklyn Academy of Music's tenth annual New Music America series. Two pre-concert articles cast his appearance as the harbinger of great things. Kyle Gann in *The Village Voice* (14 November) celebrates Moondog as against the grain. If he is a naïf, he is not so much Virgil Thomson's idea of one ("any composer who made his living outside of music") as Tristan Tzara's more exotic and suggestive definition: one who is a "private bell for inexplicable needs." Moondog discusses the program he has prepared ("A Tale of Two Cities, Paris and New York"), his growing attention to the overtone series (first published as *The Overtone Tree* but developing now into *The Overtone Continuum*, further explained in the liner notes to the 1992 *Elpmas* album) and the musical consequences of his theories:

> To describe the cosmos, I've written a 1000-part canon, *Cosmos I*. You couldn't paint the cosmos, but you can describe it in music. No one has ever attempted a piece of such magnitude. Mahler wrote a symphony for a thousand players, but it

didn't have a thousand different parts. *Cosmos I* takes nine hours to perform—not that it will ever be played, but it was something I wanted to do, to describe what the cosmos is like.

Allan Kozinn in *The New York Times* (November 16) noted that when Moondog "vanished" in 1974, "it was as if a landmark building had been taken down." He asked how Moondog's unorthodox style of conducting worked. Moondog explained: "I see my relationship with them as being first among equals, so that in a way there are 40 conductors, each in charge of his own part, and each responsible for the performance." He notes further that the musicians "respond well to that idea." Mr. Kozinn then describes how "he sits to the side of the orchestra and provides the beat on a bass drum or timpani."

The schedule, a preview on November 8, an open rehearsal at 2 p.m. on the 16th and a thirty-minute program the evening of the 16th, went off as planned. The program notes for the performance of the Brooklyn Philharmonic Chamber Orchestra, written by David Byrne, explain some of the old Moondog favorites to new listeners ("Stamping Ground," "Bird's Lament," "Good for Goodie") and contain at least one surprise. "Dark Eyes" is a *czardas* (a Hungarian dance in two movements, the first slow, the second very fast). This new form for Moondog is

part of the third movement of Hardin's Symphony no. 50 [!], The Rodzinski. This symphony, written in fond memory of Artur Rodzinski who, while conductor of the New York Philharmonic during the Forties, let Louis Hardin attend the rehearsals of the orchestra. [sic] His wife, Halina, was an inspiration also. The czardas was written with her in mind. The eight-part counterpoint consists of a double two-part canon in the strings, joined by another double two-part canon in woodwinds, the piece starting slow and ending at a break-neck speed.

Steve Reich, among others, acknowledged at the benefit preview on the November 8 how in effect so many of the avant-garde composers in America today were disciples of Moondog. In his otherwise tepid review of the concert itself in *The New York Times* (November 19), John Rockwell noted how Moondog "had a cult following among composers, chief among them Philip Glass, and it is possible to hear elements of Mr. Glass' style in Mr. Hardin's simple reiterations." This is rather faint praise for both composers, yet his response to the actual concert was not that different from even Moondog's fans in the audience: despite the publicity, it was lukewarm, though Rockwell does acknowledge that the fifty musicians were the evening's highlight: "The most charming (*Paris, New Amsterdam* and *New York*) evoked the bustle and energy of those cities on a somewhat more expansive scale than the other pieces." Peter Goodman in *Newsday* (November 18) more or less agrees: the concert "could most charitably described as disappointing," but the nine numbers "by the blind, fork-bearded Moondog (Louis Hardin) livened up the evening." The explanation might best be left to a nameless member of the audience: the orchestra did not seem to be as engaged as they might have been, the playing seemed at times sluggish, and several pieces simply ended rather abruptly, almost as if all involved agreed that enough iterations had been performed. But no Moondog concert would be complete without some worthwhile memory attached to it. Here is the final paragraph of Peter Goodman's review:

> Moondog led the orchestra by pounding a bass drum on a platform at the side of the stage. His nine little numbers generally combined that quick, steady beat with pleasant, '30s Big Band melodies treated canonically. It was alternately cheerful and gypsi-romantic, fun to hear and pleasing to watch the frail, 73-year-old composer giving cues by touching his heart.

Besieged by admirers who had missed him for fifteen years, Moondog spent much of his time granting interviews in his Upper East Side hotel (including a ten-minute segment broadcast over

National Public Radio stations throughout the country) and sitting for photo and text essays (the fluffiest appearing in *People* magazine on November 27, when he concludes "dreamily" that he would like to do "100 concerts" so that he could "buy my own castle"). He also did not forget his old friends in upstate New York; in an article by Mike Gulachok, who had followed the fortunes of Moondog since they met in the glory days of Candor, the old friend as well as the international celebrity comes through (*Tioga County Courier*, November 29).

Over fifteen years earlier, Moondog had last seen his second daughter, Lisa, when her mother brought her to Candor. Though he was unaware of what was happening at first, he was surprised to find himself escorted onto the stage by his long-lost child, and another reason to celebrate his return accompanied the applause at the end of the performance. Lisa Collins, now married, had seen an advertisement for the concert, and she worked out the arrangements with the producers behind the scenes. Now, proudly together for what was the first time, since she had no memory of her father, they celebrated. After the concert they sat up all night talking, establishing a relationship that had never been possible before. Thus Moondog was allowed the privilege of being a father once more, and although they never saw each other again for a variety of reasons (Lisa had three children, and Moondog almost immediately returned to Germany and was never again well enough for make long trips), they corresponded until his death. Such moments as these enriched Moondog's final years, bringing him full circle not only with his past work but also with his past life. This American interlude of two short weeks within the European "exile" was a triumph of spirit and a surprising testament to the endurance of his reputation and vigor through many years and over many miles.

WHEN WE DISCUSS HOW MOONDOG "knew" people, it is useful to remind ourselves that a man who lived eighty-three years, sixty-seven without sight (often without a solid home and never a slave to a paper trail) remembered by sound and touch, often with eerie accuracy. But he would not wave hello and seldom signed on the dotted line. The memories that others treasure about him also differ from those we associate with photo albums and family chronicles. What was eccentric and cute to us might have been merely habitual to him. We recollect the Viking in his costume, but he recalls Marlon Brando's quiet voice and Charlie Parker's palsied handshake. The rock star and the cab driver resonate with equal volume; the celebrity and the doorman occupy the same space. We have already seen many instances of what others called his odd habits: his sewing, plowing, hunting, writing. There will be more to come: until the end of his life Moondog made friends in a number of places other than home. But we must remember that as others looked him over, he was listening closely to them. His was a world of music, a language that cuts across geographical and cultural borders. It is hardly surprising that his best compositions are those that travel with the least amount of explanatory material. *The Creation* will be harder to produce than any Moondog piece not only because it is bigger but also because it is in a way narrower and requires a kind of supra-musical commentary, unlike "Theme" or "Good for Goodie" or "Rabbit Hop" or "Bird's Lament" or even "All Is Loneliness." His interactions with the world also demonstrate a dichotomy: to others he was larger than life; to him, others were the sounds that gave meaning to silence. He remembered them in a far different way than they remember him, and all are better off for the difference.

In the early 1990s Moondog made new friends, busy as ever. He was in England four times, all of them long visits culminating in numerous concerts and two albums: *Sax Pax* and *Big Band*. Of course, he was also elsewhere and not always pleased. In 1976, Paul Jordan had explained what the wrath of Moondog looked like if things went against his aesthetic sensibilities. More than once he stopped a concert and began anew after he could not smoothly lasso the players back into the complex patterns he demanded. He even yelled "stop" once (though he was not apparently heard) when a tuba player came in wrong and he was sitting, helplessly, a guest rather than a conductor, in the front seat. On November 27, 1990 in Munster, at the Landesmuseum, in a concert produced by WDR

Landesstudio Munster and the Westfalischer Kunstverein, he was, according to one onlooker who knew him well, "not amused." The "sold out" performance was called *Kosmos Zwischen den Stillen*, and was made up of pieces culled from one of his two magna opera, *The Kosmos*. The complex music for viola da gamba, violone, flute, fagott, oboe d'amore, oboe, bassetthorn, gong, cembalo, and timpani did not come off, because the musicians were not well prepared to play the demanding compositions.

But things did go well sometimes. In 1992, for instance, he produced one of his more unusual albums and visited England for the first time. His English excursus, which took over two years, with many hiatuses, is a microcosm of Moondog's life and work. But first he had to complete a protest first articulated in *H'Art Songs*. The eclectic *Elpmas* (1992) is the longest CD Moondog ever made, running to almost 72 minutes. Recorded in 1991 in Düsseldorf, with a Japanese and Northern European ensemble, it looks back to his most distant past as well as at time present, since many of the compositions were inspired by Native American themes and sounds. There are at least four distinct signatures the listener can discern (and the reader can decode from the liner notes): Amerindian roots (still central, still powerfully redolent of Chief Yellow Calf's lap and buffalo-skin tom-tom), Japanese analogies (Mary's influence still discernible), animal rights protest, and aesthetics. Each can be seen as independent from the other, with clear demarcations: "Wind River Powwow" and "Westwood Ho!" on the one hand, "Fujiyama 1 and 2" on the other; "The Rain Forest," "Seascape of the Whales," and "The Message" balanced by "Introduction and Overtone Continuum" and "Cosmic Meditation." But to Moondog's work such neat classifications do not apply: "If some of my music sounds like Jazz of the 'Swing' era, it is because Swing is North American in origin, coming right out of the drum beats and highly syncopated melodies of the Plains Indians," is one instance of blending; "['Cosmic Meditation'] has quite a hypnotic effect on the listener. Its unworldly sound brings one close to the essence of things, to the 'peace that passeth all understanding'" is another.

The unusual instruments and arcane appearances are still here: a one-year-old child performs, because he can sing "the highest G flat on the piano, something no soprano can do." His father plays a century-old banjo. There is his hexagonal drum, first made in 1981, the balaphone, small bells from India, a gourd in unison with a lure, plus marimba, the latter because it "sounds so realistic." Not only does Moondog fail to explain what some of these instruments are, he also fails to decode the album's title, burying the "four elpmas bands" in the same kind of explanatory prose he uses to introduce his "Overtone Continuum" and "Overtone Band."

> The Overtone Continuum is a self-contained system, consisting of the first nine overtones, which I call the Noble Nine. I used the overtone series...as a theme in my *Creation*. Little by little I achieved a breakthrough by applying diminution to the overtone series, reducing whole notes to half notes, to quarter notes, and so on. All those series could be played together, fitting perfectly, making a unique system, in accordance with the strictest laws of counterpoint. Slowly I realized that I had stumbled onto cosmic laws, such as the law governing contraction and expansion, cause-effect inversion, two-directionality of time, etc.... Each overtone represents Time and each rest between represents Space. Either the Overtone Continuum contains the message or is the message.

(For the record, "elpmas" is "sample" read backwards. It is the first time that Moondog used a "sampler," because he thought that the machine "could realize his concept of counterpoint perfectly," according to the liner notes of the posthumous *Moondog, The German Years* double CD.) Predictably, reviews were few and sketchy at best. Not many listeners have the adventurous taste that Moondog demands when in his haughtier or quintessential element. Yes, *Elpmas* is "a fiery protest against ecological outrage and treatment of Aboriginal people that blends Native American rhythms and swing jazz to heart-surging effect" (Gavin Martin, *Uncut*, March 2000).

True, it is "sweetly folksy" also (Stuart Maconie, *Q4*, 2000) and the music is "very gentle," "ethnic," and "environmental" ("children, rainstorms, some pretty badass sounding birds"), but it is an oddity all the same: Andi Thoma, one half of "Mouse on Mars," co-produced and sang, "most effectively on the charming faux horse opera *Westward Ho!*" yet the album concludes with "an ambient piece of Enoesque complex simplicity [?] and beauty" (spiderbytes.com). With such praise Moondog had often been damned before.

Moondog released two more albums before he died, though several others had been recorded and have been posthumously released. Both of these ambitious efforts were the product of what might be called his English years, 1992–1995, when he spent much time across the channel cementing personal and professional relationships that lasted the rest of his life. If Moondog had become one of the latest avant-garde composers to hit the scene in Germany, in England he was akin to a rock star. Elvis Costello, Danny Thompson, John Harle, and many others not often associated with classical music tracked him down and brought him over, though he did not need much encouragement. The Viking always loved a new audience, and this one was ready for him. He did not specifically write for the various concerts and festivals (with several notable exceptions), but he did adapt many of his stand-bys (recall minisyms and maxisyms) for the occasions and players. The results were two of his most popular and well-received albums in Europe, especially in the English-speaking world. *Big Band*, recorded in 1994, released in 1995, and *Sax Pax for a Sax,* recorded in 1993, released in 1994 and again in 1997, are the products of his Anglophilia.

Danny Thompson, on a radio program for the BBC in 2001 (*Howling at the Moon*), describes Moondog as a "saint." For those who grew to maturity knowing Moondog as the counterculture hero, this is less of a leap than one might think, though Moondog would surely have bristled at being characterized by so Christian a term. (After all, he had become a Viking at least in part because he did not want to be confused with Christ.) If he was a saint, it was of a different variety altogether, and that is how the compliment was intended by one of the founders of the group Pentangle. It was as a hero, to be more secular, that he came to England three times in three years, a cross-cultural icon of historical relevance.

To trace the arc of his *Big Band* and *Sax Pax* suites from the time they were performed and recorded in England until they were released is to chart Moondog's journeys through exposure and celebrity in the most active years of his last decade. But also, the time lapses between his concerts, recordings, and releases reveal the trickiness of the business of music and warn against trying to assign definitive interpretations to the "periods" or "development" of any composer, especially one as peripatetic as Moondog. A year before he first arrived, in 1991, his works for saxophone were performed twice in England. Additionally, away from the center of frenetic activity, his music was appearing in different places and guises. In 1992, for example, the American Ballet Theatre was performing his "Works for Orchestra" in several cities throughout the U.S.

John Harle, the noted British saxophonist, invited Moondog to England again and again. Fortunately for Moondog, the trip was short, and he had among his hosts Danny Thompson. Once in London, for the first time, he performed with the London Saxophonic at the Guildhall in summer 1992, a concert that drew the largest afternoon crowd in memory and for which he wrote several new saxophone pieces. Soon he was touring with the ensemble, heading off in August to Germany, for concerts at Bochum, Jena, Kassel, and Stuttgart, and after that to Switzerland and Austria. It is astonishing how much he was able to write while so busy and on the move. His friends, who often housed him, were not only generous with their hospitality, but also made it possible for the blind, nocturnal composer to work undisturbed. On April 25, 1993, in Witten, Germany, he conducted a new work commissioned by WDR Radio, "Alphorn of Plenty," performed by a sixteen-alpenhorn ensemble "Mytha Horns" from Switzerland. There he met Thomas Heinrich, co-founder and driving force of moondogscorner.de, the definitive website. Moondog finished this busy and exhausting touring season in Moers, Germany.

In October 1993, he was back in England for a second time to record the *Sax Pax Suite* and album at the Terra Incognita Studio in Bath (part of Newton Park College), and there, preaching to the converted as he always had on campuses, he did not disappoint his admirers with his ideas or his music. He used just two beats on the whole album, a much simpler percussion repertoire than in the past, inspired by his experience with the American Indians: "I use either the fast or running beat, as the Indians call it, or the slower, walking beat." He was also working on orchestrating what he now called his *Overtone Tree*, taking his title from his earlier treatise (not to be confused with his *Overtone Continuum*), a "symphony in one movement." "It's a thousand bars long and it has so many contrapuntal parts that you need four conductors to make it happen" (to Johan Kugelberg, *Ugly Things* magazine, 1997). Here is another finished but unrealized gargantuan work.

Moondog had less fun with the liner notes for *Sax Pax* than with those of some earlier albums. He explained that he dedicated the album to Adolphe Sax near the centennial of his death, February 4, 1894, but his instruments are not to be linked to military bands, for they "are used exclusively for peaceful purposes." But the pun on "pax" could involve not only peace but also "packs," or different sized groups in the ensemble; "Single Foot" has four, "Sandalwood" five, "New Amsterdam" seven, and "Novette No. 1" nine. Danny Thompson also receives a dedication in the form of "D for Danny," which "the former Pentangle co-founder" plays on his contrabass "named Victoria." Moondog also says that the entire album is part of a more ambitious series called "JAJAZ," jazz "in two directions"

> like a Janus-head showing two faces. There is one looking backwards into the past, represented by classical techniques of composing, and the other face turns towards the future which is characterized by a new kind of combining old and new elements in music.

Back in London in 1994, with John Harle performing, he recorded *Big Band* at the Elephant Recording studios. He had great fun with the liner notes this time, producing a commentary much like the more effusive and invigorating ones in the past forty years, couplets to accompany the music, mixing fun and high seriousness. Of the older pieces, written in the Fifties and Sixties, he reminisces fondly: "New York" is "the sweetest wine sap" and "my baby." "Paris" was written in upstate New York in his "shack, as warm as toast," while outside the snow was knee-deep. "Bumbo" is less Caribbean than a mambo because it was written in the form of double two-part canons on 52nd Street. "Shakespeare City," newer in time, is a "pair of sixteen-bar chromatics" that "represent the Bard around the world." "Frankanon" is less grandiose but more personally revealing, dedicated to Ilona's brother who, at twelve, "wanted me to stay with him for his Christmas." And so "they adopted me." "We Have to Have Hope" is a rare Moondog venture into contemporary American politics, though admittedly with a light-handed touch: the fact that Hope, where then-president Clinton had been born, and Batesville, where Louis Hardin last saw the light of day, are both in Arkansas might be a coincidence, but didn't both men share similar interests as well as a geographical proximity? "I heard he played the sax." "A Sax" is dedicated to the man who created the instrument, and "Reedroy" was written for the soloist who performed it, John Harle. The pieces played by the London Brass are quite different from those played by the London Saxophonic. These final seventeen minutes or so of the album are linked to the Moondog cosmology. "Cosmicode" explains how the universe is run, how "Megamind" is found "in the overtones from one to nine." The gong in "Black Hole" "creates an atmosphere" within which we may "contemplate in fear the awesomeness of Density's propensity." Finally, the ten-minute "Invocation," by now a signature Moondog piece, asks the sixteen players to work in synchrony in order to suggest how

Communication carries on between the living and the dead, between

The living and the living twixt the galaxies that can and can't be seen.

The Meltdown festival was Moondog's last appearance in England. Invited by one of his most influential admirers, Elvis Costello, Moondog was on London's South Bank in summer 1995, lionized by an audience more accustomed to hearing cutting-edge popular music. One fan who was there describes the moment:

> No matter your opinion of Costello ... you must needs tip your trilby in his direction for pulling off this historic Moondog coup.... Not a soul in the audience was left untouched by this performance; besides the power of the music, there were his touching remarks to the audience, revealing little glimpses of his life on the streets, his political views, his musical career, his loves. And his eccentricity: holding up a percussion instrument, he said, "This is several hundred pecan shells, in an old sock!" John Harle helped him off stage as we gave our standing ovation...and Moondog acknowledged holding aloft his drumstick in salute, a beatific smile emerging from his white whiskery face. The waves of emotion affected us all. People in the audience were crying.

In an interview with the *New York Times* jazz writer Don Heckman in 1997, Elvis Costello gave his take on the legacy of Moondog as a musical and supra-musical figure:

> When I first heard Moondog on the radio in the '60s, I thought his music was a product of those days. Little did I know that it was just one of the occasions in which the world has discovered Moondog. Recently, I was talking with my son Matt, who said, "Do you know this album" and out of his bag produced a Moondog album from the '50s. I have no doubt that in 40 years or more, a father and son somewhere will be having the same conversation about a Moondog record.

But a footnote should be appended to the nostalgia. As with his 1989 appearance in New York, those who were there felt they were seeing him for the last time. The poignancy of the moment understandably overwhelms the quality of the performance, for by the end of his life Moondog was a living symbol. It was (to many) nearly irrelevant what was played or how (though never to him), and that fact complicates his legacy. It will be a long time before those who loved him in New York and France and London and Stockholm and Germany will be able to listen to his music without also seeing the incredible man who produced it. Regardless of how much he tried, and despite his disavowals, Moondog was an electrifying performer. For his music to survive his presence it will need interpretations by diverse hands in other venues; it will have to be gently but firmly weaned away from its creator.

AFTER THE EXCITEMENT OF his Swedish years (1981–1986) and English years (1992–1995), the last half decade of Moondog's life was, for him, quieter, in part because his health was failing, and in part because personal decisions shaped his day-to-day life. In the same year as his final London appearance, 1995, he began to suffer the alarming effects of diabetes. A decade after the first diagnosis, with thousands of pills behind him, Moondog entered the secondary stage, the consequences of his persistently high blood sugar. Surrounding his eightieth year, his accelerating bladder problem (nephropathy) necessitated a urinary catheter. For the remainder of his life he was yoked to a bag at his thigh, which must have frustrated this fiercely independent man, his good humor about it notwithstanding. Even though the logistics of traveling were now more nightmarishly complicated than ever, and despite discomfort and potential embarrassment, Moondog appeared at two concerts in 1996, both times with his favorite pianist, Dominique Ponty: he often called the two of them the "DMD" (Dominique and Moondog duet). At the Rudolf-Steiner-Schule in the German city of Bielefeld-Schildesche, Thomas Heinrich and some other friends staged a concert for strings (the Stadtisches Orchester Bielefeld), choir, and piano (Ms. Ponty) to celebrate Moondog's 80th birthday. A tape made a day earlier on a Bosendorfer grand piano is (like much of what could have been his legacy) lost. At the infamous 1988 Rennes concert, Stephan Eicher, soon to become a European pop star, met Moondog, loved his music, and gave him carte blanche at the Montreaux Jazz festival in Switzerland, also in 1996. Once he had written "Mood Montreux" for the occasion, nothing was going to stop Moondog, even the inevitable accident. "Uh-oh," he said, shortly before curtain time, "I'm leaking." Everyone but him agreed that this was serious and that he had to go immediately to the hospital. The audience was alerted and remained absolutely quiet after it learned about his difficulties backstage. Moondog, however, was there to entertain, and the show went on. He went to the hospital immediately afterwards, and did not perform again until 1999, for the last time with Ms. Ponty.

American fans, in the age before Googling, would occasionally hear about him after his visit of 1989. In probably his last appearance in prose in *The New York Times* (June 8, 1997) until his obituary two years later, in the "F.Y.I." column, he said, "I miss New York. I still have a strong attachment to it." Stronger, indeed, than any attachment he may have had to his "old Viking garb": "Ilona got rid of all that years ago. She even hid my spear." Five months before he died, on April 1, 1999, one of the five featured poems printed in honor of National Poetry Month included this passage from "He Said," by Gerald Stern:

And Blake the poet, he said,
a dove both black and white, and Moondog whom he watched
night after night in the early Fifties playing
his instruments and moaning, and Amos, he said,
placed by the Gideons over the flowerpots,
who hated coldness, accommodation, extortion, oppression,
and roared in the grapes, he said, and melted mountains.

A touching piece written by Mike Gulachuk in the *Tioga County Courier* on August 26, 1998 recollects the man who charmed Candor with his eccentric genius and went on to become a celebrity without forgetting his roots. But humor, allusion, and reminiscence aside, Moondog's music, if not his ideas, was often taken seriously by serious artists, even when he was not performing it. In 1997 the Kronos Quartet, in an album called *Early Music* (Nonesuch), along with pieces by Dowland and Hildegard von Bingen, played Moondog's "Synchrony No. 2." The conceit covering such a selection was that some ancient music can sound modern and vice versa. Moondog would have been pleased to be acknowledged as a composer who, in order to make something new, carried on tradition. Numerous other examples of Moondog's works and life appear in programs, recitals, citations, and accolades; in the quiet months before he died, the world was experiencing an information explosion. In the late 1990s, especially, his name appeared frequently, sometimes in the strangest places, and his music continued to be played, sometimes in ways which might have caused him pain, but he was never out of circulation.

Moondog's personal life changed also at this time of painful adjustment to the new demands upon his body. Ilona had met the man she would later live with and marry, Ludwig Sommer, and from 1995 she spent weekends with him, returning to work with Moondog during the week. But when Ludwig's mother died, he invited not only Ilona, but Moondog also, to live in his large apartment in Munster. In 1997, then, the long sojourn at Oer-Erkenschwick of over twenty years ended when they moved north. On August 17, 1998 Ilona and Ludwig were married, and Moondog was thrilled. Both men had gotten along from the beginning, and this made his final years much easier. What in other families might have proved a traumatic change, especially to the suddenly vulnerable aging artist, turned out to be a blessing, the "two Louises" sharing mirth and mature companionship, something Moondog had rarely known in his long, peripatetic life. It would be difficult to overstate how important this was to him: his last great spurt of creative activity came about not only because he was physically more confined and limited (Moondog could write lovely music in a fierce snow storm), but also because of a happy home life with his beloved Ilona and her husband. How unusual this domestic relationship must have been, and how exciting that they were able to make it work! Moondog, who last lived with his father in 1942, had finally found an equal, extended, and satisfying relationship with a man not related to his professional life, one with whom he lived in harmony through the physical sufferings as well as the continued adulation from the world outside.

The last year of his life (1999), when Clinton was soon to step down and yet another new world order was about to be born, was painful and triumphant. In April he met the group that would perform his *Bracelli* after he died, the Ensemble Bracelli, and on August 1 he was in France more than twenty years after his first visit, at the Mimi Festival in Arles. This performance was his last, his swan song, and fittingly was essentially the DMD one more time: Dominique Ponty on the piano, Moondog on percussion and reciting couplets. At the same time, his disease moved into its final phase, gangrene due to peripheral vascular degeneration. In March the big toe on his left foot turned blue and he had to be rushed to the hospital, after the expected resistance. "No way," was his first response, and getting him there took two adults. Ultimately, the toe had to be amputated, and he seemed for a while to improve noticeably. But several months later, just before going to France, the little toe on the same foot had to be removed also. Yet Moondog remained sanguine and mobile. Even during the trip to Arles, which included an airport strike in the middle of the hot summer, he was able to move about and perform. Later that month, the inevitable arrived.

One day in late August he came out of his room in grave discomfort, saying, "I didn't know it would be like this." He had an appointment at the hospital that day. He was able to dress himself and wanted to "go out on his own two feet." On the drive he threw up and seemed to have had a stroke: he was paralyzed in one leg and his speech was slurred. (These are signs of focal neuropathy in its final stages, including Bell's palsy.) He remained in the hospital for two weeks. At one point the staff was considering cutting off his beard because it made feeding and cleaning difficult, but even at death's door certain conditions are non-negotiable. Once again, he seemed to improve, at one point flirting with a pretty nurse, at another announcing to Ilona that he had an idea for a long musical piece, at yet another telling an attendant ("laconically") that Philip Glass' music was "too artificial." The next day, however, he died of heart failure. Ilona realized that he had left at home a copper bracelet which he had worn continually for years to ward off illness—that he had known he would never return. It was September 8, 1999.

Even those who knew him marginally or had thought him long dead soon heard. Obituaries appeared the world over, in Germany first, but in the U.S. shortly thereafter. The longest in major newspapers were in the *New York Times* (by Glenn Collins) and the *Los Angeles Times* (by Jon Thurber), both on September 12. The half-page obituary by Collins was seen beside the new Columbia CD comprising his two albums of 1969 and 1971 at Tower Records in New York City for over a year. In upstate New York, his old friend Mike Gulachok celebrated his life in the *Tioga County Courier* on September 26, while the notice written by Connie Nogas appeared twice (the *Binghamton Press* and the *Ithaca Journal*, September 23). These are but a handful of the scores that flooded the presses and the Internet. Obituaries are seldom informative for those who know the person's life or work, but their number itself tells a story. He was loved and appreciated by many people from a wide spectrum of the world's population, from groupie to classical pianist to just plain folks. Perhaps the most touching memorial to his death was a long article by Carol A. Henry in the *Tioga County Courier* (November 24, 1999) in upstate New York reporting on the "Moondog Mania Night" that took place at the Candor Historical Society on November 15. The testimony of old acquaintances was moving: there was Bucky Moon, Paul Jordan, John Hitchings (of John's Fine Foods in Owego, where the bus from New York stopped), and Don Weber (who explained how Moondog knew all the dogs in the neighborhood and would "navigate his way by the dog's bark, as he talked to them in the dark"). To them, he was a warm, engaging human being who just happened to be an artist. As many of those who knew him said many times, once you were able to get beyond the daunting image you were in the presence of a happy, gentle man.

IN THE YEARS SINCE HIS DEATH his reputation has grown in odd ways and the dispersal of his musical bounty has taken some unexpected turns. In the age of the Internet, a name like Moondog is a recognizable commodity even to those too young to have ever recalled him as a living, breathing human being. A Google search gives around 645,000 hits; a *New York Times* search lists fifty instances of performances of or writings about him in the past twenty-five years in New York City alone. Almost five years after his death, the New York *Daily News* gave him a full-page profile in its Big Town Songbook Series ("Celebrating New York's Musical Heritage"). Not surprisingly, controversy has also followed him. In several car commercials in the U.S., jazzed-up versions of his "Bird's Lament" have been the background music. There is litigation pending because his estate, for instance, is charging that the rather large amounts of money being paid for the rights have been distributed to the wrong people. As Moondog knew all too well because of his experiences with production, the difference between making music and the business of music is so large that the two realities scarcely exist in the same world. Freud was reputed to have said, "sooner or later, sex." Moondog might have suggested, "sooner or later, money."

His music still lives. Three posthumous recordings in Europe he made or approved, one with two CDs, have appeared. Two of these four discs are retrospectives of his career. Numerous others have recorded his music in their own way, and many older vinyl records are candidates for redistribution. Of the many original CD releases available, three give a sense of the variety: In *New York Presence* (Summit, 2004), a brass quintet, the Extension Ensemble, performs, for the first time, "Instrumental Round No. 1" and two old favorites originally written for different instrumentation: "Sandalwood" and "Pastoral." *Un Hommage à Moondog* (Trace, 2005) is composed of renditions with varying instrumentation by younger admirers (with Stefan Lakatos). *Strings for Kings* (Ars Musi, 2006) is a selection of mainly Moondog pieces (subtitle, "Moondog Sharp Harp") played on the harp by Xenia Narati. It is revealing to hear Moondog speaking as of old on the street accompanied by newly recorded strings and other materials, or "Black Night" electronically enhanced; it is both fascinating if a bit unnerving to hear selections from *Art of the Canon* on the harp.

Of course, once the composer releases his work to the public he not only loses some input into how it is interpreted, but also, to an astonishing degree, loses control over how he is perceived by the musical establishment. If ever a composer needs performers who will be true to the vision behind the works, it is Moondog, for many of the reasons that we have seen again and again throughout the story of his life. Because he was a cult figure, and wrote music that is melodious and memorable and short, to some he will always be a writer for mass audiences and, therefore, not serious. Because the music which he composed that is unmistakably serious is also tonal, some consider him derivative and anachronistic. To get a full picture of the music Moondog wrote not only requires different modes of listening but also a wide variety of exposures. Until his mammoth sound sagas (*The Creation, Cosmos*) get a full hearing, the scope of his later career will be unknown. Moondog wrote big as well as small. Moreover, since he wrote so much, and most of it exists only in Braille, it still remains untranslated into sight-readable musical notation.

IN MUNSTER, MOONDOG'S GRAVE, designed by his old friend the artist Ernst Fuchs, alive with flowers, is a fitting tribute. The bust of his head, with full beard and chiseled profile, sits on a delicate marble column, slightly larger at the top than at the base. "Moon Dog" is carved prominently beneath his visage. He looks serene, as ever. Yet he was also driven by gods, demons, or the genii of place and time to make his life a testimony. He knew early on that invention does not rest easily with limitation. Moondog's life, from the outset, had been an adventure, from his earliest days and through the modulations, triumphs, and tragedies of his bizarre career. For him, life called for continual creative responses. Compelling causes attracted his gargantuan energies. At an age when most retire and many are content to hang on, he lived hard at being a composer, committed to his lifework in the teeth of criticism and (as with anyone attempting to make things new) against posterity's odds. That is how he had always lived, a man of convictions, patience, and staying power, fearless in the face of change, aware of fame's tenuousness, and, amid reversals and upheavals, displaying a keen and infectious sense of humor, often at his own expense. Whether the canon's gatekeepers will consider him a major artist is uncertain, but that kind of recognition is irrelevant to those who have experienced the twentieth century, even for a few moments, through the prism of his creations. That he lived an artist's life is part of the public record. Our final view of him, of course, may be that of the public celebrity and counterculture revolutionary, for surely, as long as memories of the Viking of Sixth Avenue exist, that is how he will be known to many. But if his work as well as his image endures, then we might remember him in a more intimate way: as the peaceful warrior, the bringer of good news in a stormy world. The day before he died, Moondog was, as he had been for over six decades, hard at work, lit up in his own quiet, private place, playing.

Note: For a complete and up-to-date discography on Moondog, the best source is moondogscorner.de. Not only do the devoted founders of his memory-hoard keep meticulous records, they have also located and reissued rarities long thought lost. A journey through the "Tracking List" section is an outline for a study of Moondog's career as composer and performer, and it is constantly updated and enriched. Moondog's sheet music and written works are available from managarm.com.

Appendices

Music of the Fifties

C ompared to the elaborate adaptations and arrangements of the *Suite of Eight Pieces* by Kenny Graham on MGM Records, the selections on the 1953 Mars EP, *Moondog*, are simple. With the probable exception of two, they were recorded on location, and the background noises attest to the authenticity and spontaneity of the performances. "Avenue of the Americas (51st Street)" is an "improvisation in 7/4 time on the oo." With the sound of traffic clearly discernible, the drum and the unique twang of the oo engage in a lively dialogue ("snaketime moderately") that lasts about a minute and a half. The piece is highly percussive, the melody line barely audible; Moondog performs on both the oo and his triangular drums. (The trimba, though created before 1953, was not so called until 1954; the trimbas, confusingly another instrument entirely, was created later and can still be heard in its latest incarnation on the recordings made in Europe in the 1980s and 1990s.) "2 West 46th Street" is next; called a "recorder solo in 5/8 time" on the sheet music (the time signatures do not appear on the album or in the program notes), it too runs about ninety seconds. Unlike the improvisations which underscore Moondog's spontaneity, this piece has a strong lyrical, melodic quality: drums precede the vibrant, lively recorder, which carries one of Moondog's happiest statements, certainly the cheeriest in this album, in "snaketime fast." Also in the background are maracas and bells. The haunting "Lullaby," about seventy-five seconds long, in moderate (5/4) snaketime features drums heard moments before the melodic theme is stated, first, by a samisen, a Japanese instrument, similar to a guitar, with a long neck and three strings, played with a plectrum; the recorder joins for the next statement, and finally Suzuko chants three successive cycles of the melody, each time one octave higher. True to the form of the canon that Moondog increasingly favored, "Lullaby" ends where it began, with the dialogue between drum and samisen. Of all the selections on this album, this "Lullaby" (not to be confused with a later "Lullaby," also featuring Suzuko, on the first Prestige album) is the piece that most anticipates later developments, including one of Moondog's most cherished technical achievements in the Sixties and Seventies: the perfection of the round. The street noises on West 46th Street, where it was recorded, are especially audible during the final few bars. The fourth and last piece on side one, "Fog on the Hudson," which appeared the following year in *New York 19*, was recorded near the river, on 57th Street near 10th Avenue. Like the first piece, it is almost purely percussive, a dialogue between a powerful fog horn and the oo/drum combination, the horn introducing and concluding the seventy-five seconds of improvisation.

There is a nice balance in the arrangement of the four selections on side one. The five and a half minutes of music, recorded as performed (on the west side of Manhattan, from Fifth to Tenth Avenues, from 46th to 57th Streets), open and close with improvisational percussion. Between the covers of drum and oo are the two more elaborate and ambitious, because more heavily layered, compositions. Side two, which also has four selections, and also runs to roughly five and a half minutes, has a different texture. Not only are the two percussive pieces more studied than those on side one, they also smack of the studio. The two melodic pieces come first and third, staggered rather than centered. Whereas side one is a cycle, or a loop, side two works through alternation. Although Mr. Schwartz delighted in capturing the dance of life without intervention, he nonetheless displayed a sense of design as well. On side two, two instruments are introduced by Moondog which he apparently abandoned after the Mars recording: unlike the oo and the trimba, staples throughout the 1950s and signatures of their creator, the utsu, a small keyboard in the pentatonic scale (like the black piano keys), appears in two numbers, and the uni, a zither-like arrangement with seven strings in unison, appears once here, in one selection on the Epic album a year later, and thereafter no more.

"Utsu," in 5/4 ("moderate" snaketime), is one minute long. Suzuko plays the instrument against Moondog's percussion. This selection sounds more Oriental than any other on the album and carries the simplest melody line. "On and Off the Beat" presents Moondog with drums and temple blocks in "a study in 5/4 rhythm" ("moderately"). A horn, cymbals, a triangle and the oo highlight this percussion piece. "Chant," in "slow" snaketime, is a two-part round for voice and utsu, with the uni, rather than the usual drums, serving as percussion. Moondog, throughout the experimental Fifties, used many unexpected sources for percussion, from flute to feathers, so the uni is the first in a series rather than the end of a line. Simpler than "Lullaby," and more Oriental in texture, "Chant" is a surprising and exciting piece, the mournful blending of the two unusual instruments creating in one minute what the best of Moondog's earliest music seems to evoke without coyness: simple, buoyant yet utterly refreshing musical statements. The final piece, "From One to Nine," is a formal study of percussive "snaketime." Moondog speaks briefly (a common occurrence on future albums) and announces that he will "demonstrate the quarter-beat tempos," from 1/4 to 9/4. A footnote in the sheet music explains that the drums, "tuned to various pitches," are played to "the background of the oo in perpetual motion." With the voice introduction, the last selection is by far the longest, lasting well over two minutes, bracketed by a gong.

KENNY GRAHAM'S ADAPTATION, *Moondog Suite / Suncat Suite*, is a jazz album with a Joan Miró painting on the cover. Not only is Mr. Graham called on the program a "jazz revolutionary" whose first group was the Afro-Cubists, not only is he one who "genuinely refuses to have any truck with commercialism or to write anything bad because it pays well," but he is also "greatly in demand as a powerful, swinging tenor player" or as a writer of "best-selling arrangements." This paragon and paradox is a "large, red-bearded, soft-voiced, strong man" who lives a "surrealist life." His response to having been told that he was born at eight o'clock in the morning was: "the earliest I ever got up." But he came to life when he heard the Mars record from across the Atlantic. He was so "fascinated" by the "new worlds of rhythm and tonal coloration" that he decided to "translate" Moondog's music "to the more orthodox instruments" of "a jazz combo of progressive design." The resulting "Moondog Suite" becomes "provocative" because, despite common sense and the laws of physics, the new arrangements somehow manage to capture "the spontaneity and vigor" of the originals. Fortunately, the music is better than its defense.

Moondog's bio is even more embarrassing than Mr. Graham's. Among other inaccuracies, for instance, we are told that he "grew up on an Indian reservation," that he is a "minstrel" who travels "from crowd to crowd making spontaneous music," and that the Mars record was in fact one of these "street-corner concerts." He is a legend who is a composite of Byron, Socrates, and Gandhi, "a tall, monk-like figure of ageless quality....Though the night might be cold, his feet are usually encased solely in sandals. His body is wrapped in a flowing robe fashioned from rough, brown blankets. His bearded face bears a gentle, haunting look." This "world-famous...poet, philosopher, mendicant, musician extraordinary [sic]" is noted for his "virtuosic" performing skills, his instruments ("whistles and flutes...of unusual timbres"), his ability to "create on the spot" and his wit: the night around him, as he plays, becomes "startling," "spellbinding," "imaginative."

Program notes behind them, the Satellites perform well. What is lost is the simplicity of Moondog's sound, so markedly without comforting tonal patterns, traditional instruments, familiar rhythms, and lengthy development. Kenny Graham eliminated

"Avenue of the Americas" and "On and Off the Beat." Of the nine quarter-beats Moondog illustrated in "From One to Nine," only the first five are retained, and these alternate with the longer selections: thus "One Four" precedes "2 West 46th Street," "Two Four" precedes "Chant," and so on. About three and a half minutes of the original eleven-minute suite, therefore, were dropped. The remaining selections, however, grew twice as long.

Side one of the Epic (1954) album lasts fifteen minutes and offers ten selections ranging from an elaborate quartet to percussion solos. "Dragon's Teeth" does for the eighth note what "From One to Nine" on the Mars album did for the quarter: on the trimba, "a series of ten drums, triangular in shape, used in graduated sizes," Moondog introduces his snaketime rhythms from 1/8 to 9/8 while in the background, the "composer's wife" plays the oo in perpetual motion. The tour lasts ninety seconds. "Voices of Spring," the next selection (like "Dragon's Teeth," "Tree Frog," and "Rim Shot"), probably comes from the files of Tony Schwartz. Against a background of twittering sparrows Moondog freely improvises this "short rhapsody" on the recorder after reciting "Voices of spring were in chorus / Each voice was singing a song / I could not sing in that chorus / Until I wrote me a song / I wrote my song and joined the throng."

"Oasis" is in many ways the most unusual and ambitious composition on side one. Moondog dedicated it to the wife and sister of the album's producer, "two of the country's best young concert artists," who perform on the violin and the piano. Moondog plays the trimba, maracas, and uni (which provides that "provocative twanging sound") in "a fascinating rhythm background." As the program notes accurately describe this three-minute piece, a thematic departure even for the wide-ranging Moondog, it is colored by Asia Minor, even though, in form, it is a round: percussion, piano, and violin enter, at equal intervals, develop and embellish the melody, and then depart, violin first, piano next, in a precise, modulated structure. "Tree Frog," like "Voices of Spring," is a small experiment using as its point of departure a natural sound: to recreate "the song of the tree frog in spring," Moondog taps his fingers against the holes of a recorder with the microphone close by. Since no air is forced through, he thus creates a percussive sound with a wind instrument. "Be A Hobo" is a round Moondog sang throughout the Sixties and performed on the second Columbia album (1971): "Be a hobo and go with me / From Hoboken to the sea." After a brief percussive introduction, Moondog sings, through overdubbing, this delightful song in two voices.

The one-minute "Instrumental Round," like the later "Theme and Variations," has been one of the most durable of Moondog's compositions. Here it is "an experiment in orchestration," in which Moondog plays bass, trombone, flute, oboe, and drums, weaving them together, through overdubbing, into the round that later re-emerged as the madrigal "All Is Loneliness" (on *More Moondog*, Prestige, and *Moondog 2*, Columbia, as well as in the Janis Joplin version, with Big Brother and the Holding Company (1967), and live in concert, 1972). The intriguing but minor "Double Bass Duo" is ninety seconds of what the program notes call "the free, eclectic spirit" of Moondog: having discovered himself locked out of the recording studio alone with his newly purchased bass, he used the time to "experiment"; when the sounds evolved into "thematic material" he recorded the dialogue, playing both bass parts as well as the drum accompaniment. "Why Spend the Dark Night With You," another madrigal which followed him through the Sixties and reappeared in 1971, when the two voices were his and his daughter June's, is here entirely in Moondog's hands: he sings both parts of the simple lyric against plain percussion.

"Theme and Variations" is, with "Oasis," the stellar piece on side one. In 1969, played by an orchestra, it introduced the Columbia Masterworks album. On the Epic record Moondog plays the "more than twenty voices" himself, on borrowed instruments for the most part; for three minutes this marvelous, complex round enlarges and embellishes the four-note theme into an evocative, powerful, almost mournful statement. On Epic, the title of the piece is descriptive; fifteen years later, when it is called simply "Theme," it is closer to symbolic: over two decades before he completed his sound saga, this round emerged fully matured and polished. Moondog's rounds, in which form comfortably enclosed creativity, always guaranteed a finished product in the smallest space. "Theme and Variations" is grand yet contained: it announces Moondog's procedures, it celebrates the debut of one of his most successful kinds of orchestration, and it establishes a new idiom. Snakes and dragons, howls and frogs aside, "Theme" resonates and abides. It does even more: it suggests whole worlds of sound and procedure that Moondog would later explore. The last, brief piece on side one, "Rim Shot," first appeared on the Brunswick Jazz recording of the Pythian Temple concert; it is another percussive study, this time of "acceleration" in 5/4 time. Moondog as an improvisational performer was never in better form.

The two suites on side two were the most ambitious compositions Moondog recorded in the Fifties; with the exception of three selections on the 1969 Columbia album (one of which is an expansion of the middle movement of the second suite) they were the longest he recorded in America. Using "the twelve-tone chromatic scale used by the Viennese masters," the "classic tonal structure" of the "parallel" suites "is used to evolve a five-part invertible counterpoint." Each movement is in "canon form, separate thematically from its companion movements." No. 1 is written in "minor-major-minor" sequence, No. 2 in "major-minor-major" sequence. The times of the corresponding movements are the same in both suites: 7/4 first movement, 5/2 second, 7/8 third. Years later Moondog recalled that there were many problems in the studio recording of the final (7/8) movements of both suites, for the players struggled with the rhythms.

No. 1 is scored for dragon-teeth drums, with gloves, two violas, three cellos, a set of five temple blocks and, in the last movement, Suzuko (the composer's unnamed wife) on the "Japanese drums" (not specified further). The last movement is a minute longer than either of the others, and the entire composition plays in slightly over six minutes. The music, even in the more quickly paced first and third movements, is plaintive and sober, the lower register strings (for which Moondog had a special affinity, decades later celebrated in his "bracelli" compositions), in the minor keys, an interesting and original scoring.

The second suite, all seven-plus minutes of it, traveled well: in 1969 it re-emerged as the ballet "Nocturne," performed by the Donald McKayle Dance Company, and went on tour in the Middle East under contract to the B'nai B'rith. Its second movement, on Epic two and a half minutes long, was generously enlarged into Symphonique #3, "Ode to Venus," close to six minutes of the 1969 Columbia album. In those program notes he said: "I wrote it in a month back in 1954, revised it and scored it in 1960, and added parts to the coda in 1969." Here, in 1954, the jacket notes merely describe the instruments added to the drums and the five strings: in the second movement, temple blocks and claves, in the third movement the "tuji" (which appears one other time, on the third Prestige album)—a "new and intriguing" addition to the Moondog percussion stockpile, "a sort of board with dowels mounted in rows. The dowels are fingered swiftly by the player, producing an unusual percussive sound." The music is more stimulating, varied, and complex, the contrast between the movements more dramatic (a wonderful ingredient for successful ballet music), the percussion more noticeably a handmaiden to the orchestral lushness. Along with "Theme and Variations" it marks the ascendancy of the mature Moondog, so it is no surprise that it aged better and grew more in stature through the years. So did its composer.

THE COVER OF PRESTIGE 1 (7042) presents a shadowy, slouching pariah, indefinite and awesome. Bob Weinstock, who produced all three Prestige albums, was a devotee of jazz, and the other albums he released at this time featured performers and composers such as Thelonious Monk, Gil Melle, Billy Taylor and Candido, and Django. The persona hovering over Moondog, therefore, was to some extent cast in the brooding image of a line of contemporary favorites. (The "Snaketime" Moondog, on the other hand, features a photograph of a happy Moondog playing a flute on a rooftop with Mary, smiling, sitting alongside him holding a Japanese short sword.) Although the music was the same, the image of the creative force was packaged for two different if not mutually exclusive audiences. Thus, on Prestige 1 he was a beloved "fusionist" of progressive jazz, whereas on "Snaketime" he was the street musician riding high on a rooftop. The Prestige album carried a description of Moondog and his music which emphasized the "eclectic approach to composition"; on the right was a summary of the contents. The "Snaketime" back cover presents a picture instead of prose, a fuller breakdown of the selections and, in a footnote, further strengthens a strong sense of intimacy by identifying the "friends" who did the performing.

Making music (performing and recording as well as composing) included for Moondog an evolving extended family. In the late 1950s new presences appeared side-by-side with the more familiar. First and foremost was Mary, who was always more than second percussion. Other kin included June, the infant auditor of "Lullaby," and Sakura Whiteing (Mary's mother), who recites once. Sam Ulano, who appears on Prestige 1 and 3 as a drummer, worked with Moondog until 1971, when he was cut from the second Columbia album because of internal politics. The Barrons, Bebe and Louis, lent their studio at 9 West 8th Street to record Prestige 1, and appear on Prestige 3 in speaking parts. The Barrons were his friends during the downtown period and even later, well into the 1960s, when Moondog and a new set of friends used their studio. Robert S. Altshuler, who wrote the program notes for Prestige 1 and 2, put together the program notes for the 1969 Columbia album over ten years later (and received no credit on the jacket for his efforts). Ray Malone tap-dances (or soft-shoes) on all three Prestige albums to Moondog's percussive rhythms.

Mr. Altshuler's notes describe the subtle texture of Moondog's pieces. Opposed to the "pure" or "electronic" music of a large segment of the avant-garde, Moondog "perceives music everywhere," and the "vignettes" collected in the album "are fully realized attempts to integrate music and sound." Although this drifts dangerously close to nonsense, there is a point: artificiality was the one great enemy of Moondog's muse. Pure sound, without strictures, overlays, and re-interpretations, grounded complex meditations. "The ability to find unexpectedly complementary areas of music is an essential ingredient in these miniature portraits of life's many parts." Much of the work, on oo, trimba, and other exotic percussion, is in Moondog's attention-getting mode; other pieces, especially those for strings, are as serious as anything on the Epic album. The most stimulating pieces, moreover, are not the most experimental, but those which find new sounds for old instruments.

Prestige 1 is Moondog on nature, as Prestige 2 is Moondog on love: both have lyrical, romantic leanings through the wars on the drums. "Caribea," "Tree Trail," "Frog Bog," and "Surf Session" represent the eclectic, early Moondog at his most dynamic. Featuring the "Weiner-Sabinsky Duo" (identified on "Snaketime" as David and Rosemary Butterfield) on violin, Moondog either on percussion or piano, and Mary and Tito Banques on additional percussion, these compositions successfully integrate theme (stimulus) and sound (response). The ninety-second-long "Caribea," in 5/4, features a Latin Moondog at the piano, evoking an exotic West Indies as "Oasis" had the Near East; "Tree Trail" features bird twittering as a frame and backdrop for a haunting violin duet, in 5/2, with a simple, quiet percussion accompaniment; "Frog Bog" is, by contrast, a more complex and equally haunting violin duet against the sounds of frogs and muted percussion, in 5/4; "Surf Session," also called "Euphony No. 11," is more elaborate, at six minutes by far the longest selection on the album. It is, like those on Epic, a suite in three movements, 2/4, 2/2, 2/8 (so marked on "Snaketime"; on Prestige the only signature given is 2/4, that of the first movement), framed by the sounds of the tide, moderate in pace for two minutes, more plaintive for three, with a tantalizing, subtle finale. Moondog's romantic utterances speak even through the most languid, sad statements..

Some of the other selections integrate life and art poorly. "Lullaby," featuring Mary crooning to her six-week-old daughter, seems more cutesy and contrived than the "Lullaby" on the Mars record, even though it dates from about the same time. "Big Cat," a frenetic recorder/percussion piece in 1/4, including a tiger's roar, does not really come off. Neither does the "Dance Rehearsal" at which his old friend "Naila stages a routine for her pupil, Violetta" to Moondog's flute/percussion accompaniment: this is another tape from his audio vérité repertoire. Sometimes realism cannot be made resonant; this is the kind of piece the kinder critics tend to call historically interesting. The "Tap Dance" and "Street Scene" segments, ad libbing and improvising on the sidewalks of New York, by now seem old hat, the dialogues fey. "Oo Debut" and "Drum Suite" (the latter a three-part composition in which Sam Ulano plays Japanese drums to Moondog's trimba) are stimulating to those who like polyrhythms, and to those who appreciate virtuosity. But they, too, however skillfully executed, smack of the publicist rather than the composer.

Three more forward-looking pieces underscore the power of Moondog's unadorned style. One, "To a Sea Horse," is a piano solo, in 5/4, of slightly less than two minutes. Chords and dissonances are resolved and tonality triumphs after being assaulted; on the programmatic level, the comically graceful movement of the sea horse has been suggested. The other two, "Death, When You Come to Me" and "Trees Against the Sky," are madrigals, in 5/4, short and powerful. "Death" is more complex. The lyric is a translation of a Moondog original ("Death, when you come to me, may you come to me swiftly: I would rather not linger, not linger.") into Japanese, but the words are superfluous. Oo, drums and voice create an almost pure sound poem. "Trees" ("Trees against the sky, fields of plenty, rivers to the sea: this, and more, spreads before me") pits Moondog against himself, through the magic of overdubbing, in a celebration of abundance conjured up with trimba and voice alone.

TWO ALBUMS SWIFTLY FOLLOWED Moondog, neither as interesting or daring. All of the Prestige albums were remastered (by Rudy Van Gelder), and much material had been on tape for years before being pressed. *More Moondog* (7069) and *The Story of Moondog* (7099), therefore, contain more dated music. There are fewer original compositions by the future symphonic composer; the street musician, once again, is most emphasized. For instance, all of the SMC 78s appear. On Prestige 2 there is "All Is Loneliness" (again!), "Oboe Round," and "Chant" (SMC 2528); on Prestige 3 is "In a Doorway" (in which Moondog plays "on his last set of square drums") from "Snaketime Rhythms," (SMC 2523) "Moondog's Theme" from "Moondog Symphony," (SMC 2526); "Wildwood" (SMC 2528) and "Organ Rounds" (SMC 2527). There are four oo solos (in 6/4, 2/4, 7/4), two trimba solos (5/4, 7/4; 5/8, 7/8), two more pieces with Ray Malone, one more set with Sam Ulano, four different drum compositions exclusive of those already mentioned, two piano solo improvisations, another Violetta rehearsal session (this time with a cocker spaniel, Nina, as auditor), three conversation-music amalgams, as well as several numbers from the Tony Schwartz archives (on Prestige 3, "A Duet" and "Tugboat Toccata").

As repositories for Moondog's evolving past these albums are treasures; as raw material for a catalogue raisonée of a decade's music they are invaluable. They contain some musically interesting numbers, too. An old invention is updated (the tuji, described on Epic as a row of dowels but on Prestige 3 more prosaically as "a series of mounted sticks of graduated lengths") and a new instrument, the last one for a decade, unveiled (the yukh, a "log suspended from a tripod—hit with two rubber mallets held in right hand"). On Prestige 2, "Autumn" is the most ambitious and intriguing new work, a round for brass, flute, and percussion, and, like "Theme," a development of a four-note signature, this time with the sound effects of nature that appealed to him then. He plays his trimba in one selection with ostrich feathers; he sings "All Is Loneliness," and the plaintive cries, dramatized by overdubbing, underscore the abiding sadness that generated this piece, perhaps his most famous statement, and made it authentic. The last selection, an extended "Moondog Monologue" of over eight minutes, is made up of aphorisms, madrigals and, for the first time on records, couplets, to a background of trimba and oo; in it his philosophy, or more accurately his opinions and ideas, are intermingled with his music. Moondog would always weave poetry and music afterward (on Columbia, in Germany), reciting couplets against the backdrop of, for instance, his parodic "Yankee Doodle Dixie," a genial, free-wheeling, open-ended vehicle for satire, Moondog loosening his tunic to rap.

Prestige 3 presents, in the opening selection, though not acknowledged as such, two of the four compositions he recorded with his "Honking Geese," here performed live on the corners they celebrate. In "Up Broadway," his "impression" of "Birdland" and "the Palladium" on "the great White Way," there is, first, a "dog trot" in 1/4, a jazz piece recorded on 52nd Street, the "Jazz Corner of the World," with Sam Ulano on drums; second, there is a "bumbo" in 4/4, performed on 53rd Street, the "Afro-Cuban Corner of the World," with Mary on yukh and maraca. In both works the sounds of Manhattan's streets are distinct. There are a few oddities. Moondog "gloves it" with "full" and "empty" fingers; he plays the tuji and then "skin" with ostrich feathers, in 5/8; he plays trimba with maraca and clave "exclusively." In "Two Quotations in Dialogue," he has what was probably intended to be an enigmatic exchange with his friends Louis and Bebe Barron, but this kind of thing ultimately fades in the light of his more serious efforts: "Q: What is the answer to the whole scheme of things, to know the answer, the answer, to know? A: The answer stands as kingdoms fall, there is no answer, none at all, none at all." Nearly the entire second side of Prestige 3 is either SMC reprises or Moondog on Moondog. The charming script on the cover is attributed to Andy Warhol's mother—you cannot make this kind of thing up—who had joined her son in New York to help him through the challenges that beset him at the outset of his career. The design, rearranged graphically by Andy Warhol, won an award from The American Institute of Graphic Arts in 1958.

All three Prestige albums have been reissued on two CDs with the original number code (7042 and 7069, a "double" which also includes 7099).

IN *TELL IT AGAIN* (1957), through "simple melodies and varied rhythms" Moondog's music tried "to recapture the wit and humor, charm and freshness" of the nursery rhymes by pleasing young ears with instruments (drum and flute) children tend to like. Many people have professed to admire this album, but it was neither a financial nor an artistic success. For one thing, there are more than forty different melodies, and the sheer number of pieces, each one only seconds long, fuses the sounds together in the listener's ear, creating a blurred impression of redundancy. (A similar problem occurs, some believe, in the *Moondog 2* album in 1971: the presentation of so many short rounds without change of form or pace does not set off the uniqueness of each one. The main difference is that in 1971 the quality of the individual madrigals was superior in every way to the songs of 1957.) This is one of the paradoxes Moondog and Julie Andrews must have tried unsuccessfully to solve. Unlike, say, a musical comedy, a narrative interspersed with music wherein each song has a dramatic setting, a sequence such as this, with little logic and no plot (despite the accompanying booklet) cannot avoid tedium.

The performances were fine, if uninspired at times, but on the structure (the material is divided into six categories, and between sets of songs some light banter between the two singers is interspersed) works only for a few minutes. Thus the first section, "Favorite Nursery Rhymes," is the most salutary: Bo Peep, Black Sheep, Pussy Cat, Jack 'n' Jill, Mary (both contrary and with lamb), Peter, Peter Pumpkin Eater, and friends are delicately framed. One highlight is the setting of three rhymes to the same music (Little Jack Horner by Martyn, Little Miss Muffet by Julie, and Hey Diddle Diddle by both). Suddenly, however, we are thrust into didactic songs before side one ends. Side two moves without transition from nonsense and puzzles into songs about animals and, finally, lullabies. The whole does not cohere; no part is brilliant. Moondog's music is occasional rather than resonant. Some of his work may be childlike, but it is not necessarily for children. Without the organic complexity of the canonic form, his melodies seem flat. Yes, children love repetition, learn by memorization, and revel in similitudes, but what child, even the most precocious musician, can suffer forty different rhymes freighted with exotic rhythms in a format that makes it difficult to select favorites? Unsurprisingly, this disappointing investment of great talents sat for two years unreleased.

Music of the Sixties

(the two Columbia albums)

The first selection in *Moondog* (1969) is "Theme": "*my* theme, a sort of musical signature." Recorded on the 1954 Epic album (mistakenly dated 1952 in the program notes), when Moondog himself played all the parts, it is here scored for maxisym and is still a marvelous, evocative piece, capturing a stately "haunting mood," a round of "primitive sophistication." It is a "cross between a chaconne and ground or a combination of the two" in 5/4, and a sixteen-year bridge to his earliest mature voice over much interference and noise. After a brief Moondog couplet interlude ("Machines were mice and men were lions once upon a time, / but now that it's the opposite it's twice upon a time"), "Stamping Ground" is next; although it too was written in the 1950s, it was never recorded, for want of a sufficient chorus. Inspired by the primitive Amerindian music he felt as much a part of his heritage as his other influences, it is nonetheless a sophisticated construct: the melodic line "*is* a canon," while the timpani take up "the four-note ground"; the coda ends in a "retard." *Symphonique # 3* ("Ode to Venus") was the second movement of the second orchestral suite on Epic. Fifteen years earlier this lush, slow movement lasted two and a half minutes; in 1969 it was close to six. The "Ode" is a twelve-part canon of "impressive contrapuntal texture, full of the joys and sorrows of love." It is Moondog's "implied" homage to Tchaikovsky's "None but the Lonely Heart" (the slow movement of

Symphony # 6, the *Pathetique*). The final selection on side one is "Symphonique # 6 (Good for Goodie)," a ground in "seventeen-part counterpoint": this piece is a richly textured, joy-filled three minutes in the "swing style" featuring the clarinet in its highest register, "up high like Benny plays." Its energy, delightful melodies, and variety of interpenetrating sounds celebrate the influences and credit the pupil.

Side two attempts even more daring heights. After a second (and last) couplet ("The only one who knows this ounce of words is just a token / Is he who has a tongue to tell but must remain unspoken") comes "Minisym # 1," first performed at the Village Theatre in the fall of 1967 (to a "standing ovation"), which has three "short movements, each with a middle section or trio," all in 4/4 time. The first ("jovial") and third ("vivacious") movements feature the bassoon, the second ("lyrical") the horn. "Lament 1 (Bird's Lament)" was written after he heard of the death of Charlie Parker (in 1955), one of the preeminent jazz musicians of his time.

> Bird used to stop by my doorway back in 1951-52 and talk about music. We even talked about doing a record together. One night I met him in Times Square and shook a shaking hand, not realizing that would be the last time we would meet.

The piece, only a third as long as the minisym (a bit under two minutes), is a "chaconne" with a "free melodic line over it" articulated by alto sax. (In 1966 and 1967 it was scored for strings.) Like "Good for Goodie," it is Moondog's jazz coming of age, alive and soulful as some of the work from the 1950s was not. The penultimate selection is "The Witch of Endor," at six and a half minutes the longest piece on the album. Originally conceived as part of an unperformed ballet for Martha Graham, it is, like "Thor," Moondog's program music. The first and third movements are witch's dances in 5/4, both seven-part canons in "a six-tone minor scale" that is a "feature of Asia Minor music" (like "Oasis" on Epic). They are more original than the middle movement, a trio, which depicts the struggle and death of King Saul. This music sounds more academic and derivative than the rest of the album, but not predictable or boring.

The last selection, "Symphonique # 1 (Portrait of a Monarch)," he first scored in 1960. It forms the album's finale and, as all good endings should, points ahead. The story of Thor the Nordoom was his first "soundsaga," a work with "music and sound effects, having elements of opera and play," and whose narrative is sustained in couplets. This is not only Wagner retooled; it is the earliest synthesis of what has evolved into a mammoth, multi-layered, cross-pollinating structure. From roots such as this, the poem *Thor*, finally printed in 1979, and *The Creation*, still "in progress" until his death, were nourished.

No longer was Moondog writing broadsides against the sins and abuses of modern economics. Their explanation lay behind and above the power-brokers of contemporary America, in what he would later call "poetic myth." Thor, personification of the power of the old over the new, is "Emperor of Earth," a mixture of god and man who rules absolutely and who "crushes all opposition to his will." He is "a fictitious person but nevertheless factual" (says the lover of paradoxes) who has "a monopoly on the world's gold supply," running the show "behind the scenes, by means of agents and double agents." The brief "Portrait of a Monarch" attempts to capture this imperious, absolute power, its "jocular side" as well as its "towering strength."

THE MUSIC OF *MOONDOG 2* (1971), all twenty-six bands, is among the finest that Moondog produced in America. The performances of the madrigals have their defenders and detractors. To the latter, the album is redundant in format, lacking in color, and amateurish, especially in light of the muddy vocals the listener finally hears; to the former, the purity of line and articulation more than compensates for any missing dynamics. The four-part rounds from the early 1950s are simpler but possibly more endearing than the more complex ones composed in a white heat during June 1968. Side one also has more fire and originality than side two, save the harp pastorale, but this might be due to the cumulative weight of repetition, going "around the world of sound by means of the round." Several old friends are here: "All Is Loneliness" (by now a signature), "Why Spend the Dark Night With You?" and "Be A Hobo" were on Epic; "Trees Against the Sky" appeared on Prestige 1; and "Voices of Spring," an occasional piece on Epic, is here a fully developed madrigal with a somewhat somber twist. Of those written in 1968, some of the most interesting are: "Bells Are Ringing," a five-part, joy-filled gem; "What's the Most Exciting Thing About Life?," the most complex (seven-part) and longest (two and a half minutes) and happiest of all, written after that car accident in Candor on June 6, 1968; the superb six-part "Nero's Expedition Up the Nile," whose sinuous rhythms capture the exotic mood and scene in less than two minutes; "You, the Vandal," with its feminine rhymes in ironic tension with its import; "Behold, the Willow" (a variation on a fable by La Fontaine) and "Sparrows Wake Me," two five-part works on related themes with long melodic lines and accompanying flute; and, finally, the haunting three-minute "Pastorale" for the troubadour harp, played by Gillian Stephens, for whom it was written. The other madrigals also offer surprises (the lilt of "Coffee Beans," the Oriental flavor of "My Tiny Butterfly," the popular song feel of "I Love You For Your Lovely Still Small Voice," the extended line of "Wine, Women and Song" supporting its suspended sense, the percussion retard in "Maybe," the effective repetition of the word "now" five times in "Each Today Is Yesterday's Tomorrow"). In the wake of its disappointing reception the album's real virtues seem to have been forgotten.

Both Columbia LPs have been reissued on one CD (44994).

Music in Germany

After Moondog died in 1999, some of his previously recorded performances were released. Of the dozen major releases of his music after he settled in Germany, 1977–2004, only that of the live performance in Sweden in 1981 (*Facets*) has any meaningful material from *The Creation*. He wrote an enormous amount of new music, but most of what is available is a recycling of old compositions, sometimes for new instruments, sometimes in different arrangements. On one level, this is hardly surprising: Moondog always blended the old with the new at his concerts. Also, because of the exigencies and expenses of producing live music, he had to make material available for small ensembles, and *The Creation*, as he envisioned it, can only be fully realized with a large orchestra willing to learn and play music that unfolds on a scale of hours or days in performance. Much of his music has never been performed, let alone recorded. Twelve albums in twenty-two years would be, even with the inevitable duplications, an output many composers would find adequate, but in Moondog's case, it barely touches the surface.

But what a surface it is! In little more than a year, four albums appeared: *Moondog in Europe* (Kopf, 1977), *H'Art Songs* (Kopf, 1978), *Moondog* (Musical Heritage Society, 1978), and *A New Sound of an Old Instrument* (Kopf, 1979). *Moondog in Europe* is important for several reasons, beyond being the first album he made outside the U.S. All but one of the Lögründr on side two, recorded on the organ in Herz Jesu Kirche in Oberhausen, were performed by the organist whom Moondog favored over all others during the next twenty-plus years, Fritz Storfinger. In addition, side one featured Moondog on percussion and a small ensemble playing two chaconnes, "Viking I," "Heimdall Fanfare," and several new pieces, including "In Vienna" and "Romance in G." *H'Art Songs* contains far more original material and may be considered the latest (as of 1978) stage of his unique brand of song. Moondog "shows us how it goes" on several delightful personal lyrics ("High on a Rocky Ledge," "I'm Just a Hop Head," "Here's to J.W.H."—the outlaw John Wesley Hardin who was, in imagination, if not in fact, "a relative of mine"—"I'm in the World," "Do Your Thing!" and "I'm This, I'm That") and a couple on animal rights ("Pigmy," "Enough about Human Rights," "Aska Me"). This is, like the second Columbia album, rich and entertaining, the "popular" side of Moondog. The reviewer David Keenan called these "avant-pop songs" among "the most idiosyncratic and spiritually rewarding bodies of work of the 20th century."

> The 10 superficially simplistic piano-led pop songs, with lyrics like diamond-sharp haiku, open out with each listen to reveal a musical aesthetic as melodically complex as Johann Sebastian Bach's.

The last album of Moondog's music released in the U.S. is the Musical Heritage Society's *Moondog: Instrumental Music by Louis Hardin*. Side two is identical to that of *Moondog in Europe*, with Lögründr performed on the organ by Fritz Storfinger, in a different order. Side one repeats several tracks from the earlier German album also, but adds harpsichord compositions played by Gavin Black, who was instrumental in seeing the project through: three canons and one round. Finally from this period, *A New Sound for an Old Instrument* offers thirteen organ pieces, many performed for the first time on "the king of instruments" by Mr. Storfinger. On the liner notes, Moondog avers that "an organ can do anything a jazz band can do, as good, if not better" and he accompanies the pieces on percussion to underscore the possibilities. Gavin Martin (*Uncut*, March 2000) calls the pieces "improvisations," which Moondog would never permit, however "wonderfully delicate" or "sprung with surprise and mischief" they might be. There are four Lögründr and some old favorites transcribed for a new instrument: "Oasis," "Single Foot," "Frost Flower," "Elf Dance."

Facets (Managarm, 1981), now very difficult to get, contains more selections from *The Creation* than any other collection yet released. Although the performances seem muddy and uninspired (in part because the nineteen students from the Music Conservatory in Stockholm are not well served by the tape, which barely manages to capture the allure of Moondog's huge designs), one can get a sense of where the "mammoth melody" was heading. The titles themselves inspire wonder: "Ginnungagap" (creation), "Gjallarhorn," "Black Hole," "Viking I," "Yggdrasil" (the tree of life), two "Lure" fanfares, "Magic Ring," "Sleipnir" (Odin's eight-legged horse), "The Procession of the Aesir" (the superior race of gods led by Odin). The organ pieces, recorded earlier in the church Moondog loved, better serve the composer, although only a symphony orchestra can do this music justice.

Bracelli (Kakaphone, 1986) is another half-hearted venture. The subtitle is "Moondog Conducts Flaskkvartetten," but the recording session, according to eyewitnesses, was not as controlled as the composer would have wished because the quartet was too "unconventional" for his music. One reviewer (Dean Suzuki, *Goldmine*, April 19, 1991) praised it:

> This one contains music which is dark, brooding, somber and evocative, as one might expect from the lower members of the string family. As always, the music is lovely (in fact, stunningly beautiful at times), quaint, but with that extra intangible something that makes Moondog so special.

But the album has all but disappeared.

Elpmas (Kopf, 1992) was the strangest of his German productions and in many ways the most like his earliest New York albums. That it was recorded at Andi Toma's studio called the Academy of St. Martin's in the Streets hints of old tricks up new sleeves. Moondog, like many composers who have made their livings through music since the days of the early baroque, recycled his pieces inventively. *Elpmas* "feels" like the Prestige albums, for instance, even though the music is dramatically different: unusual instrumentation, defiantly eccentric use of the human voice, theory mixed with complex musical forms, words with sound. There is the grand (twenty-four minutes of "Cosmic Meditation") and the small (the one-minute "Message"), the melodically alluring and the slowly evolving. For those who enjoy the eclectic, it is a bonanza; for those who awaited Moondog's latest phase, it was grist for the mill; but for those who were hoping to see the unified vision given full expression, it sent confused messages: too many directions, too many causes, too many disparate facets of a still unpolished jewel. *Elpmas* is as daunting as the man who composed it, like *The Overtone Tree* a little too much over the edge perhaps.

Big Band (Trimba, 1995) and *Sax Pax* (Atlantic, 1997) are the triumphs of his English period. Although *Sax Pax* was widely reviewed and praised, in part because of its wider release on a substantial label, in part because the sound is far better, it is unlike previous Moondog albums, because it is more of a piece.

Big Band, on the other hand, was much wider in scope and included more of the variety listeners had come to expect from him. The pieces for the London Saxophonic are quite different from those played by the London Brass, especially those newly written, "A Sax" and "Reedroy," which are more clearly the kind of "life-affirming music" one reviewer (Ed Pinsent) identifies as a Moondog trademark, with its "syncopated rhythms, a steady bass drum pulse...and water-tight charts for the horns." Solos by Gareth Brady ("You Have to Have Hope") and John Harle ("Reedroy," named for his soprano sax) are lovely, and the big brass compositions, drawn from Moondog's ongoing Nordic sound saga, are powerful, if at times muddy.

Old and newer favorites return: "Shakespeare City" (three times longer than the version on *Sax Pax*), "New York," "Paris," "Bumbo." A highlight of the CD is the resonant and intense "Cosmicode," "Black Hole," and "Invocation." Despite Moondog's program notes, which may or may not be taken with a grain of salt, the pieces live without program and draw you in without a supra-musical context. The unforgettable "Invocation," a triple canon on a single tone, played synchronously by sixteen horns ranging from cornet to flugel-horn to bass trumpet to euphonium (one of Moondog's favorites from childhood) to bass trombone, is what *The Creation* might sound like in miniature.

Sax Pax features the nine-member London Saxophonic, three percussionists besides Moondog, Danny Thompson on contra bass, three pianists, and assorted voices. Many of the compositions are old favorites, including two lovely piano solos: "Sea Horse" (the Moon-dog piece that most clearly anticipates Philip Glass) and "Fiesta." The mix of older, jazzier favorites ("Dog Trot," "Bird's Lament," "Single Foot") with newer, more serious works (such as the three-movement EEC Suite) has mixed results. For some, the "jauntiest jams sound like a nostalgic big band on laughing gas" (David D. Duncan). For others, "too much of one thing overpowers the listener, despite the considerable charm of individual pieces," because "each piece needs to stand alone; they are smothered by their context in proximity" (holeintheweb.com). Moreover, anachronistically if not ironically, Moondog can be seen as "new age," a "kind of garbage category" which does not serve him well (Kurt Keefner). As usual, though, many were charmed, if not by the old Moondog, then by the new one, composer of "Present for the Prez," a homage to Lester Young that answers "Bird's Lament" thirty years later, or "D for Danny," in honor of Danny Thompson. For them, the Moondog magic is in his unique synthesis, "equal parts Philip Glass and Paul McCartney." (Moondog preceded both composers, as both acknowledged.) That reviewer could not remember "the last time I heard something so utterly alien and familiar at the same time" (Ian Koss). Moondog's canons, "when played on multiple saxophones," seem more intimate and idiosyncratic and less like orchestral Romanticism" (Kurt Keefner). The "EEC Suite" is probably the least satisfying music on *Sax Pax* because it sounds precisely like recorded "classical" music and not like the unclassifiable rebel that his fans most admire.

Four albums appeared between 2004 and 2006, two in recognition of the fifth anniversary of his death, and on one we hear him for the last time at a live performance.

Moondog: The German Years, 1977–1999 (2004, Roof) is a most elaborate package of Moondog music, two CDs, one a composite of tracks from several Kopf/Roof albums over the years, and the second a recording of the last performance before his death.

Old favorites and newer creations are on disc one, with Fritz Storfinger's interpretations on organ and the big band numbers occupying roughly equal space with retellings of pieces such as "Bird's Lament," "Single Foot," and "Dog Trot." Disc two is also heterogeneous, but in a far narrower way: it is most noteworthy because the performance was the last time that Dominique Ponty played his piano music with the sensitivity and attention to detail he so admired. She ably interprets selections from *The Art of the Canon* and *Jazz Book* as well as "Mood Montreux," which she had first performed three years earlier, with Moondog on drums. The music is interspersed with his rendition of couplets.

Moondog: Rare Material (2006, Roof) is another two-CD collection. The first is a reissue of the 1995 *Big Band* album and the second yet another career overview, ranging from the SMC 78s from the late Forties to a version of a Swiss Guggisberglied first performed in 1989. These ambitious projects, with full and interesting liner notes, are probably the best place to begin if you are new to Moondog, because the pieces range in time over fifty years and cover most of the kinds of instrumentation he composed for, from piano and organ to string quartet and brass ensemble.

One can probably say the same for the thirty-six selections drawn from his entire career on *Moondog* (Honest Jons, 2005), a provocative undertaking replete with a six-page fold-out that includes pictures ranging over sixty years: these are original recordings, culled from the vast resources of his American and German albums, but with no attempt to guide the listener through the music. Thus, one would have to be conversant with the history behind each part in order to appreciate the sum of the whole, but if you know Moondog, this is another tidy package for the one-stop shopper. The disc cover even reproduces the LP design of the Snaketime Series *Moondog*, which is identical to Prestige 1: a real collector's item.

Bracelli (2004, Laska), had Moondog lived to hear it, would have afforded him the greatest satisfaction. With Stefan Lakatos recreating Moondog's distinctive rhythms on the trimba, not only as background percussion but also in the stirring "Snaketime Improvisation," the polished performances of the Ensemble Bracelli capture the dark magic of this musical idea. The two violas, two cellos, and one contrabass created for Moondog an ideal way to write canons for a string ensemble, since the viola and cello are one octave apart. On the liner notes to the 1986 album, there was this:

> The music in this collection constitutes a series of tonal pictures with tempo variations from 5/8 to 7/2. Although some of the melodies and some of the tempi are immediately congenial, their full flavour comes out on repeated listenings. This is complex music, with a sophistication that belies its seeming simplicity.

Hearing "Dark Eyes," "Gygg," and "Rabbit Hop," for instance, in this rendition, with the canonic nature of the pieces so clearly realized and the trimbas reproduced with such startling clarity, is a revelation of a new kind, because a transformation has occurred: if Moondog's music is to endure, it will be because it travels so far and ages so well.

SINCE IT WILL BE A LONG TIME before Moondog's work can be fully evaluated, in large part because much of it still awaits performance, I leave the reader with the biggest challenge the connoisseur faces when trying to do justice to so variegated a career. Upon that hearing his reputation may ultimately rest. For all the reasons discussed in the chapters covering Moondog's long apprenticeship, it is clear that he started composing in small units—canons and rounds and madrigals—out of both physical necessity and artistic philosophy. Philip Glass indicated that he considered himself in the "maverick" tradition of American composers, from Ives to Moondog, and we know that the Moondog he first knew worked primarily in miniature. As recently as 2005, in the exhibition "Contemporary Voices" at the Museum of Modern Art in New York City, Chuck Close showed among other works several "musical portraits" of Mr. Glass. In a review of the exhibition in the *New York Times* (April 22, 2005) Charles McGrath quotes Mr. Close discussing his commonality with his friend: they "were all working on the relationship of the parts to the whole and within a very severe set of restrictions." This "kind of minimalism" (a term neither liked) involved working with "very small elements...discrete bits of information that are repeated and carefully varied to create a whole." Then Philip Glass is quoted:

> If you look at some of Chuck's paintings, they're modules that are put together and shaded with different values....And I've used that idea with modular music also. But there's another aspect of it which is perhaps more important, which is that his work is really about creating art out of an exhaustive and detailed process, so that the entirety of the work is a reflection of the integrity of the process. And he wasn't the only one doing that.

I think Moondog would agree with Mr. Glass and argue convincingly that he was one of those doing that, and maybe even one of the first. Until we hear the longer and more elaborate Moondog compositions, however, he might still be classified as one of the "minimalists." When his sound sagas get their moments of exposure, we will be able to assess whether he did what he said he wanted to do: to realize in the small the immense and the profound.

Moondog Perpetual Calendar

This perpetual calendar begins with 44 B.C. and ends with 3200 A.D., though I could have taken it as far into the future as you care to imagine.

The Julian Calendar begins with 44 B.C. and ends with October 4, 1582. The Gregorian Calendar begins October 5, 1582 and on, into the future. See calendar in your encyclopedia.

Of what use is such a calendar? If you know the year and the day of the month of an event, and you wish to know the day of the week, this calendar will give it.

Since there are only seven days in a week, then there are only seven kinds of years which apply to non-leap years. See page 4, the Seven Years. Also, and for the same reason, there are only seven kinds of years for leap years; see page 5, the Seven Leap Years.

Each of the seven years has a number, from one to seven; notice that these numbers are not underlined; this means that these unmarked numbers refer to non-leap years. Compare these numbers with those of the seven leap years, each of which is underlined. In each of these 14 years, the twelve months are stacked on top of each other for compactness, in the interest of saving space. Because of this, often one month will end on the same line that a new month begins. Each calendar has seven columns, one for each day of the week, headed with the initials of the days of the week. To the left of each calendar are the initials of the twelve months, on the line where each month begins.

The Julian Calendar is on page 1 and 2. The Gregorian Calendar is on page 7 and 8. If page 1 and 2 were side by side, instead of back to back, you would see 28 columns of years, indicating a 28-year cycle. The boxed numbers at the very top are your year and leap year numbers.

Notice that in the Julian Calendar, the numbers are in solid rows, without a break, but that in the Gregorian Calendar there are repeated gaps throughout. This will be explained when you read about the calendar in the encyclopedia.

I worked this whole thing out during a period of two weeks back in the summer of 1958.

As usual, as regards the calendars, Julian and Gregorian, Caesar and Gregory are given credit, or at least, implied credit for this accomplishment, with little, if any mention of the mathematicians who made it all possible. If "hath" applies to such accomplishment, and "it" applies to the recognition of it, then the biblical quote should read, "To him who hath, it shall be taken away, and to him who hath not, it shall be added."

With this calendar you will never need another, for this year, 1972, is a leap year, number 7, underlined. Next year will be the next year number, etc.

The first day of the week you should find is the day on which you receive your calendar. Let us pretend that you received it on January 1, 1972. Find the year, 1972 in the Gregorian Calendar. Stay on the column and go up it until you find the leap year number which is boxed. Notice that the number 7 is underlined. This means that it is a leap year.

Next, find the same underlined 7 under the heading, "The Seven Leap Years," page 5. Now find the initial, J, for January, the first initial to the left of the numbers. From the J, look to the right until you find a number. It will be 1, under the initial S, for Saturday. Now check Saturday with January 1 of your wall calendar. It is Saturday also. This proves to you that the calendar is right. Next, try your birthday; then check the result with your birth certificate, hoping that it has the day of the week on it and not just the day of the month. But by this time, you will be sure that this calendar is right, even if the certificate does not give the day of the week.

Now let us find the birthday of George Washington. We are told it was February 22, 1732, another leap year. Do the same thing you did before and you will find that it was on Friday. But England did not go over to the Gregorian style until 1752, so that Washington's birthday was actually February 11, and when the new style was adopted, eleven lost days were added on to the eleventh, making it 22.

Now let us take a date under the Julian style. Magna Carte was signed on June 15, 1215, a non-leap year. The day of the week was... Don't look. Find it for yourself and then look. It was on a Monday.

Anyone and everyone will have a use for this calendar, all the way from Aunt Mildred to the most learned historian. With her it will be used in looking up family dates; with him, to give an historic day of the month an added coloring by giving the day of the week as well, the implications of the weekday. Have fun with it, and don't lose it.

— Moondog.

Julian Calendar
44 B.C. - 1581 A.D.

2	3	4	5	7	1	2	3	5	6	7	1	3	4
32	31	30	29	28	27	26	25	24	23	22	21	20	19
4	3	2	1	1	2	3	4	5	6	7	8	9	10
25	26	27	28	29	30	31	32	33	34	35	36	37	38
53	54	55	56	57	58	59	60	61	62	63	64	65	66
81	82	83	84	85	86	87	88	89	90	91	92	93	94
109	110	111	112	113	114	115	116	117	118	119	120	121	122
137	138	139	140	141	142	143	144	145	146	147	148	149	150
165	166	167	168	169	170	171	172	173	174	175	176	177	178
193	194	195	196	197	198	199	200	201	202	203	204	205	206
221	222	223	224	225	226	227	228	229	230	231	232	233	234
249	250	251	252	253	254	255	256	257	258	259	260	261	262
277	278	279	280	281	282	283	284	285	286	287	288	289	290
305	306	307	308	309	310	311	312	313	314	315	316	317	318
333	334	335	336	337	338	339	340	341	342	343	344	345	346
361	362	363	364	365	366	367	368	369	370	371	372	373	374
389	390	391	392	393	394	395	396	397	398	399	400	401	402
417	418	419	420	421	422	423	424	425	426	427	428	429	430
445	446	447	448	449	450	451	452	453	454	455	456	457	458
473	474	475	476	477	478	479	480	481	482	483	484	485	486
501	502	503	504	505	506	507	508	509	510	511	512	513	514
529	530	531	532	533	534	535	536	537	538	539	540	541	542
557	558	559	560	561	562	563	564	565	566	567	568	569	570
585	586	587	588	589	590	591	592	593	594	595	596	597	598
613	614	615	616	617	618	619	620	621	622	623	624	625	626
641	642	643	644	645	646	647	648	649	650	651	652	653	654
669	670	671	672	673	674	675	676	677	678	679	680	681	682
697	698	699	700	701	702	703	704	705	706	707	708	709	710
725	726	727	728	729	730	731	732	733	734	735	736	737	738
753	754	755	756	757	758	759	760	761	762	763	764	765	766
781	782	783	784	785	786	787	788	789	790	791	792	793	794
809	810	811	812	813	814	815	816	817	818	819	820	821	822
837	838	839	840	841	842	843	844	845	846	847	848	849	850
865	866	867	868	869	870	871	872	873	874	875	876	877	878
893	894	895	896	897	898	899	900	901	902	903	904	905	906
921	922	923	924	925	926	927	928	929	930	931	932	933	934
949	950	951	952	953	954	955	956	957	958	959	960	961	962
977	978	979	980	981	982	983	984	985	986	987	988	989	990
1005	1006	1007	1008	1009	1010	1011	1012	1013	1014	1015	1016	1017	1018
1033	1034	1035	1036	1037	1038	1039	1040	1041	1042	1043	1044	1045	1046
1061	1062	1063	1064	1065	1066	1067	1068	1069	1070	1071	1072	1073	1074
1089	1090	1091	1092	1093	1094	1095	1096	1097	1098	1099	1100	1101	1102
1117	1118	1119	1120	1121	1122	1123	1124	1125	1126	1127	1128	1129	1130
1145	1146	1147	1148	1149	1150	1151	1152	1153	1154	1155	1156	1157	1158
1173	1174	1175	1176	1177	1178	1179	1180	1181	1182	1183	1184	1185	1186
1201	1202	1203	1204	1205	1206	1207	1208	1209	1210	1211	1212	1213	1214
1229	1230	1231	1232	1233	1234	1235	1236	1237	1238	1239	1240	1241	1242
1257	1258	1259	1260	1261	1262	1263	1264	1265	1266	1267	1268	1269	1270
1285	1286	1287	1288	1289	1290	1291	1292	1293	1294	1295	1296	1297	1298
1313	1314	1315	1316	1317	1318	1319	1320	1321	1322	1323	1324	1325	1326
1341	1342	1343	1344	1345	1346	1347	1348	1349	1350	1351	1352	1353	1354
1369	1370	1371	1372	1373	1374	1375	1376	1377	1378	1379	1380	1381	1382
1397	1398	1399	1400	1401	1402	1403	1404	1405	1406	1407	1408	1409	1410
1425	1426	1427	1428	1429	1430	1431	1432	1433	1434	1435	1436	1437	1438
1453	1454	1455	1456	1457	1458	1459	1460	1461	1462	1463	1464	1465	1466
1481	1482	1483	1484	1485	1486	1487	1488	1489	1490	1491	1492	1493	1494
1509	1510	1511	1512	1513	1514	1515	1516	1517	1518	1519	1520	1521	1522
1537	1538	1539	1540	1541	1542	1543	1544	1545	1546	1547	1548	1549	1550
1565	1566	1567	1568	1569	1570	1571	1572	1573	1574	1575	1576	1577	1578

2

Julian Calendar Continued

Note

1582 is divided between Year 2 and Year 6. Year 2 is used through
October, 4th and Year 6 from October, 15th. If any one of the ten deducted
days is desired (October, 5th—October, 14th), use Year 2.

5	6	1	2	3	4	6	7	1	2	4	5	6	7
		44	43	42	41	40	39	38	37	36	35	34	33
18	17	16	15	14	13	12	11	10	9	8	7	6	5
11	12	13	14	15	16	17	18	19	20	21	22	23	24
39	40	41	42	43	44	45	46	47	48	49	50	51	52
67	68	69	70	71	72	73	74	75	76	77	78	79	80
95	96	97	98	99	100	101	102	103	104	105	106	107	108
123	124	125	126	127	128	129	130	131	132	133	134	135	136
151	152	153	154	155	156	157	158	159	160	161	162	163	164
179	180	181	182	183	184	185	186	187	188	189	190	191	192
207	208	209	210	211	212	213	214	215	216	217	218	219	220
235	236	237	238	239	240	241	242	243	244	245	246	247	248
263	264	265	266	267	268	269	270	271	272	273	274	275	276
291	292	293	294	295	296	297	298	299	300	301	302	303	304
319	320	321	322	323	324	325	326	327	328	329	330	331	332
347	348	349	350	351	352	353	354	355	356	357	358	359	360
375	376	377	378	379	380	381	382	383	384	385	386	387	388
403	404	405	406	407	408	409	410	411	412	413	414	415	416
431	432	433	434	435	436	437	438	439	440	441	442	443	444
459	460	461	462	463	464	465	466	467	468	469	470	471	472
487	488	489	490	491	492	493	494	495	496	497	498	499	500
515	516	517	518	519	520	521	522	523	524	525	526	527	528
543	544	545	546	547	548	549	550	551	552	553	554	555	556
571	572	573	574	575	576	577	578	579	580	581	582	583	584
599	600	601	602	603	604	605	606	607	608	609	610	611	612
627	628	629	630	631	632	633	634	635	636	637	638	639	640
655	656	657	658	659	660	661	662	663	664	665	666	667	668
683	684	685	686	687	688	689	690	691	692	693	694	695	696
711	712	713	714	715	716	717	718	719	720	721	722	723	724
739	740	741	742	743	744	745	746	747	748	749	750	751	752
767	768	769	770	771	772	773	774	775	776	777	778	779	780
795	796	797	798	799	800	801	802	803	804	805	806	807	808
823	824	825	826	827	828	829	830	831	832	833	834	835	836
851	852	853	854	855	856	857	858	859	860	861	862	863	864
879	880	881	882	883	884	885	886	887	888	889	890	891	892
907	908	909	910	911	912	913	914	915	916	917	918	919	920
935	936	937	938	939	940	941	942	943	944	945	946	947	948
963	964	965	966	967	968	969	970	971	972	973	974	975	976
991	992	993	994	995	996	997	998	999	1000	1001	1002	1003	1004
1019	1020	1021	1022	1023	1024	1025	1026	1027	1028	1029	1030	1031	1032
1047	1048	1049	1050	1051	1052	1053	1054	1055	1056	1057	1058	1059	1060
1075	1076	1077	1078	1079	1080	1081	1082	1083	1084	1085	1086	1087	1088
1103	1104	1105	1106	1107	1108	1109	1110	1111	1112	1113	1114	1115	1116
1131	1132	1133	1134	1135	1136	1137	1138	1139	1140	1141	1142	1143	1144
1159	1160	1161	1162	1163	1164	1165	1166	1167	1168	1169	1170	1171	1172
1187	1188	1189	1190	1191	1192	1193	1194	1195	1196	1197	1198	1199	1200
1215	1216	1217	1218	1219	1220	1221	1222	1223	1224	1225	1226	1227	1228
1243	1244	1245	1246	1247	1248	1249	1250	1251	1252	1253	1254	1255	1256
1271	1272	1273	1274	1275	1276	1277	1278	1279	1280	1281	1282	1283	1284
1299	1300	1301	1302	1303	1304	1305	1306	1307	1308	1309	1310	1311	1312
1327	1328	1329	1330	1331	1332	1333	1334	1335	1336	1337	1338	1339	1340
1355	1356	1357	1358	1359	1360	1361	1362	1363	1364	1365	1366	1367	1368
1383	1384	1385	1386	1387	1388	1389	1390	1391	1392	1393	1394	1395	1396
1411	1412	1413	1414	1415	1416	1417	1418	1419	1420	1421	1422	1423	1424
1439	1440	1441	1442	1443	1444	1445	1446	1447	1448	1449	1450	1451	1452
1467	1468	1469	1470	1471	1472	1473	1474	1475	1476	1477	1478	1479	1480
1495	1496	1497	1498	1499	1500	1501	1502	1503	1504	1505	1506	1507	1508
1523	1524	1525	1526	1527	1528	1529	1530	1531	1532	1533	1534	1535	1536
1551	1552	1553	1554	1555	1556	1557	1558	1559	1560	1561	1562	1563	1564
1579	1580	1581											

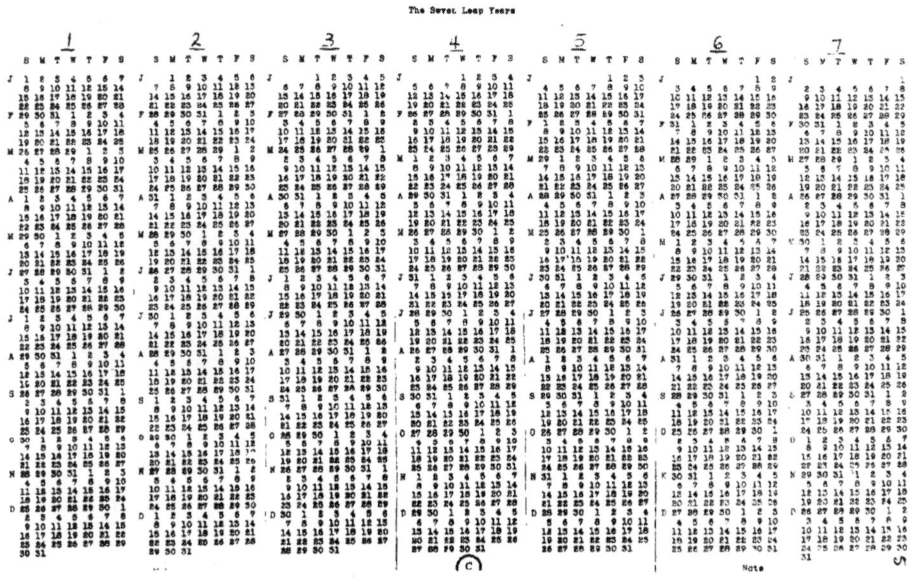

The Seven Leap Years

| 1 | 2 | 3 | 4 | 5 | 6 | 7 |

(calendar tables)

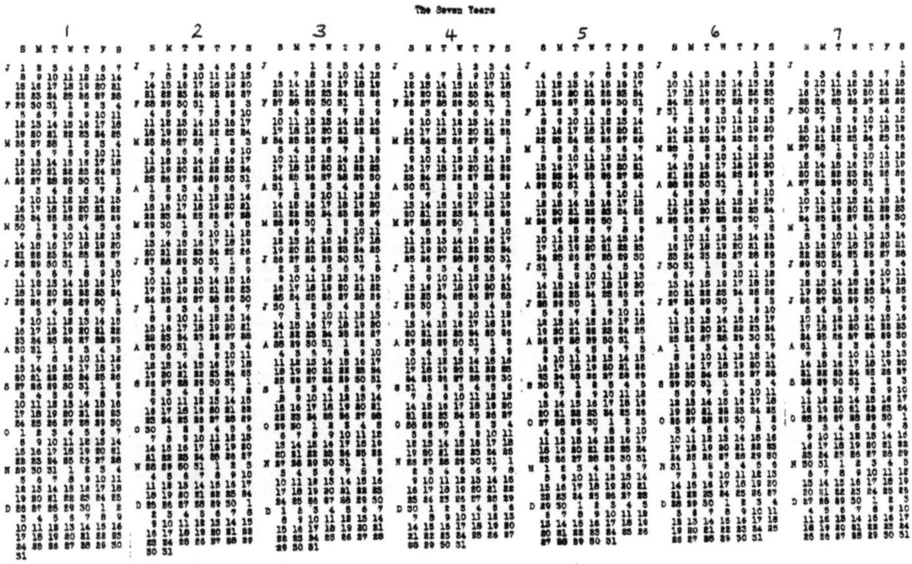

The Seven Years

| 1 | 2 | 3 | 4 | 5 | 6 | 7 |

(calendar tables)

306 / MOONDOG: The Viking Of 6th Avenue

Gregorian calendar
1583 - 3250 A.D.

2	3	4	5	7	1	2	3	5	6	7	1	3	4
										1583	1584	1585	1586
1601	1602	1603	1604	1605	1606	1607	1608	1609	1610	1611	1612	1613	1614
1629	1630	1631	1632	1633	1634	1635	1636	1637	1638	1639	1640	1641	1642
1657	1658	1659	1660	1661	1662	1663	1664	1665	1666	1667	1668	1669	1670
1685	1686	1687	1688	1689	1690	1691	1692	1693	1694	1695	1696	1697	1698
				1701	1702	1703	1704	1705	1706	1707	1708	1709	1710
1725	1726	1727	1728	1729	1730	1731	1732	1733	1734	1735	1736	1737	1738
1753	1754	1755	1756	1757	1758	1759	1760	1761	1762	1763	1764	1765	1766
1781	1782	1783	1784	1785	1786	1787	1788	1789	1790	1791	1792	1793	1794
								1801	1802	1803	1804	1805	1806
1821	1822	1823	1824	1825	1826	1827	1828	1829	1830	1831	1832	1833	1834
1849	1850	1851	1852	1853	1854	1855	1856	1857	1858	1859	1860	1861	1862
1877	1878	1879	1880	1881	1882	1883	1884	1885	1886	1887	1888	1889	1890
1900												1901	1902
1917	1918	1919	1920	1921	1922	1923	1924	1925	1926	1927	1928	1929	1930
1945	1946	1947	1948	1949	1950	1951	1952	1953	1954	1955	1956	1957	1958
1973	1974	1975	1976	1977	1978	1979	1980	1981	1982	1983	1984	1985	1986
2001	2002	2003	2004	2005	2006	2007	2008	2009	2010	2011	2012	2013	2014
2029	2030	2031	2032	2033	2034	2035	2036	2037	2038	2039	2040	2041	2042
2057	2058	2059	2060	2061	2062	2063	2064	2065	2066	2067	2068	2069	2070
2085	2086	2087	2088	2089	2090	2091	2092	2093	2094	2095	2096	2097	2098
				2101	2102	2103	2104	2105	2106	2107	2108	2109	2110
2125	2126	2127	2128	2129	2130	2131	2132	2133	2134	2135	2136	2137	2138
2153	2154	2155	2156	2157	2158	2159	2160	2161	2162	2163	2164	2165	2166
2181	2182	2183	2184	2185	2186	2187	2188	2189	2190	2191	2192	2193	3194
								2201	2202	2203	2204	2205	2206
2221	2222	2223	2224	2225	2226	2227	2228	2229	2230	2231	2232	2233	2234
2249	2250	2251	2252	2253	2254	2255	2256	2257	2258	2259	2260	2261	2262
2277	2278	2279	2280	2281	2282	2283	2284	2285	2286	2287	2288	2289	2290
2300												2301	2302
2317	2318	2319	2320	2321	2322	2323	2324	2325	2326	2327	2328	2329	2330
2345	2346	2347	2348	2349	2350	2351	2352	2353	2354	2355	2356	2357	2358
2373	2374	2375	2376	2377	2378	2379	2380	2381	2382	2383	2384	2385	2386
2401	2402	2403	2404	2405	2406	2407	2408	2409	2410	2411	2412	2413	2414
2429	2430	2431	2432	2433	2434	2435	2436	2437	2438	2439	2440	2441	2442
2457	2458	2459	2460	2461	2462	2463	2464	2465	2466	2467	2468	2469	2470
2485	2486	2487	2488	2489	2490	2491	2492	2493	2494	2495	2496	2497	2498
				2501	2502	2503	2504	2505	2506	2507	2508	2509	2510
2525	2526	2527	2528	2529	2530	2531	2532	2533	2534	2535	2536	2537	2538
2553	2554	2555	2556	2557	2558	2559	2560	2561	2562	2563	2564	2565	2566
2581	2582	2583	2584	2585	2586	2587	2588	2589	2590	2591	2592	2593	2594
								2601	2602	2603	2604	2605	2606
2621	2622	2623	2624	2625	2626	2627	2628	2629	2630	2631	2632	2633	2634
2649	2650	2651	2652	2653	2654	2655	2656	2657	2658	2659	2660	2661	2662
2677	2678	2679	2680	2681	2682	2683	2684	2685	2686	2687	2688	2689	2690
2700												2701	2702
2717	2718	2719	2720	2721	2722	2723	2724	2725	2726	2727	2728	2729	2730
2745	2746	2747	2748	2749	2750	2751	2752	2753	2754	2755	2756	2757	2758
2773	2774	2775	2776	2777	2778	2779	2780	2781	2782	2783	2784	2785	2786
2801	2802	2803	2804	2805	2806	2807	2808	2809	2810	2811	2812	2813	2814
2829	2830	2831	2832	2833	2834	2835	2836	2837	2838	2839	2840	2841	2842
2857	2858	2859	2860	2861	2862	2863	2864	2865	2866	2867	2868	2869	2870
2885	2886	2887	2888	2889	2890	2891	2892	2893	2894	2895	2896	2897	2898
				2901	2902	2903	2904	2905	2906	2907	2908	2909	2910
2925	2926	2927	2928	2929	2930	2931	2932	2933	2934	2935	2936	2937	2938
2953	2954	2955	2956	2957	2958	2959	2960	2961	2962	2963	2964	2965	2966
2981	2982	2983	2984	2985	2986	2987	2988	2989	2990	2991	2992	2993	2994
								3001	3002	3003	3004	3005	3006
3021	3022	3023	3024	3025	3026	3027	3028	3029	3030	3031	3032	3033	3034
3049	3050	3051	3052	3053	3054	3055	3056	3057	3058	3059	3060	3061	3062
3077	3078	3079	3080	3081	3082	3083	3084	3085	3086	3087	3088	8089	3090
3100												3101	3102
3117	3118	3119	3120	3121	3122	3123	3124	3125	3126	3127	3128	3129	3130
3145	3146	3147	3148	3149	3150	3151	3152	3153	3154	3155	3156	3157	3158
3173	3174	3175	3176	3177	3178	3179	3180	3181	3182	3183	3184	3185	3186

8

Gregorian Calendar Continued

5	6	1	2	3	4	6	7	1	2	4	5	6	7
1587	1588	1589	1590	1591	1592	1593	1594	1595	1596	1597	1598	1599	1600
1615	1616	1617	1618	1619	1620	1621	1622	1623	1624	1625	1626	1617	1628
1643	1644	1645	1646	1647	1648	1649	1650	1651	1652	1653	1654	1655	1656
1671	1672	1673	1674	1675	1676	1677	1678	1679	1680	1681	1682	1683	1684
1699						1700							
1711	1712	1713	1714	1715	1716	1717	1718	1719	1720	1721	1722	1723	1724
1739	1740	1741	1742	1743	1744	1745	1746	1747	1748	1749	1750	1751	1752
1767	1768	1769	1770	1771	1772	1773	1774	1775	1776	1777	1778	1779	1780
1795	1796	1797	1798	1799						1800			
1807	1808	1809	1810	1811	1812	1813	1814	1815	1816	1817	1818	1819	1820
1835	1836	1837	1838	1839	1840	1841	1842	1843	1844	1845	1846	1847	1848
1863	1864	1865	1866	1867	1868	1869	1870	1871	1872	1873	1874	1875	1876
1891	1892	1893	1894	1895	1896	1897	1898	1899					
1903	1904	1905	1906	1907	1908	1909	1910	1911	1912	1913	1914	1915	1916
1931	1932	1933	1934	1935	1936	1937	1938	1939	1940	1941	1942	1943	1944
1959	1960	1961	1962	1963	1964	1965	1966	1967	1968	1969	1970	1971	1972
1987	1988	1989	1990	1991	1992	1993	1994	1995	1996	1997	1998	1999	2000
2015	2016	2017	2018	2019	2020	2021	2022	2023	2024	2025	2026	2027	2028
2043	2044	2045	2046	2047	2048	2049	2050	2051	2052	2053	2054	2055	2056
2071	2072	2073	2074	2075	2076	2077	2078	2079	2080	2081	2082	2083	2084
2099						2100							
2111	2112	2113	2114	2115	2116	2117	2118	2119	2120	2121	2122	2123	2124
2139	2140	2141	2142	2143	2144	2145	2146	2147	2148	2149	2150	2151	2152
2167	2168	2169	2170	2171	2172	2173	2174	2175	2176	2177	2178	2179	2180
2195	2196	2197	2198	2199						2200			
2207	2208	2209	2210	2211	2212	2213	2214	2215	2216	2217	2218	2219	2220
2235	2236	2237	2238	2239	2240	2241	2242	2243	2244	2245	2246	2247	2248
2263	2264	2265	2266	2267	2268	2269	2270	2271	2272	2273	2274	2275	2276
2291	2292	2293	2294	2295	2296	2297	2298	2299					
2303	2304	2305	2306	2307	2308	2309	2310	2311	2312	2313	2314	2315	2316
2331	2332	2333	2334	2335	2336	2337	2338	2339	2340	2341	2342	2343	2344
2359	2360	2361	2362	2363	2364	2365	2366	2367	2368	2369	2370	2371	2372
2387	2388	2389	2390	2391	2392	2393	2394	2395	2396	2397	2398	2399	2400
2415	2416	2417	2418	2419	2420	2421	2422	2423	2424	2425	2426	2427	2428
2443	2444	2445	2446	2447	2448	2449	2450	2451	2452	2453	2454	2455	2456
2471	2472	2473	2474	2475	2476	2477	2478	2479	2480	2481	2482	2483	2484
2499						2500							
2511	2512	2513	2514	2515	2516	2517	2518	2519	2520	2521	2522	2523	2524
2539	2540	2541	2542	2543	2544	2545	2546	2547	2548	2549	2550	2551	2552
2567	2568	2569	2570	2571	2572	2573	2574	2575	2576	2577	2578	2579	2580
2595	2596	2597	2598	2599						2600			
2607	2608	2609	2610	2611	2612	2613	2614	2615	2616	2617	2618	2619	2620
2635	2636	2637	2638	2639	2640	2641	2642	2643	2644	2645	2646	2647	2648
2663	2664	2665	2666	2667	2668	2669	2670	2671	2672	2673	2674	2675	2676
2691	2692	2693	2694	2695	2696	2697	2698	2699					
2703	2704	2705	2706	2707	2708	2709	2710	2711	2612	2713	2714	2715	2716
2731	2732	2733	2734	2735	2736	2737	2738	2739	2740	2741	2742	2743	2744
2759	2760	2761	2762	2763	2764	2765	2766	2767	2768	2769	2770	2771	2772
2787	2788	2789	2790	2791	2792	2793	2794	2795	2796	2797	2798	2799	2800
2815	2816	2817	2818	2819	2820	2821	2822	2823	2824	2825	2826	2827	2828
2843	2844	2845	2846	2847	2848	2849	2850	2851	2852	2853	2854	2855	2856
2871	2872	2873	2874	2875	2876	2877	2878	2879	2880	2881	2882	2883	2884
2899						2900							
2911	2912	2913	2914	2915	2916	2917	2918	2919	2920	2921	2922	2923	2924
2939	2940	2941	2942	2943	2944	2945	2946	2947	2948	2949	2950	2951	2952
2967	2968	2969	2970	2971	2972	2973	2974	2975	2976	2977	2978	2979	2980
2995	2996	2997	2998	2999						3000			
3007	3008	3009	3010	3011	3012	3013	3014	3015	3016	3017	3018	3019	3020
3035	3036	3037	3038	3039	3040	3041	3042	3043	3044	3045	3046	3047	3048
3063	3064	3065	3066	3067	3068	3069	3070	3071	3072	3073	3074	3075	3076
3091	3092	3093	3094	3095	3096	3097	3098	3099					
3103	3104	3105	3106	3107	3108	3109	3110	3111	3112	3113	3114	3115	3116
3131	3132	3133	3134	3135	3136	3137	3138	3139	3140	3141	3142	3143	3144
3159	3160	3161	3162	3163	3164	3165	3166	3167	3168	3169	3170	3171	3172
3187	3188	3189	3190	3191	3192	3193	3194	3195	3196	3197	3198	3199	3200

THOR

My heart is waxing heavier these days to write of things,
not veg'table and mineral, but cabbages and kings,

whose mineral is iron and whose mineral is gold,
so hard-of-hearing to a tearing beggar in the cold,

who lumps them all together into one and calls him Thor,
the Nordoom, Emperor of Earth, he hadn't bargained for.

the more the tale I tell unfolds, the more I am alarmed
by Thor the Nordoom, Emperor of Earth, who lives in a charmed

existence. May it here and now be understood that hist'ry
is honey-combed with myth and myth is honey-combed with hist'ry,

though here it's hist'ry back of hist'ry; here I'm dealing with
a combination of the two I call historic myth.

I differ from the 'stage historians' by going back—
stage to see and hear with eye and ear through ev'ry crack

and cranny, while my colleagues never venture from the pit,
now knowing that the currency they cashed was counterfeit.

Instead, they should have spent their time in learning all about
the theatre, both on and off the stage, inside and out.

The view of Thor the Nordoom are his own and his alone,
for which I doubt if anyone could force him to atone.

If anything the Nordoom says offends you, lay the blame
on him, and not the author, for the two are not the same.

Any similarity to persons living is,
of course, coincidental. Even though the views are his,

and his alone, I must atone for him, for he is Thor,
the unatoneable; I pray you, do not ask for more.

Shakespeare should have know the world is not a stage, but rather
a theatre whose ample pit is where the masses gather

to watch the make-believers make believers out of those
who watch; but even fewer than that few on stage are those

who never grace the boards of any Globe; the few who write,
finance and stage the play prefer to function out of sight,

as does the Nordoom who is their embodiment, the Great
Compositive of all the backstage few of any State

worth mentioning in Europe from the Middle Ages on.
I'm singing, and the song I sing was written by a swan.

That such as he could ever be is due to your and my
amalgimagination. I can hear you asking, "Why

conceal the names of those you could reveal? Just play the name
game." because I'm not the sort of person to defame

the infamous who wouldn't hesitate in handing me
my head. That's why I tattle-tale allegorically.

I claim that archaeology is hist'ry at its best,
that hist'ry, on the other hand, is fiction at its best.

Think of Thor the Nordoom what you will, to me it's fiction
based on fact, unless you mean to tell me fact is fiction.

If you infer as much as I imply, I swear, the dawn
will break, for you to see just what the hell is going on,

and what the hell is going on; for what I've read between
the lines, I've written on the lines, in hopes it would be seen.

To this advice I take the opposite, as Thor will show:
"Don't tell the truth, but only tell them what you'd have them know."

Ruling from behind the scenes, the Nordoom is the Great
Puppeteer whose puppets underoperate the State.

The secret of restoring youth to keep from growing old,
he has, and, in addition, a monopoly on gold.

The time: the present, flashing back to Pepin's time, to trace
how secret money-power came to rule the world. The place:

in residence at Festnes, the redoubtable command
pose he had constructed under cover of his Grand

Scheme of Things unfolding here and now, the Teuton carries
a load of paper-work whose paper-weight a Titan carries.

The Otter's Ransom Ring is on his finger. On his crown
is Earth, encircled by the Midgard Serpent, looking down.

Hidden hilltop high within an eagle-screaming cliff's
brow, he has his lair, and from a bushy portal, sniffs

the salt-sea air that rises from the pounding surf below,
from whence is heard the tread of sentries, marching to and fro,

an area off-limits with its triple rings of gun
emplacements, radar and the rest of this petit Verdun.

Throughout his long career he's been a fam'ly man who's had
a geneology of offspring looking up to Dad,

who had the secret of restoring youth, he couldn't share
the knowledge of, especially the use, he couldn't share

with anyone, including his own progeny, on pain
of losing both, which was to him a constant source of pain,

his wives and children growing old before his very eyes,
to linger by the death-bed while another darling dies.

His culture-conscious court is full of offspring who are giving
their all, to serve their father-king which makes their lives worth living.

His kindred, faithful unto death, provide a palace guard,
a son of his had founded long ago, one Eberhard.

Even telling them he had the secret was taboo,
and, since his lips were sealed regarding this, they never knew,

though many must have wondered, never daring to express
that wonder to a father they were fearful to address.

Soliloquizing to himself, the Nordoom has to take
a penny for his thought, the only offer I can make.

Appendix F

THE SONG OF CREATION

The deep abyss was nothingness where somethingness would be,
from nothingness to somethingness inside a derial sea.

Bottomless in depth, a world that wasn't would exist,
from nothingness to somethingness, it was the World of Mist,

the World of Mist, the World of Mist, where nothing was that was,
no sky above, no earth beneath, where nothing was that was.

The fountain in the middle of the mistiness would course
the rivers nine that radiated from a central source.

With the source as hub and with the nine as radiating
spokes, the rimless wheel of water kept on inundating.

Flowing far afield the rivers froze in layers, till
the deep, which had been bottomless before, began to fill.

The rivers having done their work, the deep was full, at last;
no longer bottomless, the World of Mist was frozen fast.

Southward from the World of Light a warming wind was felt,
that caused the many-layered ice that filled the deep to melt.

The giant Ymir sprang from clouds that formed as vapours rose
from ice's turning into what it was before it froze.

The cow Audhumbla sprang from clouds as well and went her way,
licking salty stones of ice and eating hoarfrost hay.

Unwittingly her licking would expose the hair, the head,
and then the body of a man who was a god, instead.

Buried underneath receding ice that couldn't stay
her hungry tongue's persistency, the sleeping Buri lay.

Endowed with many attributes, he was the only son
of him whose name had never been revealed, the Nameless One.

Audhumbla saw the Buri was in danger, and her lowing
was meant for Ymir, for his animosity was growing.

Borr, the son of Buri, took a giantess to wife,
knowing that the giants knew how Buri lost his life.

From Ymir on, the giants hated Buri, and they slew
the oldest god who had a name, the day they ran him through.

Bestla was the giantess' name from whom would spring
the Brothers Three, not knowing what the Brothers Three would bring.

Ymir, Giant of the Frost, was doomed. His progeny
survived him when his life was taken by the Brothers Three.

Leaning on their spears the godly trio gazed upon
his writhing body in the throws of Death who'd come and gone.

The war between the giants and the gods would escalate;
because of Ymir's death, the giants would retaliate.

Regardless of the consequences, Buri's death, at last,
had been avenged in Ymir's death; a double die was cast.

The Brothers Three considered Ymir's body, finding worth
in his remains, for out of his remains they fashioned Earth.

A time in timelessness had come in which to start revolving
the giant Ymir's body, so that life could start evolving.

Certain transformations followed: of his blood, the seas;
of his bones, the mountain ranges; of his hair, the trees;

of his skull, the heavens; of his brains, the clouds, and they
were charged with hail and snow while Seasky lay a greenish-gray.

A pair of oversights would be corrected: of his eye—
brows, Midgard, 'Odin's Garden', separating sea and sky.

Ymir's transformation was complete. The Brothers Three
talked of their Creation as they walked beside the sea.

Grieving over Buri's death, Audhumbla went astray.
Grieving over Ymir's death, she went the Milky Way,

wandering disconsolately, mourning for the two
departed ones who couldn't come in to answer her moo,

that echoed on and on, as Buri's Borr and Odin's Thor
lamented in her loss, until Audhumbla was no more.

With sun and moon in orbit, Odin separated light
from darkness, light from darkness, in ordaining day and night.

He juxtaposed the seasonal successions. Fall and Winter,
Spring and Summer equaled Spring and Summer, Fall and Winter.

The trees were lonely by themselves, and so the Brothers Three
Decided all the other forms of life should come to be.

Clinging to their climates, all the other forms would be
created, spreading out, from shore to shore and sea to sea.

Midgard was in process of becoming Man's estate,
a happy hunting ground in which to kill and copulate.

That man and woman should be made, that man and woman would
be made, had been decided by the gods who found it good.

Endowed with life and motion, speech and reason, soul
and senses, ash and alder, man and woman would be whole,

Aske from an ash and Embla from an alder were
created. Lovingly she looked at him and he at her.

They lived and loved in utter innocence; the very thought
of sin was never thought of in the creed the brothers brought.

The giants constantly disturbed the gods and it was feared
the same would happen to the race of Man when it appeared.

As feared, the giants harried Man as well, but far from fighting
the enemies of god and men, the faithless fell to fighting

the gods who had created them, in whom they'd once believed,
by warring on the Gothic tribal fold who still believed.

INDEX

CD TRACK LISTING

1: Caribea (1:32)
Performer/Composer: Moondog

2: To a Sea Horse (1:43)
Performer/Composer: Moondog

3: Trees Against the Sky (.51)
Performer/Composer: Moondog

4: Oo Debut (1:09)
Performer/Composer: Moondog

5: Autumn (2:07)
Performer/Composer: Moondog

6: Moondog Monologue (8:24)
Performer/Composer: Moondog

7: Moondog's Theme (1:53)
Performer/Composer: Moondog

8: Trimbas in Quarters (1:47)
Performer/Composer: Moondog

9: I Came Into This World Alone (1:19)
Performers: Moondog, Steve Reich, Philip Glass, Jon Gibson
Composer: Moondog

10: Be a Hobo (1:22)
Performers: Moondog, Steve Reich, Philip Glass, Jon Gibson
Composer: Moondog

11: Why Spend the Dark Night With You (1:40)
Performers: Moondog, Steve Reich, Philip Glass, Jon Gibson
Composer: Moondog

12: All is Loneliness (1:38)
Performers: Moondog, Steve Reich, Philip Glass, Jon Gibson
Composer: Moondog

13: Organ Rounds (2:04)
Performer/Composer: Moondog

14: Canon in F Major, Book I (.43)
Performer: Paul Jordan
Composer: Moondog

15: Canon in B Flat Major, Book III (1:36)
Performer: Paul Jordan
Composer: Moondog

16: Canon in B Flat Major, Book I (.43)
Performer: Paul Jordan
Composer: Moondog

17: Canon in B Flat Major, Book II (.28)
Performer: Paul Jordan
Composer: Moondog

18: Canon in G Sharp Minor, Book I (.44)
Performer: Paul Jordan
Composer: Moondog

19: Canon in C Sharp Minor, Book II (1:32)
Performer: Paul Jordan
Composer: Moondog

20: 5/4 Snakebite Rattle (3:41)
Performer: Stefan Lakatos
Composer: Moondog

21: Trimbas and Woodblock in 5/2 (1:26)
Performer: Stefan Lakatos
Composer: Moondog

22: When I Am Deep in Sleep (2:17)
Performer: Stefan Lakatos
Composer: Moondog

23: Rabbit Hop (2:25)
Performer/Composer: Moondog

24: Dog Trot (2:25)
Performer/Composer: Moondog

25: Bird's Lament (2:00)
Performer/Composer: Moondog

26: Viking 1 (2:55)
Performer/Composer: Moondog

27: Heimdall Fanfare (3:06)
Performer/Composer: Moondog

28: Intro and Overtone Continuum (2:22)
Performer/Composer: Moondog

Mastering by Pete Lyman of Infrasonic